SAME-SEX MARRIAGE IN RENAISSANCE ROME

Same-Sex Marriage in Renaissance Rome

Sexuality, Identity, and Community in Early Modern Europe

Gary Ferguson

Cornell University Press
Ithaca and London

First published 2016 by Cornell University Press

Printed in the United States of America

Library of Congress Cataloging-in-Publication Data
Names: Ferguson, Gary, 1963– author.
Title: Same-sex marriage in Renaissance Rome : sexuality, identity, and
    community in early modern Europe / Gary Ferguson.
Description: Ithaca ; London : Cornell University Press, 2016. | Includes
    bibliographical references and index.
Identifiers: LCCN 2016012404 | ISBN 9781501702372 (cloth : alk. paper)
Subjects: LCSH: Same-sex marriage—Rome. | Same-sex
    marriage—Europe—History. | Gay men—Europe—Attitudes. |
    Homophobia—Europe—History.
Classification: LCC HQ1034.R6 F47 2016 | DDC 306.84/809409024—dc23
LC record available at http://lccn.loc.gov/2016012404

Cornell University Press strives to use environmentally responsible
suppliers and materials to the fullest extent possible in the publishing of
its books. Such materials include vegetable-based, low-VOC inks and
acid-free papers that are recycled, totally chlorine-free, or partly composed
of nonwood fibers. For further information, visit our website at
www.cornellpress.cornell.edu.

Cloth printing   10 9 8 7 6 5 4 3 2 1

For Jeremy, *ancora*

Contents

ACKNOWLEDGMENTS

Over the years spent working on this project I have accumulated debts of gratitude toward many colleagues, friends, and institutions from whose help and support I have benefited. The University of Delaware provided material resources in the form of a sabbatical leave in 2010–11, research and travel funds, and the aid of several graduate students, notably Anna Ogunnaike who assisted with the preparation of the bibliography. The École française de Rome could not have been more helpful in affording access to its magnificent library and accommodation for visiting scholars. Archivists in Italy and Spain, especially Michele Di Sivo at the Archivio di Stato in Rome and Blanca Tena Arregui and Francisco Javier Crespo Muñoz at the Archivo General in Simancas, went above and beyond the call of duty in responding to questions concerning collections and documents in their care.

I am particularly indebted to colleagues and friends who invited me to present my research as it progressed at their institutions: Edwin Duval, Yale University; Nancy Frelick, University of British Columbia; David La-Guardia, Dartmouth College; Kathleen Long, Cornell University; Daniele

Maira, Universität Basel; Jean-Marie Roulin, Université Jean Monnet–Saint-Étienne; and Colette Winn, Washington University in St. Louis. All of these occasions offered privileged opportunities for discussion and the refining of ideas. Particularly rich exchanges were possible in the context of a seminar at the Alice Paul Center for Research on Women, Gender, and Sexuality at the University of Pennsylvania, directed by Rita Barnard, in which she and Melissa Sanchez presented commentary pieces; at a Mellon Faculty Seminar directed by Lisa Jane Graham in the John B. Hurford Humanities Center of Haverford College, where participants discussed a precirculated paper; and during the time spent at Trinity College Dublin thanks to a short-term fellowship at the Centre for Medieval and Renaissance Studies, directed by Sarah Alyn Stacey.

I am no less grateful to scholars who, in person or via email, were willing to discuss particular points or to share their knowledge in various areas, notably Cristian Berco, Israel Burshatin, Tom and Elizabeth Cohen, Thomas Dandelet, JoAnn DellaNeva, Laura Giannetti, Paul Grendler, Ann Jones, Chiara Lastraioli, Virginie Leroux, Reinier Leushuis, Christian Moevs, Laurie Nussdorfer, Ricardo Padrón, David Quint, Michael Rocke, Guido Ruggiero, Massimo Scalabrini, Michael Sherberg, Michael Sibalis, Tessa Storey, Elissa Weaver, and Rebecca Winer. Giuseppe Marcocci generously sent me his transcript of the trial fragments, which considerably facilitated my own consultation of the manuscript, as well as the text of a forthcoming article several weeks ahead of its publication. On more than one occasion, Luisa Capodieci offered invaluable assistance deciphering documents, as did, at regular intervals, Meredith Ray, whose continued interest and inexhaustible generosity in sharing her time and expertise were crucial to the evolution and completion of the project.

Several passages of this book appeared in earlier form in "'(Same-Sex) Marriage and the Making of Europe: Renaissance Rome Revisited," in *What's Queer About Europe? Productive Encounters and Re-Enchanting Paradigms*, ed. Mireille Rosello and Sudeep Dasgupta (New York: Fordham University Press, 2014), 27–47 and 190–95.

Translations are my own except where indicated otherwise.

INTRODUCTION

Engagement

Same-sex marriage: the issue has come to prominence in many countries around the world in the late twentieth and early twenty-first centuries. In the first decade of the third millennium, the right of two women or two men to marry was granted by the ten nations of the Netherlands (2001), Belgium (2003), Spain and Canada (2005), South Africa (2006), Norway and Sweden (2009), and Portugal, Iceland, and Argentina (2010). During the same years, a significant number of other states instituted alternative forms of civil union or domestic partnership, conferring all or some of the same legal benefits; these included Australia, New Zealand, the United Kingdom, Denmark, Finland, Hungary, and France, most of which have subsequently accorded same-sex couples access to marriage.[1] At the same time, a number of jurisdictions passed laws or constitutional amendments explicitly limiting marriage to one man and one woman, in some cases preemptively disallowing all forms of partnership designed to grant the same or similar rights. This was true in the United States at the federal level and in certain of the fifty states. After a long series of legal battles, the Supreme Court declared both sets of measures unconstitutional, the former when it struck down parts of the 1996 Defense of Marriage Act in 2013, the latter in June 2015.[2] By contrast, recent years have seen laws against homosexuality introduced or strengthened in places such as Russia, Nigeria, Uganda, and Egypt. In 2014, eight Egyptians were sentenced to three years' imprisonment (reduced on appeal to one) for inciting debauchery. Their conviction followed the wide circulation on the internet of a video showing a celebration on a boat on the Nile during which two of them embraced and exchanged rings in what was said to be an informal wedding ceremony.

Yet the idea of marriage between two people of the same sex is not a uniquely modern one. In Europe, during the early modern period that is the focus of this book (broadly the sixteenth to the eighteenth centuries), the topic appears with surprising frequency in a wide variety of texts—literary, juridical, historical chronicles, memoirs, letters, and so on. In line with the flourishing of interest in antiquity launched by sixteenth-century humanists, we find references to the classical world and to ancient sources that tell of emperors marrying their favorite male slaves.[3] In the early seventeenth-century text, *L'Isle des Hermaphrodites* (c. 1605), a number of classical figures associated with male same-sex desire serve a symbolic function, including Nero and Pythagoras, a depiction of whose wedding decorates a bed canopy.[4] Although it was not published until a decade and a half after the assassination of Henry III of France (r. 1574–89), *L'Isle* is often read in part as a satire of the court of the late king. In a country torn by civil strife between Catholics and Protestants, Henry III and his *mignons* or young favorites had frequently been accused by their enemies of sexual perversion. In 1581, moreover, when the king had married his wife's half-sister to his favorite, the duke Anne de Joyeuse, with a degree of pomp never before seen, satirists denounced a court rife with every kind of secret sexual intrigue and license, including "marriages" between Henry and the *mignons*.[5]

In other instances, stories from classical mythology were reworked, such as that of Iphis and Ianthe from Ovid's *Metamorphoses*, describing the love of two young women, the former of whom had been raised as a boy, who are destined to marry.[6] In Ovid's tale, the goddess Isis intervenes to save the day by transforming Iphis into a man. A heteronormative frame is thus ultimately reestablished, although not without considerable instability since the story of sex change fed into ancient and early modern medical theories of the "one-sex body," which saw male and female as potentially shifting points on a spectrum, rather than in terms of a fixed physiological dimorphism.[7] Such ambiguities were often developed and exploited by early modern writers such as Isaac de Benserade, in whose 1634 play Iphis's change of sex occurs only after, not before, her marriage to Ianthe.[8]

Not all early modern evocations of same-sex marriage looked to classical antiquity, however. In England, Queen Elizabeth I (r. 1558–1603) received the ambassador of Philip II of Spain, Guzmán de Silva, in 1564. During this crucial meeting that reestablished diplomatic relations between the two countries, Elizabeth inquired after Philip's widowed sister, Juana, "saying how much she should like to see her, and how well so young a widow and a maiden would get on together, and what a pleasant life they could lead. She [Elizabeth] being the elder would be the husband, and her Highness, the wife."[9] Given its singular political context, the hypothetical scenario Elizabeth evokes should not be understood in too narrowly sexual or erotic terms, but in relation to the situation of a queen who would immediately have found herself subordinate to any man she had taken as a husband. Since diplomatic relations between countries frequently passed through royal marriages, Elizabeth here envisages such a union between England and Spain. Philip, in fact, had been married to Elizabeth's elder sister, Mary, after whose death he had sought the hand of the new sovereign. Elizabeth, however, had resisted. The scenario of a female–female wedding, with Elizabeth as husband and Philip's sister as wife, allows the English monarch to suggest a rapprochement between the two countries in which she avoids the personal diminishment that a marriage with Philip would have entailed and maintains her (masculine) authority and autonomy.

Marriages between women in the early modern period, moreover, were not confined solely to the realm of the imagination. A number of cases are described in sixteenth-century France by writers such as Henri Estienne and Michel de Montaigne. The former, in his *Apologie pour Hérodote* (1566), tells of a young woman from the village of Fontaines, between Blois and Romorantin, who disguised herself as a stable hand for about seven years, before marrying a woman with whom she lived for some two years while working in a vineyard. At that point, she was discovered and sentenced to be burned at the stake.[10] About fifteen years later, Montaigne recorded in his *Journal de voyage* (written 1580–81) a story he heard as he passed through the town of Vitry-le-François in eastern France, concerning a young woman who had just been hanged. Mary was one of seven or eight girls from Chaumont who "comploterent, il y a quelques années, de se vestir en masles et continuer ainsi leur vie par le monde" (plotted together a few years ago to dress up as males and thus continue their life in the world).[11] Mary had earned her living as a weaver, become engaged, though not married, to a woman in the town of Vitry, moving subsequently to Montier-en-Der, where she took a wife. Like the young woman from Fontaines, Mary was ultimately recognized and denounced to the authorities.

In *The Tradition of Female Transvestism in Early Modern Europe*, where their focus is on the Netherlands of the seventeenth and eighteenth centuries, Rudolf Dekker and Lotte van de Pol describe no less than ten cases (recalling those described by Estienne and Montaigne) of women cross-dressing and living as men, who also marry or promise to marry another woman.[12] Two of the women discussed, indeed, married twice. In the majority of cases, the cross-gendered woman courted a partner who remained ignorant of her future spouse's biological sex. Occasionally, however, the woman who became the wife was complicit with her female husband, and in one instance two women together decided that one of them would cross-dress in order for them to be able to marry, which they did in the Reformed Church of Amsterdam. Like their predecessors in France, most of the women who assumed a male identity in Holland were from the lower classes. Many of them migrants from other countries such as Germany, they acted as they did initially to escape poverty and the prospect of prostitution by opening up social options generally denied to their sex. Whenever they came to the attention of authorities, the marriages they had contracted were declared invalid, and one or both of the women were subject to punishment, in many instances some form of exile.

A case from Spain in the late 1580s is yet more complex, since it involves the question of transsexuality. Elena de Céspedes was a freed slave who lived initially as a woman, was married to a stonemason in Jaén, and gave birth to a son. Calling himself Eleno, he subsequently lived for more than twenty years as a man, working variously as a soldier, tailor, and surgeon, and married a woman. He was then recognized and denounced by someone with whom he had served in the army and who stated that Eleno's fellow soldiers had known he had two sexes. At his trial by the Inquisition, Eleno affirmed repeatedly that he believed marriage to be a sacrament, that he was not mocking the Church, that he did not think it possible or legal for two women to marry, and that when he was married to a woman he was a male hermaphrodite, his penis having emerged in the process of childbirth. Following a medical examination that reached a contrary conclusion to those that had been carried out previously, and after Eleno's admission that he had used potions to shrink his vulva, the inquisitors declared him to be a woman. They also convicted him of bigamy since, although he stated he believed his husband to have died before he took a wife, he could produce no official documentation of his widowed status.[13]

The handful of examples given here by way of illustration could be multiplied, and readers familiar with the literature and history of early modern Europe will likely recall others they have encountered. At the same time, it is clear that not all of these references to marriage have the same value or even describe the same phenomenon. Some belong to the realm of desire, fantasy, or "thought experiment"; others, forming part of lived experience, had a reality to those involved in them and perhaps also, to some degree, to their communities, even if they would not have been recognized by religious and civil authorities. My contention is that they all have a place in the history of marriage—which is to say, by the same token, that marriage must take its own place in the broader history of unions or pair bonds made, pursued, desired, or envisaged by individuals in the past. This approach builds on that adopted in relation to opposite-sex unions in medieval Europe by Ruth Mazzo Karras in her book *Unmarriages*. As Karras compellingly demonstrates, while medieval people were at times called on to distinguish between marriage and other forms of relationship, "for the most part, the line between what was marriage and what was not was not sharply drawn."[14] Thus, if the range of medieval pair bonds were to be plotted graphically this would require, more than the possibility of their being situated on a linear continuum between marriage and singleness, "a multidimensional graph that would include axes of formality, sexual exclusivity, sharing of resources, emotional involvement, dissolubility, and so forth."[15]

From the beginning of the Christian era and throughout the Middle Ages, marriage was a highly contested institution involving individuals, their families and communities, and secular and religious authorities. Who had the right to contract a marriage, how he or she could or should do so, and, in particular, who was competent to determine whether any given relationship was a marriage or not were complex and evolving questions. If medieval and early modern history offers largely a chronicle of the success of the Church in asserting its jurisdiction over marriage, this outcome was not achieved without considerable struggle. The sixteenth century was a watershed moment in this history. Partly in response to the ambiguities and confusion that frequently arose, and in particular to prevent young people from marrying in secret, the Catholic Church introduced strict new regulations at the Council of Trent (1563). In many places, however, it took several decades or longer for these to be accepted in practice. At the same time, in Protestant countries, Reformed theologians and pastors denied the sacramental character of marriage and moved even further and more decisively in the direction of strengthening the rights of parents over those of their children. The history of marriage is thus also that of the increasing disqualification and marginalization, the rendering illicit, of other forms of relationship that existed, in Karras's formulation, "in negotiation and counterpoint with marriage rather than simply outside it."[16] And this, I would argue, includes not only male–female but also same-sex relationships, although in the latter case the negotiations and the counterpoint were more tense and intricate, producing more dissonant strains.

This is the situation that appears strikingly in relation to the group of men executed by the authorities in Rome in August 1578 who form the subject of this book. Predominantly of Iberian origin, they were arrested at the church of Saint John at the Latin Gate where they had gathered, according to contemporary sources, probably not for the first time, to celebrate a wedding between two of their number. The investigation and analysis of this single set of circumstances and the people involved in them, pursued in detail, will give rise to a discussion that ranges widely over some of the most fundamental aspects of early modern European society and culture. These include not only marriage and other sorts of same- and opposite-sex relationships but also sex and gender, forms of identity, politics, migration, and social class, as well as national, ethnic, and religious boundaries and their transgression.[17]

The sources on which this study draws are principally archival—judicial and legal documents, ambassadorial dispatches, newsletters—but also personal accounts, some of which found their way into print. None of the texts concerned, however, establishes a complete and incontrovertible set of facts. In different ways, they are partial: some, incomplete and fragmentary, offer sometimes complementary, sometimes contradictory, evidence; all of them are inscribed in particular socio-rhetorical contexts (political, polemical, judicial); all serve to write their subjects, briefly and simultaneously, into and out of the record. Like the histories of other persecuted or conquered individuals and peoples, then, that of the men who met at the Latin Gate contains many holes, silences that resist our inquiries and that even the discovery of additional sources would likely be insufficient fully to bridge. Distinguished models for confronting similar problems in relation to early modern popular culture include pioneering studies such as Carlo Ginzburg's *The Cheese and the Worms* and Natalie Zemon Davis's *The Return of Martin Guerre*, both works that draw primarily on legal records. Ginzburg, in particular, described his subject Menocchio, the miller from Friuli, as a "dispersed fragment" and affirmed the need to respect the "residue of unintelligibility" of his destroyed culture.[18] The encounter with a history to one degree or another lost has also been central to postcolonial and queer studies. In the face of so fundamental an obstacle, scholars in these fields have creatively supplemented the protocols of traditional historiography, calling on the techniques and strategies of personal memoir or of imaginary projection; some have worked to turn the elisions of established narratives into murmurs of dissent or oppositional silence, revelatory of official history's ideological biases and fictionality; others have reflected on place as a bearer of memory and oblivion, presence and absence, written about processes of engagement, discovery, and frustration, or probed the historian's own affective investments.[19] Drawing on post-Hegelian understandings of history—no longer a master narrative of progress and universal meaning, perhaps a Benjaminian constellation[20]—all have striven, in a variety of ways, to undo hegemonic teleologies.[21]

The history that follows keeps the texts on which it is based clearly in view: it incorporates into its story, that is, the texts on which it draws, with all the questions they raise, including material problems related to the vagaries of their writing, conservation, and transmission. At some points, it will be necessary to hypothesize or, like hypertextual links, to suggest a plurality of possible storylines that might be pursued in different directions, through different "screens." While seeking to avoid what, in a cross-cultural perspective, Chimamanda Ngozi Adichie has called "the danger of the single story," this study is also committed to the goal of an at least partially recoverable past.[22] Where, however, its threads fail to resolve into a single narrative, this does not mean that they are bereft of all coherence or that each of them does not have something it can tell us about the early modern period and its possibilities of thought and action. A fundamental strategy, indeed, will be to bring out, to allow to be heard, the different stories that those involved in the events or interested in them were able to tell or tried to tell in varying circumstances and for particular reasons. Adopting such an approach does mean, however, that hypotheses and deductions made from the available materials will always be presented as such, never as "fact," that the process of interpreting the texts will be rendered explicit rather than occulted. It also means that some questions—even central questions concerning aspects of the nature and significance of the wedding celebrations at the heart of the inquiry—will not be fully elucidated. At the same time, the evidence uncovered will speak to issues initially unanticipated. Imbricated with that of marriage will surface, as my subtitle suggests, other (hi)stories—of sexuality, of identity, and of community.

Since this history is a textual one—that is, since the drama of reading the sources is central to the narrative that can be drawn from them—the body of the discussion is organized in two parts, each titled "Stories." The first examines various extant accounts left by contemporary observers, the second, the legal documents in which the protagonists themselves appear as (constrained) actors. The book's third, concluding part, titled "Histories," comprises two chapters. The first draws on the (unforeseen) wealth of details gathered concerning the men's sexual lives to demonstrate their importance to the history of sexuality. While it keeps the question of marriage in view, "Looking Forward / Looking Back" posits a third point of comparison between Renaissance Rome and the twenty-first century, that of eighteenth-century Paris. This introduction of evidence from a moment taken to coincide with the development of modern forms of gender identity and sexuality, in triangulation with a presumed *before* and *after*, reveals sharply how aspects of the generally accepted evolutionary chronology require reexamination and greater nuance. In opening this study with recent and ongoing efforts for the legalization of same-sex marriage, I mean to suggest the interest of pursuing engaged interactions between the sixteenth and the twenty-first centuries. Accordingly, the final chapter proposes ways in which the particular case studied might be "usable," that is, might lend itself to meaningful appropriation in the present. "Ghost Stories" brings the evidence from Renaissance Rome into dialogue with the issue of same-sex marriage from the two perspectives of LGBT politics and queer politics. It also develops lines of reflection concerning forms of desire and resistance: memory, loss, and place, sexual and social dissidence, creative and transformative appropriation, alternative temporalities, histories as yet unknown.

PART I

Stories—Observers

Chapter 1

A French Writer Visits

Montaigne's Travel Journal *and a Thrice-Told Tale*

The French essayist Michel de Montaigne does not offer the contemporary testimony closest to the events at the heart of this book, but he is the logical point of departure since his account, coming from the pen of a famous writer and thinker, is by far the most well known today; it is his version of the story that has generated scholarly interest and stimulated research. Having just published the first edition of his *Essais*, Montaigne left on a trip to Rome and Italy, via Switzerland, Germany, and Austria, that lasted from June 1580 to November of the following year. He took with him two copies of his recent book: the first he presented en route to the French king, Henry III; the second he offered, on his arrival in Rome, to Pope Gregory XIII.

As the center of Catholic Christianity and the capital of the ancient Roman Empire, Rome was a privileged destination for a Renaissance scholar. Nevertheless, it provoked a conflicted response on the part of many visiting humanists, since it offered the spectacle of architectural ruins, the symbol of a civilization definitively lost, and of a modern papal city easily perceived as corrupt and decadent.[1] Montaigne's *Journal de voyage* (*Travel Journal*) reflects on such topics. Yet what seems most to interest this traveler, strongly influenced by his reading of ancient Skeptics such as Sextus Empiricus, is the diversity of places, peoples, and customs that he encounters. In Germany, for instance, Montaigne is impressed by the general atmosphere of religious tolerance that prevails, in contrast with France, and notes with admiration the frequency of marriages between Catholics and Protestants. In each place he visits, the Frenchman is eager to see the sights and to hear notable stories— of historical events, current happenings, or unusual customs. His enthusiasm for curiosities of all kinds is such that he complains if locals fail to show him some site of interest. Montaigne confided the redaction of the first part of his *Journal* to a secretary, later taking up the writing himself, in French, then in Italian, before reverting to French in conclusion.[2] The *Travel Journal* served as a notebook on which Montaigne would later draw as he expanded and revised his *Essais* in subsequent editions; it was never intended for publication itself, however, and was almost lost to history.

When a previously unknown work by one of France's most famous authors came to light in the late eighteenth century, it was a major event. Nonetheless, the publication of the *Journal de voyage* was a contested process, since its discoverer, the abbé Prunis, to whom it was initially entrusted, found much of its content distasteful. Perhaps with the encouragement of the famous *philosophe* Jean le Rond D'Alembert, therefore, he decided to prepare an anthology of selected passages. Fortunately, Count Charles-Joseph de Ségur, the owner of the manuscript and of the castle of Montaigne where it had been uncovered, insisted on an unabridged publication and charged the Parisian publisher Le Jay with finding a suitable editor. Le Jay turned to Anne-Gabriel Meusnier de Querlon, keeper of the king's manuscripts, who, with the assistance of collaborators, brought out the first printed editions, in three different formats, in 1774. Once published, Montaigne's original manuscript was deposited in the Bibliothèque royale, from where it disappeared as suddenly and mysteriously as it had come to light.[3] A number of handwritten copies of the original manuscript were also made in the eighteenth century, one of which, by Canon Guillaume-Vivien Leydet, survives to this day. The usefulness of the Leydet copy is that it allows a comparison with the printed text, and in the many places where the latter's readings are clearly faulty or in doubt, corrections can be made. The passage concerning the same-sex marriages in Rome embarrassed Canon Leydet, just as parts of the manuscript had embarrassed his friend the abbé Prunis, and the canon suppressed most of it and translated other crucial words and phrases into Greek, thus ensuring they might be understood only by a restricted scholarly elite.[4] Meusnier de Querlon was also not without misgivings concerning the same-sex marriage story; to our great fortune he published it nonetheless, limiting himself to adding a footnote qualifying the events described as an "impiété sacrilége et monstrueuse que nous n'avons lue nulle part ailleurs" (a sacrilegious and monstrous impiety, the like of which we have read of nowhere else).[5] Here is what Montaigne relates:

> On the 18th [March] the ambassador of Portugal made obeisance to the Pope for the kingdom of Portugal on behalf of King Philip—the same ambassador who was here to represent the deceased king and the Cortes opposed to King Philip.
>
> On my return from Saint Peter's I met a man who informed me humorously of two things: that the Portuguese made their obeisance in Passion week; and then, that on this same day the station was at San Giovanni Porta Latina, in which church a few years before certain Portuguese had entered into a strange brotherhood [/confraternity]. They married one another, male to male, at Mass, with the same ceremonies with which we perform our marriages, [took communion together, read the same wedding gospel, and then went to bed and slept with each other]. The Roman wits said that because in the other conjunction, of male and female, this circumstance of marriage alone makes it legitimate, it had seemed to these sharp folk that this other action would become equally legitimate if they authorized it with ceremonies and mysteries of the Church. Eight or nine Portuguese of this fine sect were burned.
>
> I saw the Spanish ceremony. They fired a salvo of cannon from the Castle of Sant'Angelo [and the palace, and the ambassador was conducted] by the Pope's trumpeters and drummers and archers. I did not go in to watch the harangue and the ceremony. The ambassador from the tsar of Muscovy, who was at a decorated window to see this ceremony, said that he had been invited to see a great assemblage, but that in his country, when they speak of troops of horse, it is always twenty-five or thirty thousand; and he laughed at all this ado, from what I was told by the very man who was commissioned to talk to him through an interpreter.[6]

> Le 18 [mars], l'Ambassadeur de Portugal fit l'obedience au Pape du royaume de Portugal pour le Roy Philippe: ce mesme Ambassadeur qui estoit icy pour le Roy trespassé et pour les Estats contrarians au Roy Philippe. Je rencontray au retour de Saint Pierre un homme qui m'avisa plaisamment de deux choses:

que les Portugais faisoient leur obedience la semaine de la Passion, et puis
que ce mesme jour la station estoit à Saint Jean *Porta Latina*, en laquelle eglise certains Portugais, quelques années y a, estoient entrés en une estrange
confrerie. Ils s'espousoient masle à masle à la Messe, avec mesmes ceremonies
que nous faisons nos mariages, faisoient leurs pasques ensemble, lisoient ce
mesme evangile des nopces, et puis couchoient et habitoient ensemble. Les
esprits Romains disoient que, parce qu'en l'autre conjonction, de masle et
femelle, cette seule circonstance la rend legitime, que ce soit en mariage, il
avoit semblé à ces fines gens que cette autre action deviendroit pareillement
juste, qui l'auroit autorisée de ceremonies et mysteres de l'Eglise. Il fut bruslé
huict ou neuf Portugais de cette belle secte.

Je vis la pompe Espaignole. On fit une salve de canons au Chasteau Saint
Ange et au Palais, et fut l'Ambassadeur conduit par les trompettes et tam-
bours et archiers du Pape. Je n'entray pas au dedans voir la harangue et la
ceremonie. L'Ambassadeur du Moscovite, qui estoit à une fenestre parée pour
voir cette pompe, dit qu'il avoit esté convié à voir une grande assemblée; mais
qu'en sa nation, quand on parle de troupes de chevaux, c'est tousjours vingt
cinq ou trente mille; et se mocqua de tout cet apprest, à ce que me dit celuy
mesme qui estoit commis à l'entretenir par truchement.[7]

The first characteristic of Montaigne's story likely to strike the modern
reader (and contrasting with the reaction it provoked from its eighteenth-
century editors) is its lightness of tone and the absence of any expression of
condemnation or moral outrage—an attitude apparently shared by the
French traveler, his unnamed interlocutor, and a segment of the inhabitants
of the papal city, the "Roman wits." Montaigne records an anecdote he was
told on his way home from the Vatican, an anecdote intended to surprise and
amuse the worldly, cultivated visitor in search of diverse customs and unusual
happenings. If we were to take the text of the *Journal* as straightforward re-
portage, the Portuguese described would appear as men having sexual relations, convinced of and sufficiently anxious about the sinfulness of their
actions that they decided to go through a religious wedding ceremony in the
belief that this would render them blameless. This they might have done
conscious of the fact they were profaning a sacrament, but trusting that the
rite would be efficacious in spite of their sacrilege.[8] They would thus reveal
their naivety through the logical contradiction of seeking to avoid one sin by
wittingly committing another one yet more serious. Alternatively, it would
be possible to suppose that the men as they are portrayed in the story were

not conscious that their performing of a marriage was sacrilegious, and thus that the second sin, representing a blindly futile attempt to avoid the first, was the result of a no-less-naive ignorance. For the reader, this second scenario would open up the further possibility that the men in reality might not have believed they were committing a sacrilege since performing a wedding between people of the same sex might be, or should be, legitimate.

The difficulty, clearly, is that Montaigne's *Journal* records the story secondhand and in a highly self-consciously narrated form; moreover, as we shall see, other accounts of the same events were in circulation that give different details and convey different attitudes. First, then, a fundamental characteristic of the passage from the *Journal* is its ironic posture, although given the impossibility of untangling the three levels of telling, it is equally impossible to know to whom and to what degree any given expression might be attributed: the traveler composing his journal in French; the interlocutor who addresses him "plaisamment" (humorously), most likely in Italian; or the wits with whom the commentary, undoubtedly in Italian, originates. Since ironic distance is a prime basis for wit, it is easy to see the Roman raconteurs as mocking the naivety of the not-so-clever "fines gens" (sharp folk), who provide them with such good material. This expression may be more Montaigne's, however, since he employed it earlier, in his *Essais*, to describe those whose testimony he mistrusts because of their tendency to embellish.[9] Just to whom, moreover, might the phrase "esprits Romains" refer? The Italian equivalent of the French *bel esprit* would be *bel ingegno*, an expression current in the sixteenth century. According to Federico Barbierato, in certain quarters in the seventeenth and eighteenth centuries, it became synonymous with libertinism and free thinking, often in relation to sex: "One therefore became a '*bel ingegno*' (a wit) and '*galant' huomo*' (a noble spirit) by putting forward propositions, theories or simple formulations that could create a scandal, perhaps by treating subjects usually considered to be sacred lightly. . . . The *virtuosi* therefore professed a range of liberties for themselves, first of all in the sphere of thinking, then in reading and finally, almost inevitably, sex."[10] While Barbierato's examples come from Venice and a somewhat later period, many of the ideas in question, the author notes, had been circulating for at least a century, some having been shared by Menocchio the miller, studied by Carlo Ginzburg.[11]

Treating a subject "usually considered to be sacred lightly" is certainly what Montaigne is doing in this passage—and we know the profound influence his *Essais* would have on his early free-thinking readers in the late sixteenth and seventeenth centuries. It also appears to be what certain enlightened Romans were doing, perhaps with a more sympathetic than mocking attitude toward the men who provided them with such a bold example of *ingegno* and independence vis-à-vis religious authority.[12] If the wits felt any sense of superiority, indeed, this might have been the case only to the extent that they saw the Iberians as adhering uncritically to an orthodox view of sin and sex and to marriage as both institution and sacrament.[13] Such a perception, indeed, might lie behind the emphasis placed in this account on the exact replication of specific elements of a traditional wedding ceremony, a narrative element not found so clearly in most of the other early sources. In short, in terms of pinning down with certainty the opinions and motivations—and even the precise actions—of the men who met at the Latin Gate, the evidence offered by Montaigne's *Travel Journal* is rich but irreducibly slippery. In particular, we should not assume that the twice-retold words of the Roman wits echo faithfully the voices of those they concern. To one degree or another, this may or may not be the case.

Turning to other aspects of the wedding story as Montaigne formulated it, we can note that if the men involved are presented as a curious and marginal group ("certain Portuguese," "strange brotherhood," "fine sect"), they nonetheless gain a viable presence, standing as a "they" over and against a "we." Subsequently, moreover, heterosexual sex is referred to as "the *other* conjunction, of male and female," a formulation that serves to adumbrate a point of view that might be associated with "them" and from which "*our* marriages" are questioned and relativized. In its turn, however, sex between men becomes "this *other* action," so that all sexual activity here is *other*, as the narrative identification shifts between "them" and "us." Such a labile vision is quite characteristic of the skeptical Montaigne and of the appreciation of the variety of customs and of the suspension of judgment that this philosophical school advocates. The resulting attitude to unusual practices is not necessarily devoid of value judgment, however, since Skepticism also encourages the acceptance (if not the endorsement) of the status quo, of established social norms, an outlook tending to confirm the unusual and marginal as unusual and marginal.[14] We see this here in the deceptive self-evidence of an expression like "our marriages," to which I shall return; we see it also in the humorous use of religious vocabulary to describe the group of men as a "fine sect" and a "strange confraternity." Again, these expressions will be discussed in more detail later; at the outset, however, it is worth emphasizing that Montaigne does not seem to me to be using these terms in a literal way, to signal the existence of an actual confraternity, a (semi-)formal organization with a fixed structure, purpose, and shared duties and activities. The Portuguese are not described as having founded a confraternity that men can join in order, subsequently, to be able to celebrate a wedding ceremony. Montaigne is describing (as were perhaps the Roman wits) a number of men who formed some kind of group, who associated with each other, and he applies to them a religious vocabulary designed to highlight the incongruity of their actions, particularly unexpected in the city that formed the center of Catholic Christendom.

This is not to say, again, however, that the Portuguese men are subject to derision. It is notable, for example, that the marriages themselves are described in matter-of-fact terms, their serious intent implied, and they are not qualified in any way that would suggest a lack of authenticity: as "attempted," "so-called," "supposed," or the like. This serious quality to the narration has, in fact, given rise to a faulty reading, followed in a number of editions and accepted by certain scholars, notably William Beck and John Boswell.[15] The original eighteenth-century editions attribute the commentary relayed by Montaigne to "esperis romeins." Meusnier de Querlon did not follow the author's original spelling and in many instances offered readings that are obviously faulty. Since Leydet suppressed the passage in question, it is impossible to verify the phrase. Nonetheless, Querlon included a footnote to elucidate what must have appeared to him a clearly legible but potentially opaque expression in the manuscript: "Les gens d'esprit à Rome."[16] It was the *Journal*'s early twentieth-century editor, Louis Lautrey, who introduced a "correction" that was reproduced in a number of subsequent editions. Altering one letter, Lautrey transformed *esperis* into *esperts*, Roman wits into Roman experts.[17] On this basis, Beck jumped to the conclusion that theological authorities had sanctioned and performed the weddings, which leaves him wondering who could have burned the men if they married with the Church's blessing. Boswell judged that the ceremonies performed were not weddings, but Western forms of the Orthodox rite of *adelphopoiesis* or the making of brothers, whose true significance was nonetheless understood by all concerned, including the clergy. Mistranslating Montaigne so as to effect a reversal of meaning, Boswell then found evidence of an "increasing discrepancy between the (largely inexplicable) hostility of the masses and the general equanimity of the church."[18] As we shall see, such, in reality, was far from the case.

In the context of the *Journal* as a whole, moreover, the humorous distancing operated by the term *estrange confrerie* applies not only to the Portuguese men; it also works inversely to scrutinize and to relativize—to subject to an anthropological gaze—much of the religious life of the papal city, home to hundreds of confraternities dedicated to all kinds of pious activities, potentially viewed as strange—unquestionably far from self-evident to the visiting Frenchman.[19] A striking example, which Montaigne calls "an enigma," is recorded shortly afterward. The writer describes a procession of flagellants, who turn out to be mostly poor people, hired by others to scourge themselves in their stead, and who, he is told, ease their pain by greasing their shoulders with ointment. To Montaigne, however, the wounds appeared real enough; indeed, if they were not, he reflects, and the whole spectacle was a sham, what would those paying for it have been buying?[20] The passage concerning the group of Portuguese men itself focuses, to a considerable degree, on a description of ceremonies: the diplomatic–ecclesiastical ceremony of the reception of the ambassador and the "ceremonies and mysteries of the Church" represented by the alleged same-sex weddings. And it is the ceremonious nature of religious life in Rome, rather than its devotion, that strikes Montaigne in general and on which he comments several times. "Ces ceremonies semblent estre plus magnifiques que devotieuses" (*Journal*, 93) (These ceremonies seem to be more magnificent than devout [*Works*, 1144]), he concludes, for example, after attending Christmas Day mass at Saint Peter's, during most of which the pope and cardinals remained seated, their heads covered, incessantly talking with each other. Immediately following the passage concerning the Portuguese, Montaigne describes another ceremony he witnessed in a church the next day, Palm Sunday, during vespers. Close to the altar sat a fifteen-year-old youth, dressed in a long blue taffeta robe, with a crown of olive branches on his head and a burning torch of bleached wax in his hand. The boy, Montaigne learned, had murdered another youth. Following the ceremony the prisoner, pardoned, went free. On other occasions, the Frenchman witnessed executions, no less publicly orchestrated, an exorcism, an excommunication, and a Jewish circumcision, which he implicitly compared to a Christian baptism.

A final characteristic fundamental to Montaigne's account of the same-sex marriages is the way it is associated with, indeed sandwiched into, a political report concerning Portugal, Spain, and the papacy. This interwoven structure requires that we look at the two stories together. Montaigne had gone to the Vatican to watch, or at least was there at the same time as, a religious–diplomatic ceremony that generates a narrative in three stages. Directly preceding the same-sex marriage story, the first stage comprises a factual detail intended to amuse. On March 18, Montaigne tells us, the Portuguese ambassador did obeisance to the pope on behalf of King Philip; this was the same ambassador who had previously represented the deceased king and the Estates opposed to Philip. What it is necessary to understand to appreciate fully the irony of the situation is that the King Philip in question is Philip II of Spain, who, following the death of Portugal's King Henry just the previous year, had sent troops into that country to press his claim to its throne. In 1581, then, the fidelity of the Portuguese nation to the papacy was offered in the name of the Spanish ruler to whom it was in the process of being subjected. Alluding to the country's subjugated status, Montaigne's informant makes his first witticism by pointing out that this ceremony of obeisance was taking place in Passion Week, the beginning of the annual liturgical celebration of Christ's suffering and death, a time fitting for an event that involved considerable humiliation for the ambassador and his countrymen.

What is not evident from Montaigne's account is that, paradoxically, the event was also a rather humiliating exercise for Gregory XIII, since the pope had initially opposed Philip's pursuit of the Portuguese throne and consequent expansion of his domains. Throughout the sixteenth century, the relationship between the papacy and the Spanish crown was characterized by close cooperation and alliance but also rivalry, as each party constantly maneuvered to press its own advantage.[21] Spain, moreover, was the most influential power in the Italian peninsula: Philip II was also Duke of Milan and King of Naples, two territories that surrounded the Papal States to the north and to the south. The city of Rome was home to such a large number of Spaniards—from high ecclesiastics to the humblest of artisans and servants—that Thomas Dandelet refers to them as "colonizers for a form of . . . 'soft,' or informal, imperialism."[22] If Gregory XIII was opposed to Philip's annexation of Portugal, it had, in a further ironic twist of fate, been enabled in large part by the pope's own refusal to release King Henry, who was in clerical orders and a cardinal, from his vow of celibacy, thus preventing him from marrying and potentially producing an heir. By ensuring the creation of the dynastic void that Philip exploited, the pope was in no small measure responsible for the very political consequences he would have preferred to avoid.[23] Eventually, both the Portuguese and the pope were forced to accept the reality of the situation, although the latter did so first. Gregory received Philip's ambassador in mid-March; only four weeks later, at the Cortes of Tomar, would Philip be recognized by Portugal's nobility, on condition that he maintain the distinctness of the kingdom and respect many of its traditional institutions.

Montaigne watched the lavish procession of the Portuguese/Spanish ambassador, Don Juan Gomez da Silva, through the streets of the city to the Vatican, but refrained from entering the papal palace to hear the speeches and witness the ceremony. What would he have seen had he done so? Among a large company of prelates and members of the papal household, Gomez da Silva approached Gregory XIII, seated on a throne in the *sala regia* (Regal Room); as he did so, he genuflected three times. Kneeling, he kissed the pope's right foot, then his hand, and finally, as Gregory gestured to him to rise, he kissed the pope on the cheek. The ambassador presented letters from Philip that Gregory received and kissed, handing them to one of his secretaries. After the pope had removed the "precious" (i.e., ceremonial, jewel-encrusted) miter he was wearing and replaced it with a simple gold one, the king's missive was read aloud. A brief but eloquent speech was then delivered by the noted Portuguese humanist at the papal court, Achilles Statius, standing next to the ambassador, to which the pope's secretary responded on behalf of the pontiff. In conclusion, the ambassador kissed the pope's foot once again, as did a large number of those who accompanied him. When everyone retired, Gomez da Silva returned to his lodgings, where a banquet had been prepared.[24]

Such a carefully calibrated series of ritual gestures reflects the protocol of court diplomacy and ecclesiastical politics. In this case, it was also a moment of triumph for the Spanish king. Nonetheless, more than a fiction of submission to the pope was being played out. Philip had certainly gained an advantage that the reception of his ambassador was marking, yet the ceremony was equally a means of acknowledging the authority of the pope and the respect due to him; it was a way of reasserting papal dignity and embodying a certain balance of power that would allow the relationship between the two rulers to continue. At the same time, a certain number of details recorded by the papal master of ceremonies give pause for thought.

Of what significance is it, for example, that the ambassador did not dress up for the ceremony, wearing only his everyday coat, although his horse and son were decked out lavishly? Or that when the papal master of ceremonies came to receive payment for his services, Gomez da Silva offered him only fifty ducats instead of the usual one hundred? On the pope's side, what are we to make of the fact that his secretary forgot his lines, causing the master of ceremonies to reflect that even Homer nods: "nam et bonus quandoque dormitat Homerus"? Or that of all the cardinals invited by Gomez da Silva to the feast almost none attended? Or, finally, and perhaps most dramatically, that having removed his ceremonial miter, the symbol par excellence of his authority, the pope neglected to put it back on, as he should have done, when he processed solemnly out of the audience? If this was a result of oversight or forgetfulness on the part of the pope or the master of ceremonies, it is difficult for the modern reader not to think in the anachronistic terms of a Freudian slip. In this way, if a version of reality was being crafted by this rite of diplomatic reception, it was not without difficulty or without the ritual reflecting the tensions and pressures of the political problems in which it was caught up.

What Montaigne refers to allusively as the "Spanish ceremony" was thus a highly charged ritual taking place in a tense political context; it was also itself a crucial moment in the series of events that served to establish Philip II on the Portuguese throne. Montaigne concludes this third stage of his narrative with a final detail concerning another ambassador, that of the Russian tsar, Ivan IV the Terrible, who claims to find the proceedings distinctly unimpressive. Only a political actor on the edge of events, on the edge of Europe, as well as belonging to a different Church, the Orthodox, might look on with such apparent detachment and amusement. The Russian ambassador's pose was not without feint, however. As Montaigne already knew, his mission was to persuade the pope to discourage the Polish king from attacking the tsar, on the grounds that this would weaken Russia's ability to resist invasion by the Turks. The emissary thus had his own pressing political agenda to present to the pope (*Journal*, 110–11; *Works*, 1158).

What, finally, of Montaigne himself? Why did he go to Saint Peter's on March 18? Why does he interrupt his account of a diplomatic event with a sexual one? And why did he look on from outside only and not go into the Vatican to see the ceremony? As noted earlier, the *Journal de voyage* was largely a personal document, not intended for publication. Nonetheless, developing the work of Warren Boutcher and others, Philippe Desan has argued that the essayist was not a simple tourist in Rome, but was hoping to be named France's ambassador to the Holy See.[25] The current ambassador, Louis Chasteignier d'Abain et de la Roche-Posay, was a friend of Montaigne, who, on the latter's arrival, had presented him to the pope. For more than a year, La Roche-Posay had been seeking to be relieved of his functions, a request to which the French king acceded in late February 1581, without however naming a replacement. Toward the end of April, Henry III would appoint Paul de Foix to the post, but in the meantime, letters were sent on March 13 and 17, placing the king's affairs temporarily in the hands of Cardinal d'Este. On March 18, however, these letters had not yet arrived in Rome;[26] at this point then, if Montaigne was in fact hoping to receive an ambassadorial nomination, he would have been waiting in the wings, his expectations intact and at their height. In this light, the notes he was making in his journal might have been intended to serve the more practical purpose of constituting a record of information on which he might draw when composing his first dispatches to the French court.

The passage concerning the reception of Philip II's ambassador and the same-sex marriages does not constitute a diplomatic report; nevertheless, it is interesting to consider it from this point of view. According to Timothy Hampton, the *Essais* exemplify "a kind of anti-diplomacy, a private rhetoric," stressing limitation, exploration, and self-correction.[27] If the *Journal de voyage*, like the *Essais*, expresses a skeptical outlook, we can also discern in it— especially in these pages dedicated to the visitor's early days in Rome—various strategies of diplomatic writing as recommended by theorists like Machiavelli.[28] We see Montaigne positioning himself between the papal city and curia and France as an intermediary with access to people of importance, people with influence or information, relating what he sees and hears. His recounting of the "Spanish ceremony" shows him to be in contact with knowing observers, who tell him of the attitudes of the people of Rome, as well as with political figures, like the ambassador from the tsar. Philip II was France's great rival—a rivalry played out every day at the papal court. The French monarch would certainly have expected his ambassador to be able to inform him about the reception of Philip's ambassador for Portugal and the recognition this afforded; he would surely not have wanted his representative to attend any such ceremony, however, since this would have implied his approval or at least acceptance of a situation that he too had been at considerable pains to avert. In 1579, Henry III had written repeatedly to La Roche-Posay, instructing him to petition Gregory to release Henry of Portugal from his vow of celibacy in order to enable him to produce an heir.[29] As we have seen, these efforts came to nothing, and the pope never risked provoking Philip's wrath in this way. An account of the reception of the ambassador that included something of a put-down might thus have been quite to the taste of the French king.

What finally are we to make of the interweaving of the accounts of the political situation and the same-sex marriages? Might Henry III, the object of widespread satire on account of his relationships with his *mignons*, have been equally interested in both? It is true that the *Journal de voyage* often seems to revel in making unexpected juxtapositions. It is also true that the Iberian men's executions cannot be considered a mere *fait divers* without international ramifications, and they are related, as we shall see, alongside political information by a number of diplomats and commentators in their reports. Nevertheless, in the *Journal*, the political and marital stories not only sit next to each other, they are imbricated one in the other, an arrangement that is even more striking in the first eighteenth-century printings that lack the paragraph breaks introduced by modern editors.

As Montaigne presents them, the two stories are linked narratively through a series of corresponding and contrasting elements involving time, place, and national origin. On the same day as the reception of Philip II's ambassador for Portugal—according to the Catholic liturgical calendar, the Saturday in Passion Week—the station church was Saint John at the Latin Gate; in that place, three years earlier, other Portuguese men had performed other religious rituals by which they had married each other. What this means is that on the same day as the ceremony of Portugal's obeisance to the Roman pontiff, worshippers would have assembled at Saint John at the Latin Gate for a procession and mass. While historically the pope himself was usually present at the station celebrations, this may or may not have been the case at this point in time; without doubt, however, the assembled chapter of the canons of Rome's cathedral of Saint John Lateran would certainly have been in attendance.[30] In this way, the particular rites prescribed for the observance of Lent in Rome revolved around a place where, after only three years, the story of the Iberians associated with it was still very much alive in people's memories, including no doubt that of Pope Gregory. On March 18, 1581, the liturgical calendar, with its annual cyclical celebrations, thus had the effect of recalling not only Christ's passion and execution but also the more recent passions and executions of "certain Portuguese men," bringing both together with the suffering of all the Portuguese, as an ambassador offered the submission of their nation to the pope in the name of a monarch to whom they were in the process of being forced to submit.

For Montaigne's informant (and perhaps for Montaigne?) is this link grounded simply in coincidence? Or is a correspondence implied between the political subjection of the Portuguese and their marrying each other that depends on an imaginary equivalence between political submission and sexual submission? Such a correspondence seems to be mediated by the lexical nexus of the Latin *patior/patiens*, evoking suffering, subjection, (Christ's) passion, (sexual) passivity, and femininity/effeminacy. As we shall discover, a crucial historical detail that would suggest that this might indeed be the case is that only one of the men arrested and executed was actually Portuguese, another was of Albanian origin, six were Spanish. The historical reality, then, is that it was not men from a country about to be taken over who married each other, but men from the "virile" conquering nation. The occulting of the Spanish from the "male to male" marriages, the association of these uniquely with the *patient* Portuguese, goes hand in hand with—in some sense perhaps accounts for—that country's subjection. The presentation of information concerning the men's national origins thus seems to point to the ways in which their story has been inflected by political considerations; equally, and conversely, a sexual economy influences a political one as a gendered vision of erotic desire is projected onto international relations. To the extent that it establishes definitions based not on sexual practices, but on forms of desire and the objects to which desire is directed, to the extent that it associates submission with the homo rather than with male sexual passivity, such a vision resonates with ideas that will become dominant in the West under the guise of "modern" sexuality.

Chapter 2

"Our Marriages"? Male to Male / Like Husband and Wife

Among some Portuguese and Spanish men, eleven have been captured, who, assembled in a church in the vicinity of Saint John Lateran, carried out certain ceremonies, and with terrible wickedness sullying the holy name of matrimony, married each other, joining together like husband with wife. On the majority of occasions, twenty-seven of them gathered together and more, but this time it was only possible to seize these eleven, who will go to the stake as they deserve.

Sono stati presi undeci fra Portughesi et Spagnuoli, i quali adunatissi in una chiesa, ch'è vicina à S. Giovanni Laterano, facevano alcune lor cerimonie, et con horrenda sceleraggine bruttando il sacrosanto nome di matrimonio, si maritavano l'un con l'altro, congiongendosi insieme, come marito con moglie. Vintisette si trovavano, et più, insieme il più delle volte, ma questa volta non ne hanno potuto coglier più che questi undeci, i quali anderanno al fuoco, et come meritano.[1]

This second testimony comes from a dispatch of the Venetian ambassador in Rome, Antonio Tiepolo (1526–82). Tiepolo belonged to an illustrious family and had a distinguished diplomatic career. From 1564–67, he served as the republic's resident ambassador to the Spanish court. In 1571–72, he returned to Iberia as an extraordinary ambassador, meeting in Spain with Philip II and in Portugal with King Sebastian and the future King Henry.[2] His earlier professional contacts may thus have left him with more than a passing interest in the people and affairs of these nations. In Rome, Antonio succeeded his relative Paolo Tiepolo, who incurred the disfavor of Gregory XIII after Venice negotiated a treaty with the Turks.[3] Antonio Tiepolo's dispatch, dated August 2, 1578, was written after the group at the Latin Gate had been arrested but prior to the executions it announces. In many respects,

Tiepolo's testimony corroborates that of Montaigne, though not without a number of discrepancies in detail.

First, Tiepolo is less specific concerning the place where the wedding ceremonies were performed, indicating a church in the vicinity of Saint John Lateran. If this statement is not in exact agreement with Montaigne, neither is it contradictory: while the two basilicas are not adjacent, they are both located in the southeast section of the city, close to the Aurelian Walls. Saint John at the Latin Gate is less well known, but in Montaigne's *Journal*, as we have seen, it constitutes a key element of the narrative. Tiepolo had no reason to be so precise and perhaps thought it more useful to refer to the more famous edifice. As we shall see later, there are additional factors connecting the two locations that may also account for Tiepolo's privileging of the Lateran basilica.

Tiepolo diverges significantly from Montaigne, however, in his indication of the nationality of the men involved and their number. Those arrested and executed, according to the Venetian ambassador, were not only Portuguese, but Portuguese and Spanish. Tiepolo also indicates that more men were taken prisoner—eleven—than Montaigne's informant tells him were executed—eight or nine. Furthermore, the Venetian stresses that the men captured were part of a much larger group, most of whom succeeded in escaping. The rather precise figure of "twenty-seven . . . and more" might even suggest that the authorities were able to establish a list of this many names at the same time as they knew or suspected that yet others had not been identified. Tiepolo's dispatch thus invites us to envisage a sizable network of men who met together perhaps with some regularity and certainly on more than one occasion. Such a scenario raises the issue of how the men were ultimately apprehended, suggesting that their activities might have become visible to the point of triggering their denunciation.

Tiepolo and Montaigne agree that the men performed some kind of wedding ceremony. At the same time, there are differences in expression between the two writers that are significant and that go beyond the fact that the ironic tolerance of Montaigne is far removed from the ambassador's religious indignation. Tiepolo, like Montaigne, affirms that the men married ("si maritavano l'un con l'altro"), but he does not specify that they followed faithfully the ritual of a typical wedding between a man and a woman. Rather, he states that they defiled the name of holy matrimony with "alcune lor cerimonie" (certain ceremonies; literally, some ceremonies of theirs) and by joining together like husband and wife or, again more literally, like a husband with his wife ("congiongendosi insieme, come marito con moglie").

The reflexive verb *congiungersi* means to join together or to unite, here like spouses, but it also carries strong connotations of the consummation of a union through the act of sex. It is this verb, for example, that is used in the medieval Italian translation of the Bible, *La Bibbia volgare*, to describe the crime, in Leviticus 20:15–16, of a man or woman having sexual intercourse with an animal. It is also found with this meaning in the short stories of Boccaccio and Bandello.[4] The corresponding nouns, *congiungimento* (or *congiugnimento*) and *congiunzione* could have the same meaning, like their French cognate, *conjonction*, used by Montaigne, as we saw earlier, to refer to sexual relations between men and women.[5] A sexual meaning is conveyed even more explicitly, however, by Montaigne's phrase "puis couchoient et habitoient ensemble," which is why the published translation by Donald Frame—"then went to bed and lived together"—was amended in the previous chapter to read "then went to bed and slept with each other." The very logical progression of going to bed and living together is odd and should alert us to a distortion of sense. In sixteenth-century French, *habiter* is in fact a common euphemism for having sexual relations. To give only one particularly illustrative example: in the fiftieth tale of Boccaccio's *Decameron*, a wife complains that her sodomite husband neglects her sexually in order to pursue his shameful pleasures. In his 1545 French translation of the work, Antoine Le Maçon rendered the wife's accusation of her husband as "Ce malheureux laisse *d'habiter avec moy*" (my italics).[6] At no point, however, is there any suggestion of the husband leaving his wife, of his moving out of their house so that they would no longer be living together. The wife is complaining that he does not have sex with her.[7]

Whatever might have preceded, then, Montaigne and Tiepolo are in agreement that the men's actions culminated in their having sex, likely in a public or semi-public manner. While to modern sensibilities such a scenario might call to mind more the idea of an orgy than a wedding, in an early modern context it does not necessarily undermine the idea of matrimony, since the act of sexual intercourse, sometimes with only minimal privacy afforded to the spouses, was a regular part of the series of steps that made up a marriage celebration. At a particular point in the festivities, the newly wed couple would be escorted to an adjacent bedroom, from where they were not expected to emerge until the marriage had been duly consummated.

At this point, then, it will be useful to look in more detail at late medieval and early modern marriage practices more generally, as well as at other forms of relationships that existed at the time. Montaigne writes that the men joined together "male to male" in the same way that "we perform our marriages"; Tiepolo describes them as uniting "like a husband with his wife." These two formulations are not exactly equivalent, Tiepolo conveying more explicitly the clearly gendered roles that marriage involved.

In the fifteenth and sixteenth centuries, the institution of marriage was in something of a state of crisis and undergoing profound transformation.[8] Marriage involves a tension between legal and affective elements, between secular and sacred aspects, and between individual, family, community, and societal interests. At the beginning of the early modern period, the right to control marriage—to determine when one was valid and legal and when it was not—became a highly contested matter in a way that Montaigne's use of the first-person plural elides. Traditionally, two people united in marriage for a range of mostly practical reasons. At the top of the social scale noble households married their offspring in order to make political alliances and to ensure the continuation of their lineage. At a lower level, families with possessions of any kind shared similar economic concerns for their lands, livestock, real estate, businesses, and so on. Those engaged in artisanal professions often sought a partner with whom to share tasks. Marriage involved setting up a household based on a common livelihood. People with little or no financial means might well find themselves excluded from the formal institution altogether or at least until relatively late in life when they had been able to set aside some savings; such was often the case, for example, with domestic servants. Marriage was also strongly marked by a gendered asymmetry in that the rights and responsibilities it gave to men and to women were not the same. Marriage did not found a relationship of equality: husbands became the head of a household, wives were expected to be submissive; husbands gained over their wives a whole range of legal prerogatives of which the latter were deprived. In the words of Trevor Dean and K. J. P. Lowe, "marriage was understood to be a different act for women and men . . . the ideology of marriage carried within it the expression of a power relation which was convenient and pervasive . . . to the detriment of other configurations of partnership."[9]

As we have seen, a correct reading of Montaigne removes the idea of the Spaniards and Portuguese men in Rome setting up house together. Might they have married for love? Clearly for some but not all medieval and early modern spouses, marriage also involved an affective relationship. For the luckiest of these, an emotional engagement may have been present from the beginning; for others, it perhaps developed over time. In general, however, love or erotic passion was not a principal reason for entering into matrimony, and Montaigne, for one, was doubtful concerning this combination. Marriage, for the essayist, was primarily a familial and social affair, one he himself had been more carried toward than pursued: "je ne m'y conviay pas proprement, on m'y mena, et y fus porté par des occasions estrangeres" (*Œuvres*, 830) (I did not really bid myself to it, I was led to it, and borne by extraneous circumstances [*Works*, 786]). At its best, marriage should nonetheless involve an affection similar to friendship—but inferior to the perfect amity that might exist between two men—along with sexual intimacy—but of a less intense nature than with a mistress.[10]

Montaigne does not dwell on questions of the legitimacy or illegitimacy of sexual activities or of the children they might produce; these were primary concerns of the Church, however, in its regulation of marriage. The Church was also interested in the two spouses' freely given consent, insisting strongly on this requirement, even if theologians' understanding of it evolved over time. The twelfth century was a particularly crucial moment in the history of marriage, for it is then that matrimony began to be considered one of the seven sacraments. It was also debated by canonists and theologians such as Gratian, for whom betrothal was the beginning of a process of which coitus constituted the ultimate ratification. Consummation was always an important factor, yet it was never able to become a necessary and defining one due to the Church's belief in the perpetual virginity of Mary and, as a corollary, the unconsummated nature of the marriage of the mother and foster father of Jesus. For Peter Lombard, most influentially, spousal consent expressed in the present tense (*verba de praesenti*) was sufficient to seal a marriage and had immediate effect. This view came to prevail, yet coitus did not lose all importance. Discussion continued, for example, about the value of a promise of future marriage (*verba de futuro*), leaving Pope Alexander III to rule that an engagement to marry in the future followed by sexual relations was considered as having been de facto ratified in the present. Conversely, a marriage made with vows in the present but remaining unconsummated could be dissolved in certain circumstances, notably if either spouse decided to enter religious life. Subsequent popes confirmed and extended their authority to dissolve valid but unconsummated marriages.[11]

This range of beliefs and attitudes, and especially the insistence on the expression of spousal intent and the absence of a formal requirement for the presence of witnesses, traditionally afforded a degree of latitude for individual agency, a space within which men and women might maneuver. In the sixteenth century, while belief in male superiority and wifely submission remained firmly intact, the ideal of affection and companionship shared between spouses was also strengthened and developed by humanists like Juan Luis Vives in his *De Institutione feminae christianae* (1524). The issue of marriage contracted between two people, unbeknownst to or despite the opposition of one or both of their families, on the basis of their love for each other or under the influence of erotic passion, also became a major preoccupation. The literature of the time, indeed, is replete with plots that raise the question in diverse and complex situations, involving the more or less private actions of a couple and their legal validity or their perception by those around them. One of the most famous developments on this theme is Shakespeare's *Romeo and Juliette* (first published 1597), in which the couple marries in the presence of Friar Laurence but secretly and without the knowledge of their families. One of the sources of the English play was a novella by the Italian writer Matteo Bandello (1554). Other of Bandello's *Novelle* treat similar problems, such as I, 42, concerning Didaco Centiglia, a knight who falls in love with Violante, a beautiful woman belonging to a family of goldsmiths, with whom he exchanges vows privately in the presence only of her family and of a trusted servant. He later abandons her for a more advantageous match, celebrated openly in public, intending nonetheless to keep her as his mistress. To avenge her lost honor, Violante, with the aid of a slave, murders Didaco, tearing his body to pieces. When this novella was reworked in French by Pierre Boaistuau (*Histoires tragiques*, no. 5; 1559), the story raised the dilemma to an even higher pitch by having the marriage of Violente (as her name is now spelled) celebrated by a country priest ("un prestre des champs"). Despite this fact, the mother and brothers of the abandoned bride choose not to seek legal recourse against Didaco, given their lack of independent proof (they do not know the identity of the priest) and fearful of the consequences of bringing a case against a social superior.[12]

In France, the issue of secret marriages, based on vows exchanged by a couple, in one case without any witnesses, had appeared earlier in two short stories of the *Heptaméron*, a collection that Marguerite de Navarre, the sister of King Francis I, left incomplete at her death in 1549.[13] Clandestine marriage is also prominent in the most successful multivolume series of novels published over the course of the sixteenth and into the seventeenth century in France, *Amadis de Gaule*, translated from the original Spanish, *Amadis de Gaula*, of Garci Rodríguez de Montalvo and his continuers, as well as from sequels in Italian and German. The decline in popularity of the novels in the later decades of the sixteenth century, moreover, has been related to evolving attitudes among the French aristocracy and a less ready acceptance of clandestine marriage, specifically in the wake of an edict of King Henry II in February 1556. This allowed parents to disinherit a child who married without their agreement up to the age of twenty-five for a woman and thirty for a man.[14]

Perhaps unsurprisingly, since Miguel Cervantes set out to parody much of the tradition of chivalric romance—with certain exceptions, including the first volumes of *Amadis*—the issue of marriage is a major narrative resource in *Don Quixote*. At the center of the first volume of the novel, published in 1605, are three marriages of variously questionable legality: between Cardenio and Luscinda, between Don Fernando and Dorotea, and between Don Fernando and Luscinda. The first involves a private promise only, but one that the two individuals firmly maintain; the second is based on a promise, witnessed by a servant, the gift of a ring, and sexual consummation; the third involves vows made in front of a priest but with witnesses from only one of the two families and in which the young woman is constrained against her will by her parents, a fact she records on paper along with her intention, after the ceremony, to take her own life. When all the dispersed protagonists finally meet up in an inn, the two original couples re-form and everyone comes to agree that the first two marriages invalidate the third, which was, nonetheless, the only one performed in the presence of a priest and of the bride's family.[15]

These examples from fictional literature reveal the extent to which the considerable gray areas surrounding marriage were a rich source for narrative action and the representation of social and psychological dilemmas that engaged the minds and hearts of contemporary readers. It is also clear from legal records that similarly complex and questionable situations were not rare in reality and that young people used promises to marry, as well as claims to have or not to have married, to their own advantage: to persuade another person to have sex, to justify a sexual relationship retrospectively, or to do the opposite—to seek to extricate themselves from an engagement rashly or calculatingly made and known to be in one way or another questionable. People were aware, that is, of the importance of consent and manipulated the latitude for action that its contemporary understanding gave them.[16] Consent, as we have seen, was defended by the Church, but people like Ginzburg's Menocchio might also accept this basic principle while rejecting any involvement of religious authorities. In the words of the miller from Friuli, "God did not establish [marriage], men did. Formerly a man and a woman would exchange vows, and this sufficed; later these human inventions followed." Church weddings, for Menocchio, were merely part of the "merchandise" and "business" of the Church, a money-making scam that he denounced.[17]

In Protestant countries, religious reformers also denied that marriage was a sacrament, a position that allowed them to move, by contrast, firmly and decisively in the direction of strengthening the rights of parents over those of their children. For its part, the Catholic Church successfully maintained its prerogatives with respect to defining and controlling what it continued to consider a sacrament, though in many places secular authorities sought to pass legislation favoring the interests of families. In general, they did so by operating around the issue of defining who was legally able to consent, frequently seeking to raise the age of majority in order to make young people dependent on their parents for as long as possible. Reference has been made to the 1556 edict of Henry II of France. In Italy, various cities and districts passed similar laws, even if their validity was contested by the Church since canon law equated the ability to consent with the onset of puberty. The rubrics published in the wake of the Council of Trent set this at age twelve for females and fourteen for males.[18] Nonetheless, in one of the final sessions of the Council in 1563, the Catholic Church did respond to the concerns of secular authorities as well as follow its own avowed desire to prevent the sinful irregularities that might occur when someone abandoned a marriage contracted privately for a public one. The decree *Tametsi* did not impose the requirement of parental agreement and reaffirmed that marriages termed clandestine for this reason were valid; it did, however, institute a number of other legal and ritual conditions, without which a union would henceforth be considered canonically null and void. Principally, the Council of Trent reaffirmed (following the Fourth Lateran Council) that a marriage must be preceded by the publication of banns and added the new requirement that it take place not only in the parish church of one of the spouses but also in the presence of the parish priest (or his delegate or the ordinary) and of two or three witnesses.[19]

Despite the new Tridentine legislation, attitudes toward marriage and the practices surrounding it evolved slowly and unevenly across Europe. As much can be surmised from the literary sources discussed earlier, a number of which, like Cervantes's *Don Quixote*, were written several decades after the promulgation of the 1563 decree. In Italy in particular weddings frequently continued to be celebrated not in church in front of a priest but at home in the presence of a notary, whose role was to draw up the contract between the spouses and their families. In well-to-do circles in Italy, furthermore, marriage was not generally seen as being effected instantaneously by two individual expressions of will nor as requiring any sacerdotal blessing or ecclesiastical intervention; it remained a process involving the families and community that proceeded from the engagement negotiations and agreement, to the formal signing of the contract, to the procession of the bride through the streets with the possessions she was bringing to the new household, some stored in specially decorated marriage chests, to the reception of the wife by her husband into the conjugal dwelling, a celebratory banquet, and, finally, to the consummation of the union through sexual intercourse. Conversely, even if a priest witnessed a marriage but one or both of the families were not party to it, it might still be possible to find a way to have the marriage declared invalid. This is reflected in the situation of Boaistuau's Violente, whose brothers, despite the religious ceremony they witnessed, fear their inability to win a suit on behalf of their sister against a man her social superior whose family was excluded.

In his story of the Portuguese and Spanish men, Montaigne presents the elements of a wedding as involving mass, communion, and sexual consummation. The reality of marriage negotiations between families who had any form of wealth, however, was usually vastly more complex—as indeed it had been in Montaigne's own case when, in 1565, he had agreed to marry Françoise de La Chassaigne, whose dowry was paid out over a period of three-and-a-half years. It is also the case that a religious ceremony was a much more well-established marriage custom in France than it was in Italy, so that Montaigne's notion of how "we" perform "our" marriages might reflect something of his own typically French attitudes and assumptions.

Corroboration of certain aspects of Montaigne's account comes, however, from another early source, a series of anonymous manuscript newsletters or *avvisi* sent from Rome to the German family of international bankers, the Fuggers, as events unfolded, on August 2, 9, 16, and 23. The first of these, composed on the same day as Tiepolo's dispatch, refers to a wedding performed by "un certo Heremita malvagio, ilqual dopo celebrata la messa sposava loro con l'annello a coppia a coppia, come marito et moglie" (a certain evil hermit, who, after the celebration of mass, married them with a ring in couples, like husband and wife).[20] The writer immediately adds, however, "tirandossi anco de fanciulli, dequali si servivano nefandamente" (dragging along also some boys, whom they used most shamefully), the final adverb, from the Latin *nefandus* (literally, unmentionable or unspeakable), being a term commonly used to designate sodomy.[21] Here, then, is additional evidence of the celebration of a mass by a hermit and of a marriage ritual, now said to involve several couples and the giving of rings. These actions are once again associated directly with sexual activity, however—indeed with the sexual exploitation of young boys in a way that, as we shall see, reflects a contemporary pederastic structuring of desire and its expression. As we shall also discover shortly, similar sexual scenarios are portrayed in other early sources. Before turning to these, given the complexity and the variety of ideas and practices concerning marriage, we can ask whether this situation might have encouraged in the Iberians in Rome a sense of autonomy—a belief in their ability to marry in the way they desired, comparable to that of two people of the opposite sex. At the same time, as we shall see in the next chapter, a desire to marry, as opposed to contracting some other form of relationship, and especially to marry in a church, might conversely reflect their conformity to a newly emerging hegemony. We shall also examine a broad range of attitudes and social practices with which such a project might resonate.

Chapter 3

Marriage—Rites, Analogues, Meanings

Since, from a legal point of view, marriage was first and foremost a contract, it can be compared to other forms of contractual and affective relationships current in late medieval and early modern Europe. Most notably, it shared important characteristics with the *affrèrement*, or adoptive brotherhood, that was common around the Mediterranean in France, Italy, and Spain.[1] *Affrèrements* sometimes involved several or even many men, related or not by blood, and, if they were married, their wives and any children; they might also be entered into, however, by an unrelated couple, again generally men.[2] Such arrangements were for life, but could be dissolved, either by mutual agreement or subject to the payment of a specified penalty by the party or parties to be released; they involved holding financial resources in common and frequently inhabiting a single dwelling.

The question requires further historical investigation, but the *affrèrement* seems also to have been related to sworn or wedded brotherhood or friendship. John Boswell described Eastern Orthodox liturgies of *adelphopoiesis* as a form of same-sex union that, in some cases, might well have involved a sexual relationship.[3] There is evidence of the existence of similar ceremonies in the West: an *ordo ad fratres faciendum* (order for the making of brothers) is attested in fourteenth-century Dalmatia, for example. And in France in the fifteenth century, brotherhoods were sworn solemnly in church; they became increasingly rare, however, and it is difficult to know how common they might have remained in any Catholic country in the sixteenth century, especially after the reforms of the Council of Trent.[4]

As we noted earlier, Boswell considered that the Iberians in Rome, described by Montaigne, were involved in performing a brotherhood ceremony. In large part, this hypothesis was based on an altered text of the *Journal de voyage*, which led the historian to believe he was dealing with a description of official ceremonies performed by the Roman Catholic Church. Without following Boswell's reading of Montaigne, I also suggested in a preliminary discussion of the topic—on the basis of Tiepolo's less specific account—that the ceremonies in question might be best understood in the context of the tradition of sworn or wedded brotherhood/friendship and that they might not have reproduced exactly—as Montaigne's informant claims—a wedding between a man and a woman.[5] At this point, however, we can appreciate that a ceremony involving an exchange of vows and perhaps the taking of communion together in church would have constituted a ritual, if not identical in nature, at least very similar to and fulfilling the principal conditions of a marriage according to a traditional pre-Tridentine understanding (which did not require the presence of a priest). It is perhaps for this reason that, even though such a union would not be recognized by religious or civil powers, both Montaigne and Tiepolo write of the Iberians as in fact marrying.

The closeness of marriage to other forms of relationship was reinforced theologically by its being made by mutual consent and the union of souls, and not necessarily by carnal union—ideas developed in no small part, as noted earlier, in conjunction with or response to the belief in the nonsexual nature of the marriage of Mary and Joseph. It is in this context, moreover, that the French theologian Jean Gerson (1363–1429) could discuss directly, if briefly, the idea of marriage between two men or two women:

> Let us also consider that from what is said we cannot conclude as some have sought to argue, namely, that marriage could be between two men, since it is sufficient for marriage that the bodies give themselves to each other without carnal use or that the souls are united. Master Hugh of Saint Victor wrote a

treatise to refute this frivolous objection, demonstrating that between two men or two women there can be no sacrament of marriage because what is signified would be absent, that is, God and Holy Church on the one hand and God and the soul on the other hand. For in marriage, in one of the parties there must be authority and perfect and as it were active virtue, as are in the man, which represents God; and in the other party there must be lack and as it were passive virtue, as are in the woman, which represents Holy Church and the soul. Now this combination and concord cannot be found between two men or two women, as will be evident to anyone who thinks about it. But marriage by its nature also brings with it the conjoining of male and female for the purpose of generating offspring, even if some accidental case may arise as a result of which this end is not achieved, such as old age, illness, or sterility, or a devotion to maintain chastity or virginity.

Considerons encorez que par ce que dit est on ne peut conclure ce que aucuns vouloient arguer; c'est que mariage porroit estre entre deux hommes puis que il souffit a mariage que les corps se donnent sans usage charnel, ou que les ames soient d'un accort. Maistre Hugues de Saint Victor fit un traictie pour responde a ceste frivole obiection, et monstre que entre deux hommes ou entre deux femmes ne peut estre sacrement de mariage pour ce que la signification fauroit, qui est de Dieu et saincte Eglise d'une part, et de Dieu et de l'ame d'autre part; car en mariage doit estre en l'une des parties auctorité et vertus parfaite et comme active, qui est en l'omme, et represente Dieu; et en l'autre partie doit avoir indigence et comme vertus passive, qui est en la femme, et represente saincte Eglise et l'ame. Or ne peut estre ceste conbinacion et concorde trouvee entre deux ommes ne entre deux femmes, comme c'est cler a cellui qui y pense. Mais aussi mariage emporte de soy conionction de masle et de femelle pour avoir lignie, combien que puisse avenir cas accidentel pour le quel ceste fin ne se ensuit point, comme vieillesse ou maladie ou sterilité, ou par devocion de garder chasteté ou virginité.[6]

For Gerson, two reasons exclude the possibility of same-sex marriage. Copulation for the purpose of producing offspring is evoked, but in second place and as a hypothetical condition only, which serves to reduce considerably its force. Gerson acknowledges that a variety of factors, be they voluntary or involuntary, can intervene to prevent the conception of children. In the first category, we find physical limitations causing infertility, which were not recognized by the Church as grounds for the dissolution of a marriage (although impotence or the inability to have sexual relations was).[7] Gerson's second category, however, involves a willful decision on the part of spouses to refrain from sexual relations for spiritual reasons. This was believed to have been the case with Mary and Joseph, who were held to have exchanged vows with the intention of never consummating their relationship physically. Despite this notable example, such a course of action represented "a problematic position under medieval canon law."[8] Undeniably, then, we are here in a gray area of contested opinion—which inevitably undermines further the prescriptive force of Gerson's overall argument concerning intercourse and procreation.

The first and primary impediment that Gerson alleges against the wedding of two people of the same sex is of a more theoretical and hierarchical order. Like all sacraments, marriage has a signified, which is the union of God and the Church or God and the soul. Consequently, Gerson affirms, it requires two parties: the one perfect, authoritative, and active, that is, male; the other lacking and passive, that is, female. In this instance, the argument is clearly tied to historical understandings of gender that very few women or men at the beginning of the twenty-first century in the West would accept. Similarly, it is not a vision that would resonate with present-day understandings of same-sex relationships in terms of equality. Historically, it would have aligned well enough with a pederastic (age/rank-graded) model of male–male sexual relations, though Gerson does not envisage this possibility, thinking probably in essentialist terms of male accomplishment and female lack. Nonetheless, it is striking that this vision of marriage does not require as its fundamental condition a male and a female; it requires inequality. Maleness and femaleness fulfill this requirement secondarily and to the extent they are considered ontologically perfect and imperfect.[9]

Such a vision was certainly shared by many late medieval and early modern Europeans, but there were also voices, mostly female, such as those of Christine de Pisan (c. 1363–c. 1430) and Montaigne's posthumous editor, Marie de Gournay (c. 1566–1645), who strenuously contested it. Another aspect of Gerson's treatment of the issue that might well have been contested is the nonsexual nature of the same-sex unions envisaged. Undoubtedly, for the theologian, carnal relations between men or between women would have constituted the sin of sodomy. It is therefore a relationship like friendship or brotherhood that Gerson can envisage as proximate to a chaste marriage. Gerson is not following his own train of thought here, however; rather, he is responding negatively to unnamed others ("aucuns"), who have advanced this argument. It is not clear to whom Gerson is referring specifically and whether he has in mind published opinions or ideas circulating orally. It might be the case that the "frivolous" proposition is evoked in a purely hypothetical manner.[10] Even so, it would seem justified to conclude that such a heterodox view must have had sufficient purchase, in the late fourteenth and early fifteenth centuries, to merit rebuttal by the chancellor of the University of Paris in a devotional tract designed to promote the veneration of Saint Joseph. It also seems quite possible that, even if Gerson limits his discussion to this scenario, not all those who formulated such arguments would necessarily have thought only in terms of chaste same-sex marriage.

While brotherhood contracts and ceremonies form part of the wider context of possible relationships within which late medieval and early modern individuals might have situated marriage, the fact remains that all of the contemporary sources relative to the Iberians in Rome speak of them as marrying and that *affrèrements* and sworn or wedded friendship or brotherhood were unquestionably in the process of disappearing. The gradual effacement of these traditional forms of relationship coincided with the increased assertion of control over marriage by secular and ecclesiastical authorities. This is no coincidence. Affirmation of Church–state control over marriage and the limiting of permitted relationship contracts to marriage went hand in hand as two sides of a single process. The Portuguese and Spaniards in Rome might thus be seen as reflecting an authoritarian evolution in their desire to marry, as much as exploiting more traditional liberties in deeming that it lay within their power for them to do so.

If the Iberians did marry in a way that followed the main elements involved in a religious wedding between a man and a woman, what is that likely to have entailed? As we have seen, the Catholic Church issued a decree concerning the reformation of marriage in 1563. Following the conclusion of the Council of Trent, liturgical texts began to be reedited, with the new missal appearing in 1570. By 1578, the rite it prescribed would have represented the standard form for the celebration of mass in Rome. The revised Roman ritual, however, containing the rite for the solemnization of matrimony would only be published several decades later in 1614. The scenario presented by Montaigne in fact presumes a wedding accompanied by a nuptial mass, *missa pro sponso et sponsa*, since only at mass would a passage from the gospels have been read and communion administered. In its post-Tridentine form, the rite laid down for the sacrament of matrimony is short;

indeed, it takes up fewer pages in the printed ritual than do the instructions setting out the preliminary verifications to be made by the priest to ensure that the couple has the right to marry and is doing so in conformity with the new precepts.[11] The rite itself consists of three main elements, the first and most important being the exchange of vows. The priest asks the bride and groom separately, in their native tongue, if they desire to take the other as their legitimate husband or wife, according to the rites of the Church. Each is to respond that he or she does ("Volo": I so desire; It is my will). Following this exchange of consent, the priest has the couple join right hands and pronounces the formula "Ego coniungo vos in matrimonium. In nomine Patris, et Filii, et Spiritus sancti. Amen" (I join you in matrimony. In the name of the Father, and of the Son, and of the Holy Spirit. Amen). Finally, a ring is blessed and given to the husband, who puts it on the ring finger of his wife's left hand.

The rite, as prescribed in the Tridentine ritual, constitutes the essentials of an early modern Church ceremony. At the same time, and especially before the first decades of the seventeenth century, considerable local variation existed from one place to another. Later in this study we shall discover links between some of the men arrested at the Latin Gate and the Spanish Netherlands. A couple marrying in this region would have done so in a way similar to that described in the *Pastorale* of the Archdiocese of Malines or Mechelen.[12] As issued in 1589, this text incorporated the new guidelines adopted by the Council of Trent and prescribed the same principal gestures. Nevertheless, the ceremony is considerably more elaborate and contains a number of significant differences. Preceding the publication of the Tridentine ritual, the *Pastorale* can be seen as a transitional document, one in which traditional regional customs have been updated in the spirit of Trent but not yet superseded by the new normative rite.

First, the *Pastorale* rubrics state that a wedding must be preceded by a formal betrothal at which relatives (or their representatives) of both parties are present. This is a requirement more in line with secular concerns than strictly religious ones. The rite of marriage itself subsequently gives a greater role to the couple. At the outset, the priest asks both to state their name and if they come of their own free will for the purpose of contracting marriage. Following a response in the affirmative, the bride and groom join right hands, around which the priest wraps his stole. He then has each intended

spouse pronounce his or her vow to the other. This is done in the vernacular, with versions given in both Flemish and French. A francophone couple
would thus have said, "Je N. donne ma foy de mariage à vous N. que je tiens
par la main, et je vous prens pour ma leale espouse / mon leal espoux devant
Dieu et sa saincte Eglise" (I, [name], plight my troth in marriage to you,
[name], whom I hold by the hand, and I take you for my faithful spouse in
the sight of God and his Holy Church). After this, the priest pronounces the
words, "*Et ego tanquam Dei minister*, vos in matrimonium coniungo: in nomine Patris, et Filii, et Spiritus sancti" (my italics) (*And I, as God's minister*,
join you in matrimony: in the name of the Father, and of the Son, and of the
Holy Spirit). The priest next asks if there is a ring for the woman. If there is,
and it has not already been blessed, he blesses it and puts it on the ring finger of the wife's right hand, saying "Accipe annulum fidei matrimonialis, in
nomine sanctissimae Trinitatis; ut illum portans, sis armata virtute caelestis
defensionis, et proficiat tibi ad salutem aeternam" (Receive the ring of mat-
rimonial fidelity in the name of the most holy Trinity, so that, wearing it,
you may be armed with the virtue of heavenly protection and advance toward
eternal salvation). Finally, there is a series of prayers, devotions, and blessings at the altar.

While the Malines rite is essentially a more complex version of the one
that would be prescribed as part of the Tridentine reforms, the two individuals contracting marriage according to it have a more developed role. If, in
this rite, the priest rather than the bridegroom places the ring on the bride's
finger, it is also clear that this is a less important part of the ceremony. Indeed, the giving of a ring to the woman is optional, and it is accompanied by
a moment of prayer/admonition to her to remain mindful of and faithful to
her promise. The implication is that she has greater need of such aid to
maintain her virtue. On the other hand, in this rite the husband and wife
exchange vows in which they express directly to each other, while holding
hands, their will to take the other in marriage; that is, they do more than
merely assent to a question addressed to them by the priest. The latter here
is more clearly a witness, and the first part of the formula that he pronounces
subsequently (italicized in the quotation) also suggests this is the case. The
degree to which the agency of the couple is evident here reflects a traditional
understanding. While after the Council of Trent, Catholic theology continued to teach that a man and a woman marry each other with the priest

acting as a witness, the liturgical rites by which the sacrament was administered in church tended to obscure this fact, emphasizing the role of the priest at the expense of that of the spouses.

If a wedding ceremony was followed by a nuptial mass, as the Tridentine rubrics recommended, then the Eucharistic rite would include prayers for and a blessing of the couple, as well as (as at every mass) a reading from one of the New Testament epistles and a gospel. If the Iberians did actually follow this ritual sequence, they would have heard the following reading from the Gospel of Saint Matthew:

> Some Pharisees came to [Jesus], and to test him they asked, "Is it lawful for a man to divorce his wife for any cause?" He answered, "Have you not read that the one who made them at the beginning 'made them male and female,' and said, 'For this reason a man shall leave his father and mother and be joined to his wife, and the two shall become one flesh'? So they are no longer two, but one flesh. Therefore what God has joined together, let no one separate." (Bible, New Revised Standard Version, Matthew 19:3–6)

> Et accesserunt ad eum pharisaei tentantes eum, et dicentes: Si licet homini dimittere uxorem suam, quacumque ex causa? Qui respondens, ait eis: Non legistis, quia qui fecit hominem ab initio, masculum et feminam fecit eos? Et dixit: Propter hoc dimittet homo patrem, et matrem, et adhaerebit uxori suae, et erunt duo in carne una. Itaque iam non sunt duo, sed una caro. Quod ergo Deus coniunxit, homo non separet. (Bible, Vulgate Version)

The nuptial gospel, in which Jesus quotes from Genesis, emphasizes a male–female binary, going back to humanity's creation, which offers both a rationale for the necessity of marriage and its moral justification. As such, it hardly represents a text that many same-sex (and no doubt some opposite-sex) couples would select for a wedding today.[13] Nonetheless, in its emphasis on male and female, the gospel reading is in line with a characteristic of printed wedding ceremonies as a whole, which refer constantly not to the couple but to the bride and groom (*sponsus* and *sponsa*) or to the husband and wife (*maritus* and *uxor*) with, at times, different roles being prescribed for each. In other words, a wedding, as a ritual event, and marriage, as a relational model, might seem likely to appeal only to a same-sex couple that adopted and conceived of itself, at least to some degree, in gender-differentiated terms.

Tiepolo, as we have seen, reflects precisely this understanding of marriage when he writes of the Iberians joining together not only like man and wife, but, giving priority to the former, "like a husband with his wife." The verb he uses, *congiungersi*, even parallels the priest's *coniungo vos*, though, as the reflexive form of *congiungere*, it emphasizes the men's own agency and takes on, as was noted earlier, strongly sexual connotations, present also in Montaigne's noun *conjonction*. By contrast, Montaigne's expression—"Ils s'espousoient masle à masle" (They married one another, male to male)— escapes this gendered and hierarchical vision, suggesting rather gender likeness, equality, and reciprocity. That Montaigne could conceive of marriages between two men in this way is itself significant and indicative of an originality and broadness of vision on the part of this educated, skeptical observer. For such characteristics were not typically associated with marriage for most early modern men and women, as is evident in the cases in which the spousal model was sometimes transferred in the popular imaginary to a male–male relationship.

The prevalent form of sexual relations between males in early modern Europe continued to follow what can be termed a pederastic model, inherited from antiquity, that involved an older or socially superior male taking an active (i.e., penetrative) sexual role with a younger or subordinate and sexually passive (i.e., receptive) one. Such relationships, simultaneously subject to legal prosecution and thoroughly implicated in current patriarchal power structures, far from being reserved to a small minority of males, might potentially involve any man or youth. While it is not the case that all early modern male–male sexual desire and activities took shape in a pederastic (age/rank-graded) form—a fact to which I shall return later—this was unquestionably the dominant cultural paradigm. As Michael Rocke notes in relation to fifteenth-century Florence, "sodomy was inextricably enmeshed in broader forms of male association and sociability in this community, from youth-group camaraderie to neighborhood ties, from occupational solidarities to patron–client relations, from kinship bonds to networks of friends. In the intensely homosocial world of Florence, *l'amore masculino* . . . was one of the threads that helped to create and reinforce bonds between males and to fashion the texture of their collective life."[14] In terms of the categories developed by Eve Sedgwick, this kind of sexual practice was thus *universalizing* as opposed to *minoritizing*.[15] "Ruler and courtier, nobleman and page, teacher and pupil, artist/craftsman and apprentice, ship's mate and cabin boy were so many power relations within which the sexual might find expression."[16] Considering the specific roles expected of each partner and the fact that sodomy was both common and a crime, it is not surprising that pederastic-type relationships were associated for many males with a particular stage in life, typically finding expression between a young adult in his twenties or early thirties, as yet unmarried, and an adolescent in his teens. A common trajectory of male sexual initiation, therefore, involved a youth being at first passive with an older male, then later adopting an active sexual role, perhaps initially with a younger male partner, before having access to sexual relations with a woman, ideally his wife.[17]

To the twenty-first-century observer, age/rank-graded relationships between males are unlikely to call up readily a comparison with marriage. Yet this is precisely what happened in early modern Europe when these relationships were maintained over time. References to such couples in terms of "man" and "wife"—sometimes clearly intended ironically or contemptuously—are documented in both Italy and Spain. Michael Rocke notes that in Florence, for example, "[c]laims that a man kept a boy explicitly 'as a wife' (*per moglie* or *come sua donna*) are common in accusations, and the more frequent remarks that a boy was kept 'as a woman' (*come donna*) or 'for use as a woman' (*a uso di donna*) probably had a similar 'conjugal' sense."[18] Many of the men involved were unmarried artisans—bakers, hosiers, dyers, and the like— who were known to be "keeping" a boy, often an apprentice, whom they lodged, fed, and supported and with whom they had sexual relations. It is precisely this situation that is illustrated in the second 1557 condemnation for sodomy, also in Florence, of the famous goldsmith and sculptor Benvenuto Cellini. Although at the time Cellini might already have been involved or even living with the woman he would later marry, his judges found him "guilty of keeping Fernando," an adolescent working in his shop, probably as an apprentice, "in his bed as his wife and using him carnally very many times in the nefarious act of sodomy for about the last five years."[19]

In seventeenth-century Spain, exactly the same expressions are found in descriptions like that offered by Carlos Charmarinero, an employee of the city of Valencia. Meeting some of his neighbors one day, Carlos

indicated and made known to them a youth who was there, of about sixteen or seventeen years of age, named Miconet . . . the accused [Carlos] saying that that youth served him as a woman, or was like his wife, or that he used him as if he were, and that whenever he wanted he would take advantage of him by paying him a Valencian *real*.

les mostró y dio a conocer un moço que allí estava de hasta diez y seis o dies y siete años llamado Miconet . . . diciendo el reo que aquel moço le servía de muger o que era como su muger o que se servía del como si lo fuera y que siempre que quería se aprovechava del con un real valenciano que le dava.[20]

In another case, a fourteen-year-old servant, involved in a sexual relationship with his master, argued with a second boy in the household over his master's attentions, telling his rival to keep away from his "husband."[21]

Going beyond same-sex relationships perceived as being like a marriage, a case in Florence, described by Rocke, involved two men, the elder supporting the younger (aged twenty-two), until they exchanged vows in church over a Bible at the altar, each promising fidelity to the other.[22] It is quite possible that they understood this commitment as a marriage; it is also possible that they thought of their relationship in terms inflected by ideas of friendship or brotherhood. And the idea of friendship, even if in a context of inequality, was not always absent, as we have seen, from the way some men and women conceived of marriage.

A final issue can be raised at this point in relation to Tiepolo's account. The Venetian ambassador describes the men as defiling marriage and uniting like husband and wife, yet he does not state explicitly, as does Montaigne, that they imitated faithfully a wedding ceremony. Indeed, his more derisory expression "alcune lor ceremonie" (some ceremonies of theirs) opens up the question of the "reality" of the Iberians' weddings: that is, the extent to which they were intended as, and were seen as intended to be, serious in nature, or whether Tiepolo might be describing gatherings involving some kind of parody of a wedding ceremony, followed by sexual activities.

A case that offers precisely such a parodic scenario has been identified in Naples in 1591. Here, the Inquisition tried a group of clerics, youths, and boys, members of an academy under the leadership of the priest Giuseppe Buono, known as Abate (Abbot) Volpino.[23] The members would meet regularly for pleasurable—frequently licentious—recreation and trips into the countryside involving singing, drinking, masquerades, card games, and so on. On one occasion, at Buono's house, they celebrated sham weddings between at least two Augustinian friars and two prepubescent boys, the former of each couple being referred to as "uncle" (*zio*), the latter as "aunt" (*zia*).[24] Abbot Volpino presided, the couples expressed their consent, the boys were given rings, "et poi se bugeravano o vero montavano come marito et moglie" (and then they buggered one another or in truth had sex like a husband and wife).[25] The intention of these ceremonies was evidently not to effect a marriage in reality, but this does not mean, as Giovanni Romeo and Pierroberto Scaramella underscore, that the parodies were devoid of serious critical intent, especially in light of a fake vice-regal decree drafted by the group. Scaramella notes that one of the brothers was judged suspect of heresy for having believed "che . . . fosse lecito contrahere matrimonio tra maschio et maschio" (that . . . it was licit to contract marriage between two males) and emphasizes the "appiglio teorico, per quanto elementare, e però sufficientemente forte da sfidare in prima persona il simbolo dell'Inquisizione a Napoli" (theoretical underpinning, albeit elementary, and yet strong enough to challenge head on the creed of the Inquisition in Naples).[26] Romeo summarizes the academy's activities as follows:

> They spent their days frequenting the world of urban comedies, in amorous pursuit of each other, often with furious scenes of jealousy, but also reacting with irony and irreverence toward the intolerance of ecclesiastical authorities. In this charged atmosphere, they hatched their most surprising decisions, which it is not rash to see as an attempt—half serious, half joking—to legalize male homosexual relations: two marriages between gays and the customary of an imaginary vice-roy, which authorized only limited sodomitical relations between a man and a woman but was presented to the "academicians" as a full-blown declaration of intent in favor of the legalization of male homosexuality.

> Passavano le giornate frequentando gli ambienti delle commedie cittadine, amandosi, spesso con furiose scenate di gelosia, ma anche reagendo in modo ironico e dissacrante all'intolleranza delle autorità ecclesiastiche e secolari. In questo clima elettrico maturarono le loro decisioni più sorprendenti, che non è azzardato leggere come un tentativo, tra il serio e il faceto, di legalizzazione dei rapporti omosessuali maschili: due matrimoni tra gay e la prammatica di un immaginario viceré, che autorizzava solo limitatamente rapporti sodomitici tra uomo e donna, ma era presentata agli "accademici" come una vera e propria dichiarazione d'intenti a favore della legalizzazione dell'omosessualità maschile.[27]

The ludic marriages and related ideas elaborated in the context of the Naples academy constitute a particularly developed and rich example, yet they are not unique. About a century later, an academy was founded at the University of Padua named "The Atheist Truth." Bringing together students, clergy, and laypeople, the group went so far, according to Inquisition documents, as "granting the authorization to contract marriage between people of the same sex."[28] Such ideas, moreover, were part of a broad cultural mentality, resonating, as we have seen, with the ways in which contemporaries viewed—partly seriously, partly ironically—established or continuing age/rank-graded relationships in terms of *husband* and *wife*. As we might expect, they are also reflected in literary texts of the time.

In a late fifteenth-century neo-Latin poem in praise of the recently deceased and later to be canonized Franciscan, Giacomo della Marca, Giovanni Battista Petrucci describes a scene in which the friar is approached by a youth, repentant at having been involved in a sodomitical marriage: "Nam veluti mulier sum desponsatus ad usus / enormis veneris spurcaeque libidinis actus" (For like a wife I was married for practices / of an irregular passion and acts of a filthy desire). In shame, the youth hands over a ring, the sign of his former marriage, that, when the friar casts it away, is snatched up by demons.[29] It is in dramatic productions, however, that we find the most frequent and suggestive examples.

In the Italian theater in the first half of the sixteenth century—as in England until the seventeenth—women were not allowed on the public stage and boys cross-dressed to play female roles. In England, women characters within plays cross-dressed as young men (conveniently for the boy actors), but the inverse was not the case.[30] In Italy, by contrast, youthful (beardless) male characters frequently cross-dressed as women. Whereas female characters disguised themselves as the opposite sex in order to enter and act in the public sphere, their male counterparts did so to gain access to an interior, domestic space—and, in general, to a particular woman inhabiting it. While cross-dressed, however, such youths sometimes attracted the attentions of an older male, whose ultimate humiliation would then be set in train. Two well-known comedies play with the idea of male–male marriages.

In Niccolò Machiavelli's *Clizia*, Nicomaco, the head of a household, falls in love with Clizia, an orphan he has raised as a daughter. Nicomaco's plan is to give a portion of his property to a servant, who will then be able to marry Clizia, but who will allow his master to sleep with her before doing so himself. The play ends with a "shaming charivari-like moment" as Nicomaco climbs into the marital bed, in which another male servant, Siro, stands in for the bride.[31] Not only does this "bride" fight off Nicomaco's advances but the latter also receives, during his night of "nozze . . . maschie" (male marriage), five or six sexually suggestive blows under his tailbone ("sotto el codrione") from something hard and pointed ("una cosa soda ed acuta").[32]

Machiavelli's play thus stages the humiliation of a wayward patriarchal figure, whose behavior is brought back into line; it also parodies the generic conventions of the comedy, in particular the wedding with which it traditionally concludes. Pietro Aretino's *Il Marescalco* also parodies "the required marital resolution of comedies," while mirroring closely the scenario of pederastic desire and relationships discussed earlier.[33] Here the Master of the Horse of the Duke of Mantua has a sexual relationship with his young servant Giannicco and feels no desire for women; he thus resists strenuously his master's decision to arrange his marriage. Giannicco, meanwhile, is becoming an adult and makes it clear that he would be happy if his master were to marry, since he would then be able to give up his passive sexual role and assume an active one with women. He even envisages that his master's young wife might attract youths, with whom the *marescalco* could take his pleasure instead of with him; then he could sleep with the neglected wife, to the equal satisfaction of all. Ultimately, the comedy is resolved when the bride that the duke destines for the *marescalco* turns out to be an attractive boy dressed as a woman. Aretino's play thus offers a serious representation of its protagonist's pederastic desire, which is socially accommodated. At the same time, the comedy plays knowingly with the fact that all brides on stage were acted by boys, the boy bride here functioning overtly as both. The play was also conceived and performed for the first time in 1527 during carnival. It was thus in this particular festive context of temporary ludic inversion that a pederastic marriage could be represented, and a form of desire—an attraction to young males and an aversion to women—in the process of becoming increasingly problematic could be turned into a source of general amusement.[34]

Another literary example is offered by Pietro Aretino who, a few years later in the mid-1530s, published fictional dialogues, in a salacious and satirical mode, in which a prostitute, Nanna, explains to her daughter, Pippa, the secrets of her trade. In the course of her instruction, the older woman twice uses the term *husband* with reference to clerics (in particular friars and priests). In the first example, Nanna complains that it is impossible to arouse this kind of client unless their husbands also come and lie with them: "non se gli rizza fino a tanto che non si corcano seco i lor mariti" (it doesn't stand to attention until their husbands come and lie with them). This provokes the incredulous response: "O hanno marito i frati e i preti?" (Eh, do friars and priests have husbands?).[35] Using a second term that suggests that the husbands also expect to receive material gratification, Nanna goes on to claim that the churchmen like to see their catamites (*bardassoni*) engage in anal sex with the woman (p. 85). In a later passage, the prostitute expresses her appreciation for lower class clients, whose demands are straightforward and easy to satisfy. In contrast, wealthy nobles seek more esoteric pleasures, such as special positions, oral and anal sex, or the voyeuristic/exhibitionist excitement of having their "husbands" or "boys" ("i lor mariti, i lor giovani") look on or take part in a threesome "in the priestly manner" ("a l'usanza pretesca") (p. 157).

If the lexicon in Aretino's dialogue replicates what we have observed so far, the gendered dynamic it inscribes differs from the earlier cases of masters and servants/apprentices and from the Naples academy, where it was the older man who was regarded as the *husband*, the youth as his *wife*. In this case, it is the youths, the recipients of favors, who are qualified as the *husbands* of the putatively older clerics. One reason for this difference might be that if Nanna were to refer to the priests' *wives*, the reader would assume she was referring to their mistresses, as when she exclaims, "Così avessero eglino moglie" (Oh, would that they had *wives*) (p. 84). Nonetheless, it seems likely that the same gendered assumptions are at work here as in the other cases and that Nanna is suggesting that the priests are sexually passive and let themselves be penetrated by the youths they keep, rather than the other way round. We note, for example, that when these youthful husbands are introduced for the first time, they are presented as playing an active sexual role, penetrating a female prostitute anally in order to excite the priests and friars unable to become aroused. The implication seems to be, then, that these clerics are not so virile and their boys may well be their *husbands* in bed. This reading finds additional support in the fact that the second passage from the

Ragionamenti takes aim at "gentiluomini, signori e monsignori" (gentle-men, lords, and monsignors) (p. 155), desirous of many forms of pleasure and who have both *husbands* and *boys*. If we do not take these two terms to be synonymous, they would designate males expected to play different sex-ual roles. Sexual passivity is moreover referred to elsewhere by Aretino as a habit of the great: "Ma poi che 'l cazzo in cul tutto volete / come voglion i grandi . . ." (But since you want the cock all the way up your ass / like nobles want it . . .).[36]

In relation to courtesan culture, finally, similar euphemistic slang is found applied to a relationship between a woman and her male client.[37] Tessa Sto-rey has emphasized the extent to which relationships with prestigious cour-tesans, far from being hidden, were acknowledged openly with pride and even celebrated with public rituals and display. Storey describes the case of Maddalena Saltarella, who left Florence for Rome in 1539. Her movements were observed and communicated to her former lover in Florence by Marco Bracci, secretary to the ambassador of the Duke of Tuscany. Maddalena was accompanied by two men, both of whom enjoyed her favors. On the way to Rome, however, one of them is described as having married her: "C'è molti che ne fanno disegno e maxime il compare Lactantio [Lattanzio] che troverà che ha maritato la sua e la alloggia con seco, per quanto intendo, insieme con il cavalier de Buondelmonti che l'aspecta questa sera" (There are many who have designs on her, and most of all our friend Lactantio [Lattanzio], who will find that he has married her and is lodging her with him, as far as I understand, along with the cavalier de Buondelmonti, who is expecting her this evening).[38] As Storey concludes, "[a]lthough no explanation of the term 'marriage' is made, it seems to have been a festive ritual which signified that a courtesan was temporarily allied to a certain man, conferring upon him certain 'rights' and responsibilities in his relationship to her."[39]

In a second case, the evidence for a marriage with a courtesan involving a festive ceremony is yet clearer. Writing from Rome in 1545, Lelio Capilupi addressed a letter to a friend in Urbino, in which he described his "solemn nuptials" with an unnamed Neapolitan courtesan. Capilupi, who had evi-dently been enamored of the woman for some time, invited for the evening a large number of friends, some of whom were already very familiar with her; they included distinguished churchmen as well as Tobia Pallavicino, banker to the Holy See. Capilupi recounts that "Oltre il piacer del letto hebbi grandissimo passatempo a cena et dapoi, perchè invitai molti gentiluomi et feci nozze solenni" (As well as the pleasures of the bed, I had great fun at dinner [and] afterwards, because I had invited many gentlemen and had a solemn wedding).[40] Again then, we find nuptial imagery applied to the moment at which a man establishes publicly a relationship with a courtesan and the latter receives him into her bed. As Capilupi concludes, "Finita la comedia gli sposi andaron a letto" (After the play acting, the newlyweds went to bed).[41] The sexual relationship here is integrated into the context of a celebratory gathering involving a ludic imitation of at least some of the aspects of a wedding, most likely the more secular festive ones such as banqueting, gift giving, and so on. Once more, then, we observe the mobilization of a language based on marriage, here playfully and self-consciously hyperbolic (*nozze solenni, comedia*), yet behind which stands a social reality: a number of established practices serving to ritualize a relationship with a courtesan (involving the exchange of sex and money) in order to confer on it a degree of honorability, even if, as in this case, the "marriage" lasted no longer than the night and the following day, due, in large part, to Capilupi's limited funds.

It is not surprising, finally, that, even in the absence of any accompanying social ritual, the terms *husband* and *wife* might be used to refer simply to a sexual encounter. Thus, in a poem by Curzio Marignolli, a dissolute friar seeks to seduce a professed nun in the following terms:

> No law prohibits fucking,
> For if you are the mother, the father [= also priest] am I,
> We are, necessarily, husband and wife!

> Nessuna legge il fottere ci toglie,
> ché se madre sei tu, padre son io,
> siam per necessità marit'e moglie![42]

Sixteenth- and early seventeenth-century Italy thus offers a range of examples involving the idea of marriage that includes both euphemistic linguistic uses and ludic practices that are nonetheless both socially and intellectually significant. We find these two scenarios, moreover, in both male–male and male–female contexts. People from a wide social spectrum figure in these examples, from nobles and prelates to teachers and their pupils or artisans and their apprentices. Two categories of individuals appear with particular frequency, however, both to some degree sexually marginalized, although in different ways: people profiting from or exploited for sex—courtesans, youths, "boys"—and clerics. We shall encounter more such individuals in the pages that follow.

Chapter 4

OTHER WITNESSES, OTHER STORIES

Like those sent to the Fugger family, a series of newsletters (*avvisi*) were sent from Rome to the Duke of Urbino, Francesco II della Rovere, the first of which, written on July 30, 1578, is the earliest known to exist. As the case developed, the duke's informant drafted updates on August 9 and again on August 13, the day of the arrested men's execution.[1] While they corroborate various aspects of the story as recorded in the other sources, these accounts also introduce variations that complicate the picture. The initial arrest is described as follows:

Some Portuguese and Marranos, who had gone to the sacred font of their own accord, were also captured in a vineyard outside of the Latin Gate. They took with them some youths of their country, and after eating and drinking to excess and becoming drunk, going beyond all imaginable pagan immorality and marrying each other, they went to bed together. Since His Holiness is extremely angry, it is believed they will be burned alive.

Furono anco presi in una vigna fuori di Porta Latina alquanti Portughesi et Marani, iti al sacrofonte co' propri piedi, liquali conducevano seco alcuni giovani paesani, et doppo haver sopra modo mangiato et bevuto, ebri divenuti, quelli fuori d'ogni inaudita gentilità sposando seco si coricavano, et credesi per essersi grandemente Sua Santità alterata che saranno abbrugiati vivi.

Characterized by an attitude of unqualified condemnation, the Urbino report confirms, in concise and straightforward language, that the men arrested had married and then had sexual relations. To describe those relations, the writer has recourse to the euphemism *coricarsi*, to lie down or to go to bed. This association of marrying followed by sex echoes closely, as we have seen, the accounts of Montaigne (*coucher, habiter ensemble*) and Tiepolo (*congiungersi*). In contrast, no detail is given here of what kind of ceremony, if any, might have been performed, and there is no mention of the church of San Giovanni. Instead, we have a story involving men taking some youths to a vineyard outside the city and eating and drinking to excess, indeed to the point of complete inebriation. Communal feasting, as we have seen, was certainly part of the usual festivities surrounding a marriage; in fact, it often formed the context in which a newly wed couple was expected to consummate its union. The scenario presented here also aligns the events with a different kind of story, however, one in fact told frequently in courts of law at the time. According to Michael Rocke, Florentine judicial records offer insights into the shared activities of groups of men, perhaps accompanied by "their boys," including communal eating, drinking, and gambling in workshops, homes, or taverns and outings together to the countryside on holidays.[2] Evidence from Rome attests to the prevalence of more sinister variants of such forms of socializing, as Marina Baldassari has shown in her analysis of the many cases in which boys were abducted for sexual purposes by older youths or adults, sometimes operating at the head of a gang (*banda*). These groups themselves were organized hierarchically, according to a typical pederastic structure, whereby the younger members would submit to the older in return for a degree of protection. Such violent kidnappings often involved victims being taken to a remote or secluded location, such as a vineyard or garden located at the edge of or outside the city.[3] In positing a group of men who control events, gathering and taking along with them in this way some youngsters, of whom they take advantage once everyone is drunk, the writer evokes a storyline that early modern Romans would readily have recognized. As we have seen, a similar scenario would be evoked a few days later in the August 2 report to the Fuggers, although without the reference to excessive eating and drunkenness. While it is impossible to know exactly what information these commentators had at their disposal before putting pen to paper or to verify its accuracy, their versions clearly present a story that could plausibly be told, one that provided a context for understanding the events giving rise to the arrests. This familiar cultural scenario of pederastic exploitation, or even of abduction and rape, might also, we need to allow, reflect the reality of at least certain aspects of the relations between the members of the group and of their actions.

Two further details draw our attention. First, the pope himself, Gregory XIII, is said to be personally involved in the case and particularly outraged by it.[4] From the outset, then, those arrested seem destined to be burned alive, a particularly severe form of punishment. Second, where Montaigne writes of Portuguese men and Tiepolo of Portuguese and Spaniards, the newsletter refers to Portuguese and Marranos; that is, to *conversos* or so-called New Christians—Iberians of Jewish descent converted to Christianity, often under compulsion, sometimes adhering secretly to their ancestral faith but generally suspected of doing so and kept under close surveillance. The Jewish community in Rome, one of Europe's largest and most ancient, was afforded a certain degree of tolerance; at the same time, its members were the target of frequent expressions of popular hostility and, since 1555, had been forced to live in a ghetto and submit to regular attempts to convert them.[5] This situation was nevertheless preferable to conditions in Spain and Portugal, where, from the 1490s onward, Jews had faced the stark choice of conversion or exile, the former course frequently resulting only in further discriminatory measures and persecution.[6] In Rome, Jews were not de facto under the authority of the Inquisition, since they could not be held to standards of orthodoxy in a faith they did not profess. Any Jew who was baptized, however, but gave rise to doubts about his sincerity or who returned to his original religion became an apostate, and the Inquisition was on the lookout for and vigorously prosecuted all such cases. In the July 30 newsletter, the men are presented as having gone to the "sacred font"—that is, they had been baptized—but as subsequently behaving with untold *gentilità*, a noun with two principal meanings: nobility, distinction (as a synonym of *gentilezza*) and, collectively, the Gentiles or pagans or their religious beliefs and practices.[7] In the latter context, moreover, it sometimes referred to pleasures or the idea of a license in behavior associated with the pagans.[8] If it is clearly the second meaning that is intended here, this is explained by the fact that, from a Christian point of view—that of the religion that saw itself as representing a New Covenant, superseding the Old—Jews could be cast into the same category as pagans, the category in which the former themselves placed all non-Jews.

At the same time, it must also be remembered that *Marrano* was to some degree a term of abuse that could be hurled at Spaniards in general, who were present in large numbers, as has been noted, in sixteenth-century Rome. The ubiquity of immigrants from this country was not without provoking tensions and resentment on the part of the local Roman and Italian populations, especially in the decades following the sack of the city by Charles V's imperial armies in 1527. This is seen on two occasions, for example, in the *Life* of Benvenuto Cellini. When a group of Spaniards comes to retrieve a silver vase Cellini has worked on, refusing to pay him and attempting to take it by force, the artist calls them Marranos and traitors (*marrani, traditori*); people in the vicinity approach and take up the refrain: "Amazali pur questi marrani" (Go on, kill these Marranos). Given that the men in question are servants of the Bishop of Salamanca, it seems unlikely that all of them would be "New Christians." Calling them Marranos is thus simply a means of vilification. Similarly, Cellini later terms a Spanish goldsmith with whom he is in dispute "un disonorato marrano" (a dishonorable Marrano).[9] Since the Urbino report is the only early source that describes the Iberians arrested as Marranos, we might understand it in the same way as the preceding examples.[10] On the other hand, as James S. Amelang notes, Spanish *conversos* at this time were indeed a highly mobile group, often constrained to move from places where they had been stigmatized or to take to the road in search of better economic opportunities.[11] Moreover, as we shall see, further evidence will emerge of connections between the group meeting at the Latin Gate and Rome's Jewish community. The question of whether some of those arrested might have been of Jewish origin is thus best left open.

The second newsletter to the Duke of Urbino, dated August 9, refers once again to Portuguese and Marranos, who are said to have been condemned already to the stake, but who it appears are to be examined by the Inquisition regarding matters touching the Christian faith. The involvement of the Inquisition in addition to that of the pope, if again this statement is accurate, would not be surprising and could be justified both by the question of the men's views concerning the sacrament of marriage and by their allegedly Jewish origins.[12] Unfortunately, with some notable exceptions, few records of trials (*processi*) by the Inquisition survive from the sixteenth century, a great many of the Roman documents having been either lost when they were removed to Paris on the orders of Napoleon or destroyed rather than repatriated following the emperor's fall in 1815.[13] The Roman inquisitors met regularly on Wednesdays; on Thursdays, usually in the presence of the pope; and, as necessary, on Saturdays. In 1578, August 13 fell on a Wednesday. The inquisitors thus met on the day the Portuguese and Spanish men were put to death, as well as on the following day with Gregory XIII. It is hard to imagine that the topic of the exceptional execution of so many individuals for so unusual a crime was not part of their conversation at that time and in the days and weeks preceding; if it was, however, it remained within the secret part of their meeting, leaving no trace in the *decreta* or minutes of their deliberations.[14]

The account in the second report to Urbino also confirms the assertion of Tiepolo that many more men were involved than were captured, a good number having succeeded in escaping: "erano in molto maggior numero ma con la fuga per hora hanno proccacciata la vita" (they were much more numerous but have saved their lives for the time being by fleeing). In contrast, no mention is now made of the question of marriage. This disappears from the account, leaving only the men's "enorme, abominevole et nefando vitio" (enormous, abominable, and unmentionable vice), the expression *nefando vitio* again constituting a clear reference to sodomy.

When the Duke of Urbino's informant returned to the same topic on August 13, it was to notify his readers of the execution of the "accursed Portuguese and Marranos" ("si è fatta la giustitia de' maladetti Portughesi et Marrani"). Now, however, the writer specifies that seven such individuals were executed along with an Italian boatman ("un barcarolo italiano"). Contrary to what earlier reports had led us to expect, moreover, the prisoners were not burned alive; rather, they were hanged and then transported by cart to the Latin Gate, where their corpses were thrown onto a pyre: "liquali doppo essere stati impiccati furono sopra due carrette portati a Porta Latina, et ivi abbrugiati" (who, having been hanged, were taken on two carts to the Latin Gate, where they were burned). The unusual ritual devised for the men's execution thus involved a return to the Latin Gate. In this way, their crime was expiated in part by the burning of their bodies in situ, no doubt to cleanse that place of the defilement it had undergone. We shall discuss this ceremony of execution in greater detail in the next chapter. Finally, we learn that, in addition to the eight men executed, a number of others remained in prison who were expected to suffer the same fate: "si cuoceranno ad altro forno" (they will be baked in another batch). Again, as we shall see later, while more men had been arrested, they do not appear to have been executed.[15]

The ambassadorial dispatches to Venice and the newsletters to Urbino found a resonance not only in Montaigne but also in a polemical text involving Venice, composed exactly forty years after the events. In 1618 Giacomo Castellani published his *Avviso di Parnaso*, a work that took up and refuted an earlier satire, attributed to the Spanish writer Francisco de Quevedo, which had attacked the Venetian Republic and Charles-Emmanuel of Savoy.[16] Responding to the depiction of Venice as a new Sodom, Castellani retorts that while the inhabitants of the biblical city gave themselves over to every sort of bestial lust ("ogni sorte di lussuria bestiale"), they did not attempt to dress up evil as something good and right. In contrast,

> the Spanish have reached a point, beyond which not even the devil from Hell might pass, since they tried to transform the unmentionable vice into the sacrament of matrimony. Go to Rome, to Saint John at the Latin Gate; there you will see depicted—if in the few years since I saw it, it has not been erased—the story of those Spaniards who, having taken with them some youths of their country, dressed them as maidens in order that they might not be recognized, and in that holy church got married to them as if they were women. For this, they paid the penalty in the flames here on earth; and now they must be enduring eternal punishment in the flames of Hell. Can you find anything like this in another nation, among as many as exist in the whole world, except in yours? Take the Jews, the Turks, the Scythians, the Cannibals, and as many Barbarians as walk the face of the earth; I am certain that among them you will not find an evil so great.

> gli Spagnuoli sono arrivati a termine, che più oltre non potrebbe arrivare il Demonio dell'inferno, poiche del vitio nefando hanno voluto far Sacramento di matrimonio. Andate in Roma a San Giovanni ante Portam Latinam, dove vederete, se da pochi anni in quà che io la vidi non è stata cancellata, dipinta

l'historia di quegli Spagnuoli, i quali, havendo condotto seco alcuni giovanetti della lor natione, accioche non fussero conosciuti gli vestirono come donzelle, e in quella Santa Chiesa si sposarono con essi, come fussero donne. Di che pagarono le pene temporali quà nel fuoco; et hora deono patir l'eternali in quello dell'inferno. Trovatemi Voi una cosa tale come questa di altra natione, fra quante sono in tutto il mondo se non nella vostra? Pigliatemi li Giudei, li Turchi, gli Sciti, gli Antropofagi, e quanti Barbari sostenta il suolo della terra; son sicuro che frà essi non mi troverete una malvagità così grande.[17]

A first point that can be made is that this version of the story contains no reference to the men's possibly Jewish origins or status as *conversos*. It is clear, moreover, that, whether the writer had heard this allegation or not, it would have made little sense to repeat it in this particular polemical context, since his aim is to paint the Spanish as more depraved than any other nation, including Jews, Muslims, and pagans. The satire here is purely anti-Spanish. While this narrative distances itself from the reports sent to the Duke of Urbino in this respect, in another it resembles them much more closely. For if Castellani describes marriages, he also emphasizes the vice of sodomy ("vitio nefando"), which he situates in the pederastic framework of a group of Spaniards who take along a number of youths ("giovanetti") under their influence or control. The later writer even uses the same verbal expression as the first report sent to Urbino—*condurre seco*—both texts resonating in this way with the *tirandossi* of the August 2 newsletter to the Fuggers, quoted in chapter 2. Like the two earlier sources, then, the *Avviso di Parnaso* evokes a typical pederastic scenario, even an abduction scenario, that, as we have noted, was quite familiar in the papal city. In Castellani's account, moreover, it is the age/status difference of a pederastic relationship that is plotted onto a marital framework as the youths are assimilated to women ("come fussero donne"). As we saw earlier, this was also a common way of conceiving of and referring to such relationships, perhaps in derision, especially if they were continued over a certain duration of time. A final detail of particular note, one that takes us yet further in this direction and beyond anything found in the other accounts, is the claim that the men actually dressed the youths up as women. The transvestism described may refer to the occasion of the wedding ceremony itself, in which case it would resonate with the boy-bride scenario that concludes Aretino's *Marescalco*. Yet this is not necessarily the case, since the cross-dressing is explained primarily in terms of the youths not being recognized ("accioche non fussero conosciuti"); it thus seems to evoke first and foremost a strategy of disguise related to the abduction scenario.

Without being able to determine with certainty whether the cross-dressing narrative has any historical accuracy, a number of elements serve to call it into doubt. First, this account is the only one extant that includes this claim, and it is also the farthest removed chronologically from the events themselves, which it postdates by no less than four decades. Consequently, it might be seen as representing the culmination of a process of elaboration undergone by the stories concerning the marriage ceremonies. If the *avvisi* sent to the Fuggers described a ceremony with rings following mass, Montaigne's account, composed three years after the events, is the first to specify the celebration of a nuptial mass with gospel reading and communion. At an even greater temporal distance, the *Avviso* is the first and only text to portray marriages with boys dressed as maidens.

Furthermore, while Castellani bases his description on a painting he claims to have seen at the church of Saint John at the Latin Gate, he also prevaricates by stating that it might no longer exist ("se . . . non è stata cancellata"). Even more tellingly, no painting is mentioned by any other source, yet had one existed already in 1581, Montaigne and his informant would surely have referred to it. If it ever existed, then, it too must have been commissioned and executed at some chronological remove from the events themselves. Giuseppe Marcocci suggests that the painting in question might be a very late example of a *pittura infamante*.[18] If so, however, a number of factors would make it extremely unusual. This kind of painting, in fact, was common only in the later thirteenth and fourteenth centuries. In the fifteenth century, it was on the decline, and the latest examples cited by scholars all concern Florence and end in 1537. In addition, the paintings themselves almost always depicted men of the upper classes or at least of significant social standing, individuals with a reputation whose loss would bring them disgrace and deprive them of legal rights. Such men were almost always alive, but out of reach of the justice system—hence the compensatory nature of the shaming punishment imposed. The crimes involved were most commonly those of treachery, rebellion, murder (especially political), embezzlement, counterfeiting, or (false) bankruptcy. Finally, except for a few late examples, the shaming images were not painted in the place where a crime was committed but on the outside walls of some civic building, such as the palace of the Podestà; by the same token, the practice does not seem to have been common in Rome, being associated with cities with more communal forms of government.[19]

At the same time, painted representations were sometimes made of executions (i.e., in addition to the imposition of capital punishment), such as that of Girolamo Savonarola. These were usually created to shame a family, however (as in the case of a mural painted on the side of a church next to the main square in San Gimignano in 1274), or else to celebrate the victory of a commune against a particular rebel or traitor (as with Azzo del Frignano in Bologna in 1243). Two examples seem closer to the situation of the group of men at the Latin Gate in that they involve sacrilege, yet again there are important differences. In Prato, in 1312, a lawyer's son named Giovanni stole the city's most important relic, the cincture of the Virgin Mary, in order to take it to Florence. The series of ten painted scenes that the city of Prato commissioned for the inside of its *duomo*, however, recorded not only the crime and its punishment; it also celebrated the miraculous intervention that had prevented the theft and saved the city from humiliation. Similarly, in Florence in 1501, a young nobleman, Antonio di Giuseppe Rinaldeschi, was executed for hurling dung at an image of the Virgin Mary after getting drunk and losing money at gambling. The panel with nine painted scenes representing the events seems to have been commissioned by the clergy of Santa Maria de' Ricci to commemorate an event that made the church both notorious and a place of pilgrimage. For the panel also served to convey a particular religious message—that of the power of the defiled image and of divine providence—since Antonio repented and made a good death, so that, in the final scene, angels fight off devils in order to bear the soul of the redeemed sinner to heaven.[20]

In the case of Saint John at the Latin Gate, then, while it is perhaps not impossible that a *pittura infamante* might have been made at some point, we must ask what would have been the purpose of doing so. For no one would have been susceptible to being shamed. The men executed were dead, and unlike Giovanni or Antonio, they were not from noble or influential families; on the contrary, as we shall discover, they were men of little or no social standing at all. Nor, in this case, was there any miraculous intervention to celebrate, no venerable image to promote along with its salvific properties. Would it have been sufficient to celebrate the mere fact that the men had been captured and executed? Or that the church's defilement had been expiated? Moreover, who would have had an interest in commissioning such an image, whose effect would have been diametrically opposed to the authorities' all-but-certain desire to erase the events from memory? If such a picture were to serve a shaming function, the most likely scenario might be that it was designed to shame the Spanish nation. While Spanish leaders in Rome would no doubt have protested such a move, this is the precise goal of the *Avviso di Parnaso*. Might it rather be the case, then, that the text's author presented his information in the form of an imaginary ekphrasis in order to render it more vivid and to heighten its credibility?

Let us return, finally, to the question of youths dressed as maidens, as described by the *Avviso*. Cross-dressing in order to promote discretion might appear to have been a self-defeating strategy, since a group of men with adolescent girls would have been more, not less, likely to attract attention in public and raise questions than a group of men and youths. Does the satirical text exaggerate here, then, to make its point? This seems quite possible. If the writer did indeed see a painting at San Giovanni, however, then two other explanations might be proposed. The first is that, in order to communicate visually in a painting that what was being represented between a group of male figures was a wedding, the painter had recourse to dressing some of them as female brides. The second, whose pertinence will become evident later, is that the youths were depicted wearing not dresses but some form of religious habit.

If Italian diplomats and commentators considered the events at San Giovanni a Porta Latina worthy of being reported to their masters, what of the Spanish ambassador in Rome, Juan de Zúñiga?[21] The bundle of documents with the shelf-mark *Estado, Roma, legajo 933* in the Spanish National Archives in Simancas contains many of Zúñiga's dispatches to King Philip II during the days and weeks in question. The catalog of the papers from the Roman embassy was printed in 1936, transcribed from an earlier manuscript inventory prepared in 1819 by Canon Tomás González, "Comisionado especial por el Sr. Rey D.ⁿ Fernando 7.º para el reconocimiento y arreglo del expresado Real Archivo" (Special Commissioner of the King Don Fernando VII for the inspection and ordering of the aforementioned Royal Archive). The description of the contents of *legajo* 933 includes the following: "El Papa manda quemar a ocho españoles convencidos de pecado nefando, porque el embajador se negó de todo punto a interceder por ellos" (The pope ordered to be burned eight Spaniards, convicted of the unmentionable sin, since the ambassador refused absolutely to intervene on their behalf).[22]

Here then is proof that the Spanish ambassador was apprised of events and that he relayed information concerning them to his king; here too is evidence that he refrained from intervening in any way to offer assistance. Again we find reference to the "unmentionable sin"; on the contrary, there is no allusion to the performing of marriages, but Canon González might well have chosen to omit this from the inventory, had the subject been discussed in the dispatches. Unfortunately, those dispatches, attested in 1819, no longer appear to be present. None of those currently in the *legajo*, excluding oversight on my part, corresponds to the catalog description. This is not the last time we shall encounter documents absent from archives, documents very likely removed or destroyed deliberately.

Archives themselves also become inaccessible. Only at the very end of researching this book and in haste was I able to access the Archive of the Spanish Embassy to the Holy See, part of the General Archive of the Ministry of Foreign Affairs and Cooperation, which had been newly transferred to the Archivo Histórico Nacional in Madrid. The boxes corresponding to the period in question did not yield any relevant evidence.[23] During my time in Rome, the archives of the Collegio Spagnolo, attached to the Spanish National Church, were closed indefinitely for renovation.

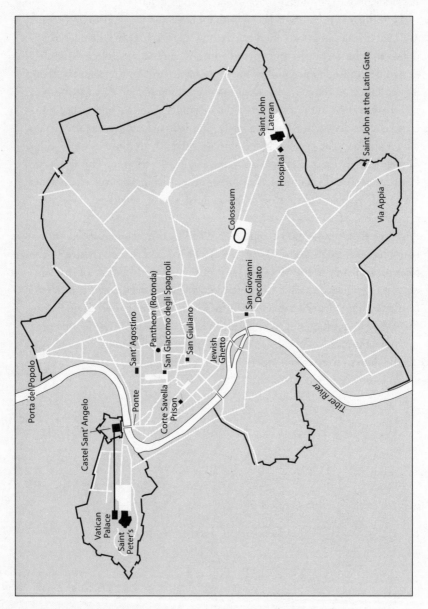

Map 1. Rome in the Sixteenth Century

Figure 1. Detail of a sixteenth-century plan of Rome showing the center of the city. From Mario Cartaro, *Novissimae Urbis Romae accuratissima descriptio* (1576); photo from Amato P. Frutaz, *Piante di Roma* (Rome: Ist. Nazionale di Studi Romani, 1962).

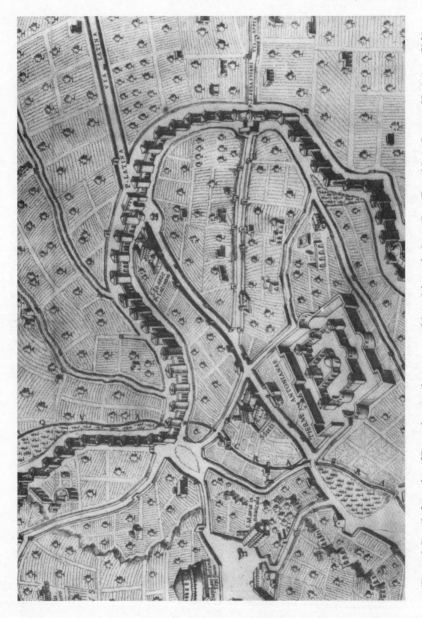

Figure 2. Detail of city plan of Rome showing the area around Saint John at the Latin Gate. From Mario Cartaro, *Novissimae Urbis Romae accuratissima descriptio* (1576); photo from Amato P. Frutaz, *Piante di Roma* (Rome: Ist. Nazionale di Studi Romani, 1962).

Figure 3. Member of the Confraternity of San Giovanni Decollato holding a *tavoletta*. Photo from Corrado Ricci, *Beatrice Cenci* (Milan, 1923; New York: Liveright, 1933).

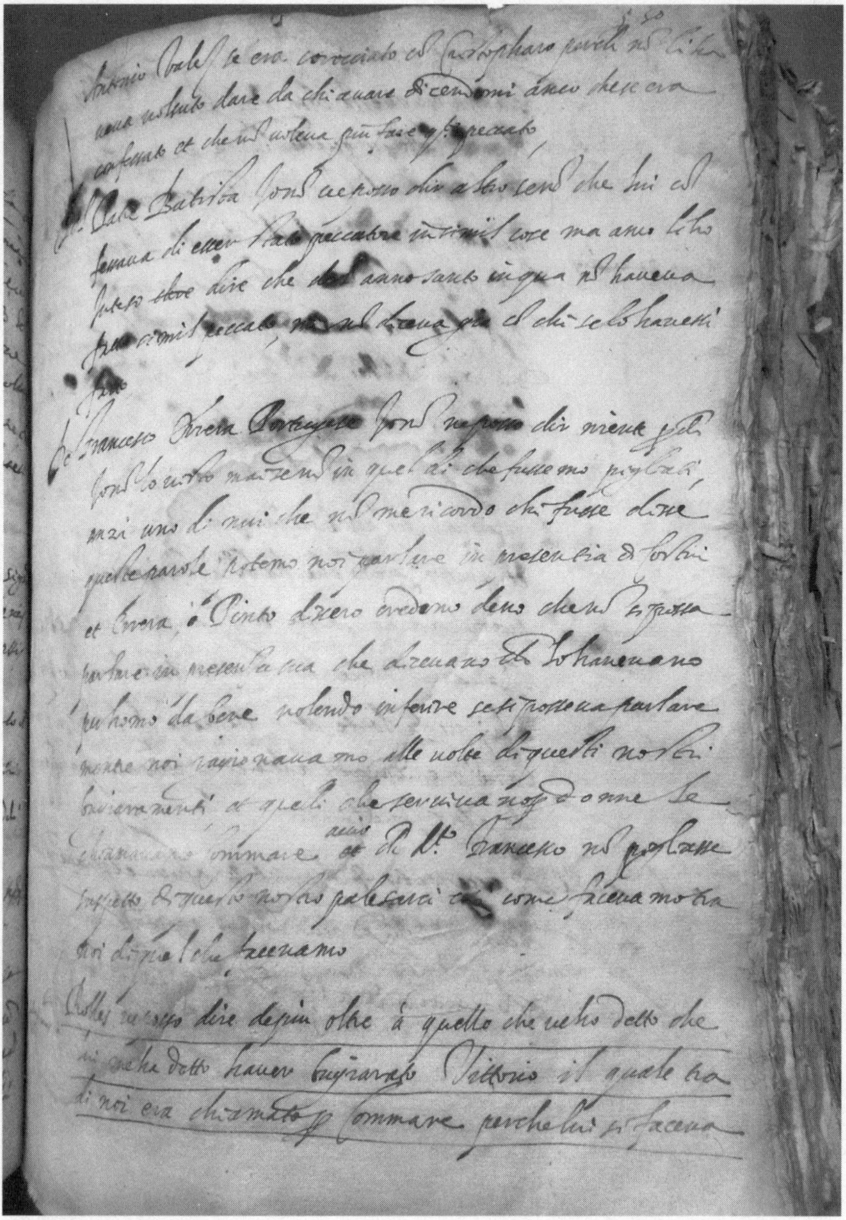

Figure 4. First page of the extant trial transcript. Rome, Archivio di Stato, Tribunale Criminale del Governatore, *Processi*, busta 168, n. 2, fol. 550r. Su concessione del Ministero dei Beni e delle Attività Culturali e del Turismo, ASRM 29/2015.

Figure 5. Church of Saint John at the Latin Gate. Photo: "Église San Giovanni a Porta Latina2" by LPLT - Own work. Licensed under CC BY-SA 3.0 via Wikimedia Commons.

PART II

Stories—Actors

Chapter 5

FINAL HOURS

Wills and Execution

The execution of criminals was a process that evolved in significant ways in late medieval and early modern Italy, becoming increasingly surrounded with pious action and communal involvement, notably through the foundation of various confraternities that took charge of condemned prisoners in the hours leading up to and following their death. The earliest such confraternities were established in the mid-fourteenth century in Bologna (Santa Maria della Morte) and Florence (Santa Maria della Croce al Tempio). In Rome, the Confraternity of San Giovanni Decollato (Saint John the Beheaded) or della Misericordia (of Mercy) was organized by a group of Florentines in 1488 and officially approved by Innocent VIII in 1490; among its members until his death in 1564 was one Michelangelo Buonarroti. The building of the association's church and its decoration were gradually completed over the course of the sixteenth century; the fresco of the beheading of the titular saint above the high altar was completed by Vasari in 1553.[1]

The mission of the Confraternity of San Giovanni was thus to minister to condemned prisoners, to "comfort" them, as described in the confraternity manuals produced to aid the brothers in their work. The principal activity of these lay "comforters" was to talk with the condemned men in order to bring them to acknowledge their guilt and the justice of their fate and, in particular, to make their confession and receive communion before dying. Prisoners would be handed over to the confraternity the day before their execution; brothers in robes with pointed hoods would exhort them to repent, pray with them, and, if they were cooperative, help them make their final dispositions, such as writing a letter to relatives and dictating a simple will, bequeathing whatever property they owned, liquidating their debts, either arranging for them to be paid or begging for them to be forgiven, and providing for the return of any items they had on loan. Ideally, from the point of view of the brothers, prisoners might leave some money in gratitude to the confraternity itself. The following morning, still dressed in their hooded robes, the brothers would accompany prisoners to the site of their execution, continuing to exhort them along the way with pious words, singing psalms or hymns, and holding up to their view portable devotional images depicting the crucifixion or the death of a martyr. The purpose of these hand-held *tavolette* was twofold: first, to shield the prisoner to some extent from the surrounding crowd and, second, to encourage him to continue to focus his attention on spiritual matters and thus to find a positive meaning in his suffering and death by uniting it with those of Christ and his saints. Finally, after a criminal's death, confraternity members might collect his corpse in order to deliver it to his relatives or friends or else take it for burial in the cloister of their church.

About six weeks after his arrival in Rome, Montaigne was witness to a spectacle of this kind accompanying the execution of a famous bandit named Catena. His secretary recorded the following description:

> Besides the formalities used in France, they carry in front of the criminal a big crucifix covered with a black curtain, and on foot go a large number of men dressed and masked in linen, who, they say, are gentlemen and other prominent people of Rome who devote themselves to this service of accompanying criminals led to execution and the bodies of the dead; and there is a brotherhood of them. There are two of these, or monks dressed and masked in the same way, who attend the criminal on the cart and preach to him; and one of them continually holds before his face a picture on which is the portrait of Our Lord, and has him kiss it incessantly; this makes it impossible to

see the criminal's face from the street. At the gallows, which is a beam between two supports, they still kept this picture against his face until he was
launched. (*Works*, 1148)

Outre la forme de France, ils font marcher devant le criminel un grand cru-
cifix couvert d'un rideau noir, et à pied un grand nombre d'hommes vestus
et masqués de toile, qu'on dit estre des gentilshommes et autres apparens de
Rome, qui se vouent à ce service d'accompaigner les criminels qu'on mene au
supplice et les corps des trespassés, et en font une confrerie. Il y en a deux de
ceux-là, ou moines, ainsi vestus et couverts, qui assistent le criminel sur la char-
rette et le preschent, et l'un d'eux luy presente continuellement sur le visage et
luy fait baiser sans cesse un tableau où est l'image de Nostre Seigneur; cela fait
qu'on ne puisse pas voir le visage du criminel par la rue. À la potence, qui
est une poutre entre deux appuis, on luy tenoit tousjours cette image contre
le visage jusques à ce qu'il fust eslancé. (*Journal*, ed. Rigolot, 97–98)

To many prisoners, whose life was soon to end, the brothers of San
Giovanni Decollato must indeed have brought a degree of solace and support.
The process of "spiritual comforting" was also a coercive and self-interested
one, however. In order to obtain a prisoner's compliance, for example, the
brothers might have recourse to both positive and negative arguments. On
the one hand, they would offer practical incentives, such as the opportunity
to dictate a will or even the possibility of a less painful means of execution.
Admitting culpability would generally allow an individual to avoid being
burned alive, this particularly terrible form of death being reserved for those
who refused to accept their error or their guilt, unrepentant heretics like
Macario, the Greek Archbishop of Macedonia, in 1562 or Giordano Bruno
in 1600.[2] On the other hand, the reluctant prisoner might well be threatened with the fire and eternal torments of Hell, described to him in vivid
detail, or, in anticipatory warning, feel the pain of a candle's flame brought
close to his flesh. The ultimate beneficiaries of the confraternity's ministry
were thus the brothers themselves and society at large, since its effect was to
confirm the legitimacy of the religious and social process of taking a human
life through the condemned individual's acquiescence, his own acceptance
of and (willing) participation in it. Bringing a sinner back into the body of
the Church before expelling him definitively from the body of society, offering him the possibility of eternal life in exchange for his life on earth, served

to reinforce social cohesion, justifying and reaffirming established norms. In this way, the brothers' work of "comforting" was as much a part of the process of social regulation as the subsequent execution itself.

A similarly dual dynamic is evident in the short notices in the form of wills that the confraternity recorded for each of the men who received its ministrations. As we have seen, the brothers' object was to bring their charges to make what they considered a "good" death and thus potentially save their soul in the afterlife. The only alternative outcome was that of the "bad" death of the impenitent sinner. This "good" story that they tried to orchestrate or the "bad" one that they tried to avoid was what they subsequently recorded in the prisoners' wills. What we might term the genre of these short texts allows for only the one or the other of these two possible narrative trajectories. At the same time, since they record a moment in which the prisoner was allowed to speak, they also open a space for certain elements of a life to be represented: details of geographical origin, references to relatives or acquaintances and places of frequentation, and the listing of possessions. Very occasionally, they allow the echo of a voice to be made out in the form of a mediated statement.

In the case of the men executed on August 13, 1578, there are two sets of entries. The first, in the *Giornale*, busta 5, vol. 10, in an untidy hand and subsequently struck through with a diagonal line, seems to have been taken down hastily as the prisoners were interviewed. A carefully written and more formal text is found in the registers of *Testamenti*, busta 16, vol. 34, and was published by Domenico Orano.[3] In the *Giornale*, introductory and concluding statements surround summary entries in the form of a name followed by the items bequeathed or discussed. In the *Testamenti*, each entry stands separately and is introduced by a similar statement describing the fact of the man's detention in the Corte Savella prison (located in what is now the Via di Monserrato) and his state of mind, followed by the testament itself. The entry concludes by describing the execution that followed the celebration of mass. The *Testamenti* texts are thus much easier to read and more detailed. By the same token, they reveal clearly the process of elaboration of the "good" story of the prisoners' deaths; they also obscure fundamental information by introducing errors into the transcription. The geographical origins of the men, for example, are frequently deformed beyond recognition: "de la Mata, diocesi di Tortosa" becoming "de la Malta," "di Toledo" becoming "di Raditoldo," and "di Madrid, diocesi di Toledo" becoming "di

Madis"; "di Viana, diocesi di Ebora" is rendered as "di Vienna" and "di Monzon" as "di Maenza." We can easily imagine the brother assigned the task of writing up the clean copy of the wills in a state of tiredness or else in a hurry to be done with his pious but tedious task, perhaps less than convinced of its utility for the reprobates in question (in any case now dead) and quite likely eager to return to his family and the supper waiting for him at home. I will thus refer in the first place to the *Testamenti*, but complete or correct this information when the *Giornale* clearly offers a more accurate reading.

Most fundamentally, the registers of the Confraternity of San Giovanni Decollato indicate that the group executed was made up of eight men, thus confirming the figure given by the newsletters to Urbino and the account of Montaigne. They also confirm the Spanish origin of six of those involved, three of whom were Castilian, two from Toledo and one from Madrid; of the others, two were Aragonese/Catalan—one from Monzón, the other from the region of Tortosa—while the last was an Andalusian from Seville. The Spaniards were thus characterized by both commonalities and a diversity of regional attachments, which, while retaining significance in a foreign context, likely became secondary to a shared Iberian culture.[4] Of the two remaining friends, one was Portuguese, from Viana do Alentejo, near Évora; the other is said to come from "Pastrovichi in Albania" (rendered in garbled form in the *Testamenti* as "Patronichi" and "Frastonichi"). This man, who will elsewhere describe himself as a Slav, thus came from the region of the eastern Adriatic that the Italians called Schiavonia. Part of Venice's *Stato da mar*, including Dalmatia in the north and Albania farther south, the territory was subject to historic and ongoing disputes between the Republic, the Serbs, and the Ottoman Turks. According to Stephan Karl Sander-Faes, the cities of Budva (Budoa) and Bar (Antivari) in present-day Montenegro became part of Venice's Albanian province in 1405, Bar being lost again in the early 1570s. The area in between, ruled by the Serbian clan of the Paštrovići, came under the government of the Republic in 1423.[5] If we compare the information contained in the confraternity registers with the sources examined earlier, we see that Tiepolo was reasonably accurate in identifying men from Portugal and Spain. The informant of the Duke of Urbino wrote of Portuguese and Marranos, but also of an Italian boat- or ferryman. As we shall discover later, it is to the person from Venetian Albania that this last designation refers.

Each of the wills ends with a version of the formula "Poi fu menato in Ponte dove fu appiccato e poi fu posto sopra una caretta e portato a Porta Latina dove fu abruciato" (Then he was taken to Ponte, where he was hanged, and afterward put on a cart and conveyed to the Latin Gate, where he was burned). Once more, this confirms the information contained in the last newsletter report to Urbino. We learn in addition, however, that, before being transported by cart to the Latin Gate where they were burned, the prisoners were hanged "in Ponte"; that is, in the square adjoining the Aelian Bridge, facing the Castel Sant'Angelo on the opposite side of the Tiber, a common site for the carrying out of executions. This detail also allows us to appreciate fully the particularly spectacular nature of the ritual enacted on August 13, 1578. For not only was it highly unusual for as many as eight individuals to be put to death at one time but also, on this occasion, the lifeless bodies of the hanged men were paraded through the streets of the city, traversing its entire breadth from the northwest to the far southeast. This division of the pageant of death into two parts—hanging on one side of the old heart of the city, followed by a long procession to its remotest gate where a pyre was prepared—was unprecedented. When the authorities decreed that a corpse should be burned, it was generally done immediately after execution in the same place or nearby. On the occasions when bodies were moved, this was inevitably intended to convey a symbolic meaning, as in the case of a Dominican friar beheaded in jail and then taken to the Campo de' Fiori, where his corpse was burned along with his heretical books.[6] As Allie Terry notes, early modern penal justice was based on the public and violent punishment of offenders in ways seen to correspond to the offense committed. Thus, in Florence, "[t]he route of the criminal procession was lengthened depending on the crime that was committed, since, in order for the punishment ritual to be truly efficacious, the entire community needed to stand as witness against the criminal."[7] This was certainly the effect desired by the Roman authorities in August 1578, the performance of justice in this case pointing both to the extraordinary nature of the crime being expiated and its association with the Latin Gate.

Given that the Spanish men and their Portuguese and Albanian companions were not burned alive but first put to death in a less painful manner, we might assume that they cooperated with their judges and "comforters." That this was in fact the case is confirmed by the opening sentence of each entry, which states that the prisoner recognized his guilt, wishing to die a good

Christian, made his confession, and took communion. In the first entry, for example, we read that the prisoner "si rese in colpa de sua pechati et confessatosi si comunico et disse voler morir volentieri da buon christiano et perdono a chi l'haveva offeso, et domando perdono a tutti" (acknowledged the guilt of his sins and, having made his confession, took communion and said he wished to die willingly as a good Christian, and he pardoned anyone who had done him offense and asked pardon of all). While, as we have noted, the condemned men had every incentive to cooperate with the carceral and penal system, it also seems quite possible that some of them at least may have expressed genuine piety. Two of the Castilians reveal an association with their national church of San Giacomo degli Spagnoli;[8] all but two of the men left goods or money to charity or to the confraternity, four asking for a mass or masses to be said for their soul, of whom two specified a mass at a privileged altar (of which there was one in the confraternity's own church of San Giovanni Decollato). Moreover, and while again we must remember that this is the story the brothers wanted fervently to tell, all but one of the condemned men is said to have received communion "con gran devotione" (with great devotion).

A final characteristic shared by the prisoners is their low social status, which was undoubtedly a factor both in the way they acted and in their arrest and treatment by the police and courts. If a couple of them appear to have been a little more comfortably off and better established, none of them was wealthy and some were even recipients of charity from the Spanish church. Whether or not these circumstances were connected for any of them with a particular socioreligious heritage, some or most of them likely came to Rome in the hope of improving their economic prospects. Their situation was thus typical of that of a large segment of the city's inhabitants in the second half of the sixteenth century, a period during which its population doubled.[9] Most of these new immigrants were men, who outnumbered women in the central districts by a ratio of seven to three.[10] This skewed demographic was not due simply to the presence of numerous unmarried priests and religious; it was also the result of the current job market. In addition to the skilled legal and secretarial professionals they employed, Rome's many ecclesiastical households were staffed almost exclusively by male servants (cooks, grooms, coachmen, footmen, valets, and so on).[11] Beyond the domestic service sector, the city offered men unskilled or semiskilled work in the areas of agriculture and construction, as well as other forms of general manual labor (for example, porters). Much of this work was temporary or seasonal and characterized by a high rate of turnover so that workers were obliged to change jobs frequently, often needing to survive periods of unemployment, with some living in a state of quasi-permanent mobility. The majority of this male population was also single, living in less-than-stable lodging arrangements or else occupying a room in the house of a master or sharing an apartment or building with a group of coworkers. While some of the men who made their way to Rome in such straitened circumstances were able, over time, to accumulate the resources necessary to marry, for many this goal remained out of reach. Perhaps not wholly surprisingly, it is men from exactly the same demographic background who found themselves most frequently in court accused of the crime of sodomy—men of the lower classes, many of them single servants of various kinds, subject to one degree or another of marginality and mobility.[12]

In the San Giovanni Decollato registers, then, we first meet Baldassare or Battista, the Albanian. He bequeaths nothing but his cloak, which he asks be given to charity. The wills of two other members of the group are equally devoid of possessions: Gasparo di Vittorio, from Monzón, leaves nothing behind; Francisco d'Errera, from Toledo, leaves only what he is wearing, an "abito lionato," that he says belongs to the Spanish church and should be returned there. This tawny-colored garment might be some kind of coat; alternatively, it might be a religious habit. Also from Toledo, Girollimo/Geronimo leaves to charity a hat or cap made of sarcenet (a kind of silk) and the modest sum of thirty-four and a half baiocchi for a mass.[13]

Antonio Valies, from La Mata (Tortosa), is more talkative and seems to have closer ties to a number of people, including family members with whom he is in contact. What he has to leave behind, however, is a string of debts that he begs his parents to cover, after asking for their forgiveness. In this way, Valies admits to owing fifty-four gold scudi to a certain Pedro Galliano (lent to him ten months earlier in Milan), ten scudi to his grandfather, and to his uncle's widow the cost of various measures of black velvet and satin and a used black jacket of fine cloth. In addition, he owes eight reali (= 8 giuli) to a priest and has taken two or three measures of grain from the store his father shares with friends. Finally, he asks his parents to give ten gold scudi on his behalf to the poor. Accordingly, if Antonio himself was devoid of cash, we must assume that his immediate family, whose members would seem to be nearby, was not without resources. Given the extent to which expensive kinds of cloth and items of clothing figure in the list, we might also wonder whether some of his relatives, notably his aunt and late uncle, were not tailors or involved in the garment trade. Materials died black also tended to be particularly costly. Was this black velvet and satin destined for a clerical wearer? Or did Antonio have made for himself, without ever paying for it, a very handsome set of clothes?

Bernardo or Bernardino d'Alfar, from Seville, also owed money in the amount of four scudi to a certain Manuel de Errera, living near the residence of the French ambassador. He asks Errera to forgive him the debt and, moreover, to have two masses said for him at a privileged altar. Alfar bequeathed only a small amount of cash—thirteen baiocchi—to the confraternity, again for a mass for his soul. The short cloak of black Florentine cloth that he left at the prison he gives to charity.

The two remaining men arrested and executed appear to have been the best established, having the most in the way of material possessions; it is perhaps unsurprising, then, that we will find them to have been at the center of the group and its activities. Alfonso di Rogles, from Madrid, left a number of items of clothing in the prison that he donates to charity.[14] He has additional clothing, including boots and a shirt, in the room that he rents from a certain Lucia near the church of Saint Augustine; these he gives to the confraternity, to which he also bequeaths a giulio for them to say a mass for his soul. In a city in which accommodation was often hard to come by, finding a bed could, in and of itself, prove to be a challenge. Robles had trestles and boards on which to sleep, along with a mattress, but he did not own them; they belonged to the church of San Giacomo, to where he asks they be returned.[15] To his landlady, Lucia, he leaves a copper pot, which she already has, in lieu of the five giuli he owes her for rent. Finally, Alfonso states that he has left a letter in the oratory of the prison that he asks be sent to Flanders, to his wife.

Marco Pinto, the Portuguese member of the group from Viana do Alentejo, lived in rooms at Saint John at the Latin Gate. As a result, we can see that he formed the link between the other men and this church. He also has to his name considerably more possessions than any of his companions, all of which he gives to the confraternity to distribute as alms for the good of his soul. These include various pieces of furniture—two tables and a dresser or sideboard—and household goods contained in a (or three) chest(s), including napkins, tablecloths, and a cooking pot with feet. He also has a large stock of poultry: sixty chickens, twenty hens, and twelve cockerels.[16] Pinto also lists two items of clothing—a canvas jacket in his rooms at San Giovanni and a pair of leather above-the-knee breeches left in the prison ("un paro di calzoni di corame").[17] Finally, Marco Pinto donates thirty and a half baiocchi to the brothers to say a mass for his soul at a privileged altar.

These, then, are the men whose actions set in motion the wheels of Roman justice and generated stories that would spread throughout Europe, stories that converge and diverge, stories heard today only in a murmur. In their final hours of life, these men were "cataloged" in the registers of a pious confraternity. We learn where they came from, of some of their relationships with families and friends, of the few ordinary and meager possessions they had managed to acquire, and of the material preoccupations they expressed— mostly the recognition of obligations unfulfilled and the surrendering of basic objects and items of clothing to others as poor or poorer than themselves. If I have dwelt on the details contained in the wills recorded by the Confraternity of San Giovanni Decollato, it is in part because they offer elements that become meaningful in relation to other information, elements that contribute to our increased understanding. However, I dwell on these details not only for what they might tell us but also for what they do not tell us, to preserve what is gratuitous and accidental, what cannot be recuperated into narrative, to adumbrate what is lost.

The effect on me of reading these documents was akin to that described by Michel Foucault as he worked on the brief case summaries recorded in the prison archives of the Hôpital général and the Bastille. Evoking "the resonance I still experience today when I happen to encounter these lowly lives reduced to ashes in the few sentences that struck them down," Foucault confides: "these 'short stories,' suddenly emerging from two and a half centuries of silence, stirred more fibers within me than what is ordinarily called 'literature' . . . owing, no doubt, to the mere fact they are known to have lived."[18] Like those of Foucault's "infamous men," the obscure lives of these early modern immigrants to Rome were suddenly transformed by their encounter with power, an encounter that focused on them a brief but intense beam of light, generating "fragments of discourse trailing the fragments of a reality they are part of," but also characterized by a "rarity and not prolixity that makes reality equivalent to fiction."[19] The depositions made only hours before the condemned men were executed are both legal documents and pious fictions, momentarily illuminating lives that they serve to write out of history, literally preparing them for and justifying their extinction. Their rapid and highly controlled entry into and erasure from history thus form a single, poignant movement.

And so I feel the vain imperative to preserve what flotsam of these sunken lives manages to traverse time's ocean and wash up on our twenty-first-century shore. Objects precious and useless, so many reality effects, at once compelling and ineffectual, significant pointers to an external materiality and random signs stripped of meaningful context.[20] Before going further, these objects invite us to pause, to let our imagination dwell on some of their queer legacies: a bed borrowed from and returned to a church, no doubt harboring memories of illicit desire and illicit pleasure; a letter to a wife, left behind yet not altogether forgotten; expensive black cloth, velvet and satin, acquired on credit, never paid for; a pair of fancy leather breeches, apparently donned for a celebration, removed and laid aside in jail.

Chapter 6

Voices on Trial

Beginning with Battista the Boatman

It is in the fragmentary remains of the transcript of their trial that we hear most clearly the voices of the group of men arrested at Saint John at the Latin Gate on Sunday, July 20, 1578, and executed some three weeks later. Again these documents contain much information that points to historical realities at the same time as they fail to answer some of our keenest questions. Most importantly, the voices on trial are transcribed according to judicial protocols. As with the other sources examined, then, the court records relay, more or less clearly, stories that must be discerned and interpreted: stories in the form of the accounts of events presented by the accused, as they no doubt try to minimize their guilt and perhaps even to incriminate others; stories that their tellers revise when confronted with information elicited separately from other prisoners; stories that respond to the formulation of questions and statements by the judge that reveal his own attitudes and presuppositions; stories of individuals broken down by torture.

Of the three fragments recording the court proceedings brought to light by Giuseppe Marcocci, only one, unfortunately, is substantial.[1] The greater part of the transcript, including the beginning and the conclusion of the trial, is thus missing and almost certainly deliberately destroyed in order to suppress its contents. The remnants that survive, moreover, would seem to represent not the originals but a copy, if the information sent to the Fuggers on August 16 is accurate: "Il giorno inanzi furono giustiziati gli Spagnoli sendo stati abbrug-giati i corpi et i processi loro nel luogo dove furono presi per estinguerne a fatto la memoria" (The previous day the Spaniards were executed, their bodies and their trial records having been burned in the place where they were arrested in order to erase all memory of them).[2] The surviving fragments were rebound, out of order, so that the series of interrogations recorded appears as follows:

fols. 550r–569v	3) Bernardo de Alfaro (end of interrogation)
July 27–31	Hieronimo de Pacis [cf. earlier Geronimo] (seemingly first interrogation)
	Bernardo de Alfaro
	Fr./Br. Battista (G.-B.) Caviedis (seemingly first interrogation)
	Antonio Valez [cf. earlier Valies] (seemingly first interrogation)
	Battista (seemingly first interrogation)
	Marco Pinto (beginning of interrogation; transcript breaks off)
fols. 570–572	4) missing
fols. 545r–546v	1) Gasparo Vittorio (end of interrogation)
July 27 or earlier	Bernardo de Alfaro; confrontation with Francesco [or Francisco] Errera (beginning of interrogation; transcript breaks off)
fols. 547–549	2) missing
fols. 573r–574v	5) Alfonso Robles [cf. earlier di Rogles] (unable to
August 3	appear in court)
	Antonio Valez; confrontation with Francesco [or Francisco] Errera (beginning of interrogation; transcript breaks off)

If we compare these names to those that figure in the registers of San Giovanni Decollato, we see that all the men executed are represented here, although no testimony is recorded from Alfonso Robles, who is described as being unwell (possibly due to the effects of having been tortured). As we shall see, the situation is complicated by the apparent presence in prison of two men with the same name, Francesco Errera, one Spanish, the other Portuguese. Finally, a certain Brother or Father Caviedis is interrogated, and reference is made to Cristopharo Lopez, also among the arrested. In this way, we can conclude that if Montaigne and the informant of the Duke of Urbino were correct in referring to eight men executed, Antonio Tiepolo was also accurate when he affirmed that eleven men had been arrested.[3] Three of those held were apparently not sentenced to death (a fact corroborated in part, as we saw earlier, by the final newsletter report to Urbino).

The criminal case was heard by the judge Paolo Bruno in the Court of the Governor (*tribunale del Governatore*), the judge's questions being recorded in Latin, the prisoners' responses in the Italian vernacular. In sixteenth-century Rome, the prosecution of sodomy was usually dealt with by this court or else that of the Vicario, the Inquisition becoming involved only in cases where there was a suspicion of false belief.[4] Following the Council of Trent, however, all cases involving marriage—such as the relatively frequent accusations of bigamy—would be dealt with by the Inquisition since, for the Catholic Church, they involved a sacrament called into question by Protestant Reformers. That the San Giovanni group was not tried by the Inquisition might imply that this body was not convinced that the men were guilty of holding heretical ideas about matrimony. At the same time, the severity of their sentencing to death, relatively rare for convictions of sodomy without violent or aggravating circumstances, certainly suggests that this was not an ordinary case. Marcocci speculates that the Court of the Governor could act more quickly and discreetly than the Inquisition, thus assuring the swift punishment of the accused and avoiding a longer trial, which likely would have been more embarrassing for the Church.[5] Whatever the case, it seems all but certain that the Inquisition and the pope must have been involved in the decision to adopt this strategy, as is affirmed, as we have seen, by the newsletters to Urbino and to the Fugger family.

Taking the transcripts in chronological order (section 1 in the list), we first meet Gasparo Vittorio, briefly, who signs his name at the conclusion of his testimony. Gasparo is followed by Bernardo de Alfaro. Alfaro admits to being a friend of Alfonso Robles and the other Spaniards who were often at San Giacomo. (This may be a mistake for San Giovanni, or it may refer to the men meeting also at their national church of San Giacomo degli Spagnoli, with which, as the wills reveal, at least Robles and Errera had connections.) When asked if he has ever had sex with or at least slept in the same bed as Robles (*coabitare*; *dormire*), Alfaro denies the charge, the words recorded paralleling in the vernacular the judge's Latin (as well as recalling the expression of Montaigne, in particular the verb *habiter*): "io non son dormito mai ne habitato insieme con Robles" (I've never slept or had sex together with Robles). The court does not believe this and warns Alfaro to tell the truth, since not only Cristopharo Lopez but several other witnesses have testified to the contrary. When Alfaro maintains his denial, the court brings in one of these other witnesses, Francesco Errera, to confront him. Errera confirms his earlier testimony, repeating that Alfaro had buggered a certain Agilar ("Agilar si faceva bugiarare da Alfaro" [Agilar used to get buggered by Alfaro]) and that many times he had also slept with and buggered Robles, as the witness had been told by Robles himself ("Alfaro qui presente bugiarava Robles che questo me lo diceva detto Robles") [Alfaro, here present, used to bugger Robles; that this the said Robles told me]. The scene turns into a series of repeated accusations and denials.

When we next hear Alfaro, however (section 3 in the list), he is spilling the beans about his own sex life and that of his friends. In his final brief extant interrogation (later in section 3), we discover the reason for Alfaro's change in attitude when he refers to his deposition of the previous day— "doppoi che io fui levato dalla corda" (after I was hoisted up with the rope)— and the judge requires that he confirm his earlier testimony "postquam fuit depositus a tortura" (after he was subjected to torture). We thus see the working of the court's methods of interrogation, which include the infliction of pain by means of the *strappado* or *corda*.[6] While this use of torture must obviously make us suspicious of some of the statements produced, it does not invalidate them in their entirety since the court is usually looking for confirmation of specific details it has already elicited from one or more of the other prisoners. These are drawn from members of the group as they are interrogated separately from each other and led to reveal different pieces of information in response to particular questions. It also appears that whereas some of the men tried to say as little as possible, a couple of them, from the beginning, decided that their best strategy was to cooperate with the judge and to volunteer sensitive information. In doing so, they no doubt hoped not only to secure favorable treatment from the court but also to minimize their own role and involvement in the versions of events they presented. Two men in particular seem to have followed this course, Cristopharo Lopez and one of the two men named Francesco Errera.

In the remaining extant depositions, in addition to statements by Errera, we hear testimony from five of the other men: Hieronimo or Geronimo de Pacis (no doubt Paz in Spanish); Battista Caviedis, referred to alternatively as Father or Brother; Antonio Valez; another man named Battista; and, finally, Marco Pinto. Let us turn now to these, beginning with the background stories they offer, one of the most complete being that of the layman Battista (not Father Caviedis).

When asked about his arrest, Battista paints a domestic picture of that Sunday afternoon at San Giovanni: he was putting water on to boil to pluck some chickens, Pinto was sweeping the room, a Roman youth was sitting in a chair. When asked why he thinks he was arrested, Battista reveals that he works as a boatman, ferrying people across the Tiber, and that, about a month ago, on Saint Peter's Day, he was involved in a brawl. When another ferryman ran into his boat, he hit him over the head with a piece of wood. The story Battista tells is evidently about establishing an alibi, incriminating himself in a minor way in order to feign ignorance of any other possible motive for the arrest. Later he will reveal more details of interest in relation to this altercation, but first the court asks him to state when and why he came to Rome. Battista explains that he is a Slav (or Serb, "sciavone") from Pastrovichi or Paštrovići and that he came to Rome in the Holy Year of 1575. Lacking money, he stayed for only five days, however, moving on to Terni where, for a month and a half, before getting into another fight, he worked an olive press. He left and supported himself in the same way, he says, for four or five months in Torni, after which he returned to Rome. Battista goes on to detail the different locations where he has lived in the city and the people he has worked for. When asked about his friends, he names Robles, whom he used to visit at several places: where Robles lodged with his aunt, Anna Lopez, the hospital of San Giacomo degli Incurabili, when he was ill, and, most recently, at his room in the house of Lucia. During much of his time in Rome, then, Robles has been dependent for accommodation on women. Renting out rooms was, in fact, a ready way available to women to generate income since they were not required to own the space they let, but might themselves be tenants. The men who typically took advantage of such arrangements practiced, as likely did Robles, low-level, semiskilled, or unskilled trades or were laborers.[7] Battista also reveals that Robles's current landlady, to whom he left a copper pot in his will, is a courtesan ("cortegiana"). This connection of the Spaniard and his friend to the world of prostitution is significant and suggestive of the fact that they likely shared in aspects of the life of this milieu. The church of Sant'Agostino, near which the rooms Lucia rented out were located, moreover, was an address particularly favored by courtesans.[8] At the very least, lodging with a prostitute in this area would seem potentially to afford a degree of freedom from the moral surveillance that a more "respectable" landlady or landlord might impose.

The judge next tells Battista to detail his relationship with Robles from the very beginning. At this point, Battista admits that he first met Robles fourteen or fifteen years earlier in Flanders, a fact of which the judge is aware, since it was revealed to him by Alfaro in his testimony after being tortured. In around 1563 or 1564, then, Battista was working on two ships being built for the Genovese, while Robles ran an inn ("faceva l'hostaria") where Battista went with friends to eat on holidays. The reference to Flanders raises the question of whether Robles was living with his wife at this time. Battista is silent on the matter, yet it would seem that obtaining a position as an innkeeper or publican would have been easier for a married man than for a bachelor. Moreover, while it is possible that Robles's wife might have accompanied him from Spain, the fact that she remained in Flanders after her husband left might suggest that she was a native of or resident in that region. The reasons for Robles's departure will be discussed shortly. At this point, however, and while it is impossible to be certain, we can see that Robles's ability to establish himself in such a key role within a community, of which he was not a native, might well have been a consequence of marrying a local woman. While we do not know the precise nature of the work Robles obtained in Rome, his living arrangements suggest that he was not able to achieve there the same level of social integration and economic success as he had earlier. If Robles did indeed marry in Flanders and the wedding took place in church, the ceremony must have resembled closely that of the rite of Malines/Mechelen described in chapter 3. His wife must also have belonged or had ties to the Spanish community—numerous as a result of Spain's control over the Low Countries at this time, but resented by many

Netherlanders as representatives of an occupying power. Indeed, the Dutch War of Independence or Eighty Years War would break out only a few years later in 1568, with seven northern provinces gaining their independence in 1581.

After remaining in Flanders for about eight or nine months, Battista left, following a quarrel over his wages with the captain in charge of the ships. Going first to London, he sold exotic goods, such as rosewater and balls scented with musk, that he claimed to have brought back from the Levant. Setting out for Seville on a ship attacked by English pirates, he ended up in Brittany, where he enlisted in the army of the King of France. After eight or nine months in a garrison in Nantes, he was involved in a campaign, after which he went to Tours where the company was disbanded. Making his way to Paris, he then worked for four months as a groom before enlisting in the army of the King of Spain and returning to Flanders, no doubt to fight against the Dutch who had taken up arms for the cause of independence. During this second stay, Battista specifies, he did not have any contact with Robles. At this point in his interrogation, however, the prisoner made a strategic error by adding of his own accord ("ex se"), while the scribe was still writing, that the record should state that he did not meet up with Robles because he did not go looking for him, that he had gone to Flanders because of the war. In wanting to emphasize that he did not seek out Robles—and thus evidently to minimize their familiarity—Battista says more than is required, and the judge, picking up on his defensiveness, presses him to say why he feels compelled to justify himself in this way. Battista can find no better explanation for his misstep than to respond that they had asked him about Robles repeatedly. In fact they had done so only once, although specifying that he should give a full account.

Resuming the narrative of his past, Battista reveals that after eight months in Flanders as a soldier, he returned to Paris, where he reenlisted in the army of the French king for a period of about four years. Next he fought with the Venetians for one year in Crete. At that point, he returned to his home region for a year before coming to Rome, as he described earlier, for the Holy Year indulgence. While Battista's career was thus particularly vivid and itinerant, it illustrates well the situation of a number of his companions, which was that of many (im)migrants in Rome. These men, poor and of low birth, often moved around extensively in search of precarious, unskilled work. Robles, too, as we have seen, had been in Flanders and perhaps other countries after leaving Spain. Others of the men reveal that they have served as soldiers; several describe periods working as servants.

Having learned the history of his movements, the judge proceeds to ask Battista about Robles and about his reason for being at Saint John at the Latin Gate on the day of the arrests. In response, Battista returns to the story of his brawl with another boatman, disclosing that in its wake he had taken refuge in the house of a cardinal, Giovanni Girolamo Albani, in order to benefit from its legal immunity ("franchitia").[9] On the Thursday preceding the Sunday of the arrests, Robles came and found him, accompanied by two youths dressed as hermits ("dui gioveni vestiti da romiti"), now among those in prison. Robles advised Battista to go to San Giovanni and, when the latter replied that he did not know the way, told him that the two youths would act as guides. This they did, before returning to Rome one after the other. In this way, Battista reaffirms his alibi of having gone to San Giovanni to evade the hand of the law following his public fight ("per scansarmi dalla corte per questa cortione"). He then adds, referring back to the opening scene evoked in his deposition, that the chickens he intended to pluck had been brought, he believes, by Robles, not by himself, again evidently seeking to minimize his own involvement in the day's activities. The question of the exact nature of these activities, we will leave aside for the present in order to explore a number of other points.

First, it is clear that Battista's relationship with Robles is of interest to the judge; no less evident are Battista's nervousness about this and his desire not to deny the relationship's existence (no doubt impossible to do) but to minimize its importance. At the very end of his interrogation, the court will ask Battista if he has a history of previous convictions or been investigated for any crime. When the boatman replies in the negative, he is informed that the court knows he has been imprisoned several times for sodomy, twice regaining his liberty through the intervention of Robles. In response to further questioning, Battista also denies that Robles ever sought to sodomize him or that he sodomized Robles. Again, however, the judge informs Battista that the court knows very well that he has been sodomized by Robles for many years. Battista, for his part, repeats his denial that he ever buggered Robles or Robles him. Just before introducing this line of questioning, the judge had asked if Battista knows Bernardo Alfaro, which he had also denied. The reason for this question is that, after being tortured, Alfaro told the judge that when Robles left Flanders he was fleeing from the law, having been accused of sodomy and other crimes committed in gangs ("bande"), that Robles had kept ("tenuto") and buggered ("bugiarato") Battista for fourteen years, and that, on two occasions, Robles had succeeded in saving Battista from being burned at the stake.

Since the bond between Battista and Robles has been and is close and goes back some fourteen or fifteen years, should we think of them as forming a couple?[10] Even if the two men have known each other for a relatively long period of time and apparently had an intimate sexual and affective relationship in Flanders, it is difficult to say exactly where things stand between them at the moment of the trial. Robles is apparently still looking out for and helping Battista, but that he is "keeping" him and having sex with him is affirmed only by Alfaro, under the effect of torture, who also affirms that Robles has sodomized Gasparo Vittorio. Moreover, as was noted earlier, the two main prisoners cooperating with the court, Cristopharo Lopez and Francesco Errera, have both testified to the fact that Alfaro himself regularly has sexual relations with Robles, Errera maintaining in his confrontation with Alfaro that Alfaro has buggered both a certain Agilar and Robles many times. Later Alfaro himself will admit to the judge that he has buggered Agilar twice but also "io sono stato bugiarato da Robles et io ho bugiarato lui et havemo fatto la pugnetta insieme" (I've been buggered by Robles and I've buggered him and we've jerked off together). In all these descriptions, as throughout the trial, the specific sexual roles played by each man is clearly indicated, one being active in anal sex, the other passive. It is true that the court is anxious to establish the precise actions of each prisoner. Yet completely role-neutral expressions, such as the modern "to have sex" or even "to fuck" with a plural subject ("we fucked" as opposed to "I fucked him"), were less current in this world where sexual role was the primary conceptual and habitual category. At the same time, there exist other sexual activities, such as masturbation, here referred to colloquially, and the language used to describe them is couched in terms of mutuality.

According to these statements, then, both Robles and Alfaro were alternatively active and passive—in modern terms, versatile. Both had penetrated other individuals (Battista and Vittorio in the case of the former; Agilar in the case of the latter), but they were also alternatively active and passive with each other—and the fact that Alfaro discloses the information about his own passivity with Robles, whereas Errera had spoken of him as being active, makes this all the more credible. The insight we are accorded here into sixteenth-century sexual practices is as important as it is rare. For we meet two men whose sexual activity does not limit itself to one role nor to a youthful object; in this way, it does not conform to the pederastic paradigm that was in some sense the "norm"—both outlawed and criminal and institutionalized, part of habitual male sexual culture. Versatility among and between adult males has often been presented by historians as a unique characteristic of "modern sexuality," defined in terms of the sex of the object of desire rather than in terms of sexual role, as it develops from the later seventeenth or eighteenth century onward. Robles and Alfaro require that we revise this view. Specifically, they demonstrate the existence in the late sixteenth century of a flexibility and diversity of sexual practices, which, in some instances, were less rigidly codified than a historiography of dominant cultural paradigms has recognized.

From this perspective, Battista, too, is an interesting figure. The boatman was not only an adult, like Robles and Alfaro; he was, in addition, a big, brawny individual. At one point, Antonio Valez refers to him as "grande"; as we have seen, he served frequently as a soldier and had a penchant for getting into fights. Battista is also said to have been sexually passive. As such, he represents another kind of person that the history of sexuality has not frequently been able to identify in the past and has often associated with modernity. Unlike other members of the group whom we shall meet later, Battista was neither a youth—for whom sexual passivity might be accepted or even expected—nor was he an effeminate male, rejecting or giving up to some degree on masculine gender expectations and identifying, at least in terms of sexual role, with women. Again, then, he challenges us to rethink or to nuance some ingrained historiographical notions.

Although Robles and Battista had known each other for many years, evidence is lacking to designate them a "couple." Indeed, Robles may have had more of a current sexual relationship with Alfaro, whose strategy in incriminating Battista might have been to deflect attention away from himself. Perhaps, he might even at some level have been less than fond of Battista, this man from Robles's past whom Robles continued to frequent and help—despite his tendency to get into trouble—choosing to maintain a friendship and, perhaps also, sexual contact. This scenario, while clearly hypothetical, would nonetheless fit with the information recorded and take account of where it comes from and under what circumstances. In the end, and under the effects of torture, Alfaro would denounce not only Battista but also Robles as a disreputable character: "è un tristo et un homo di mala vita" (he's a bad person, a man of evil life).

Returning, in conclusion, to Battista's report of being guided to San Giovanni by two youths, it is striking that this directly reverses the pederastic scenario of adult men taking with them or abducting boys for sexual purposes, a scenario that, as we have seen, shapes the accounts contained in the newsletters to Urbino and to the Fuggers and the *Avviso di Parnaso*. While, as he does elsewhere, Battista is no doubt trying to stress his lack of familiarity with the church, the story he tells of Robles's visit and his taking refuge there to lie low is not without plausibility. The fact of the youths being dressed as hermits is intriguing, though it clearly represents a disguise intended to justify their presence at the church. Most intriguing, however, is the evidence of a man of Battista's lowly station having a connection of some kind with a high-ranking cardinal or, more likely, with some part of the prelate's household. What is more, the titular church of Giovanni Girolamo Albani (the particular Roman church attributed to him as a cardinal) was none other than the basilica of Saint John at the Latin Gate. Since, as we have seen, Marco Pinto lived at this church, Battista's access to such an influential figure or to his entourage must undoubtedly have been through him. When Battista arrived at San Giovanni, he met Pinto, whom he claims he knew only slightly; when he tells Pinto that Robles has sent him, Pinto gives him food, drink, and shelter. At this point, then, let us turn our attention to the church of San Giovanni a Porta Latina and the member of the group who lived there, Marco Pinto. A question that will remain unanswered, but that should not be forgotten as we proceed, is the extent to which a prince of the Church might have been familiar with Pinto or aware of what was going on in his residence and, even more so, at his titular church.

Chapter 7

Saint John at the Latin Gate

Marco Pinto

The church of San Giovanni a Porta Latina, which has the rank of a basilica, is an important Christian site since it marks the supposed place of the martyrdom of Saint John the Evangelist—or rather the attempted martyrdom, because, according to legend, boiling in oil failed to kill Christ's "beloved disciple," who was subsequently exiled to Patmos where he wrote the Book of Revelations.[1] The Latin Gate is also a strategic point of entry into and exit from the city, through the Aurelian Walls, along the ancient Via Latina. In the sixteenth century, despite its symbolic and strategic importance, this part of Rome was an extremely remote and marginal place. Up until the nineteenth century, when the area was drained, it was a marshland frequently infested with malaria and exposed to attacks by brigands and criminals who made raids from the surrounding countryside. It is the isolation and inhospitability of the location that account for the fact that, over the years, a succession of different religious orders have been given charge of the church, but until recently, none of them ever remained for very long.[2]

Legally, moreover, the church had a peculiar status. In the twelfth century, it was made dependent on the Lateran canons—the chapter of the Roman cathedral church of Saint John Lateran, located some distance to the north. The canons received income from Saint John at the Latin Gate, but remained in general rather disengaged. From 1517 on, Saint John at the Latin Gate had been the titular church of a cardinal; it was also supposed to have a defender or commendatory abbot, appointed from among the canons and charged with its maintenance, and an archpriest, responsible for its everyday running. In 1578, the titular cardinal and archpriest were men of the highest importance. The former, as noted in the previous chapter, was Giovanni Girolamo Albani (named in 1570); the latter (since 1565) was Mark Sittich von Hohenems, the nephew of Pope Pius IV. If Albani financed some renovation work on the building, including the commissioning of a painting of the martyrdom of Saint John for the high altar in 1570, it is likely that he visited the church only occasionally for particular ceremonial occasions. For his part, Mark Sittich had an illustrious military and diplomatic career, taking part in campaigns against the Turks and acting as legate to Avignon and as governor of various towns in the Papal States. His interest in what for him was a very minor charge must have been extremely limited. The standard histories of the church record no name of a defender between those appointed in 1544 and 1630, which leaves an obvious gap for the years that interest us. They do, however, refer frequently to the presence of hermits taking care of the church on a day-to-day basis.

Saint John at the Latin Gate was thus an important church, but also a remote and somewhat neglected one. Both geographically and legally, it represented a marginal place, especially in the late sixteenth century in the apparent absence of the formally required defender. As we have seen, the Portuguese man Marco Pinto was living at San Giovanni, where he seems indeed to have been well established, with a number of pieces of furniture, various household goods, and a flock of poultry. Since the defender of the church was supposed to be appointed from among the Lateran canons and to hold the rank of commendatory abbot, this was clearly not Pinto's role at San Giovanni. It seems probable, however, that he served in some capacity like that of a lay caretaker or perhaps a sacristan, charged with the daily running of the site. It is this position and the particular legal and geographical situation of San Giovanni that Pinto was able to exploit to foster a very different kind of marginal culture, introducing "hermits" of an unaccustomed sort.³ As Alfaro puts it, after being tortured, "Pinto teneva quel loco a San Giovanni per bugiarare" (Pinto ran San Giovanni as a place for buggery).⁴

As we saw in the previous chapter, Battista related that he was guided to San Giovanni by two youths dressed as hermits, who accompanied Robles and were among those held under arrest in prison ("dui gioveni vestiti da romiti che sonno prigioni"). One of these youths was the Spanish Francesco Errera; the other was likely Geronimo de Pacis. Both were involved sexually with Pinto.

In his interrogation, Geronimo initially adopts the familiar strategy of trying to minimize his involvement in the day's events, saying that he was sick in bed ("io stava in letto amalato") and went to San Giovanni a Porta Latina on his way to the hospital at San Giovanni in Laterano. Battista later corroborates Geronimo's condition and his young age, but also suggests a link with Pinto, when he refers to "un giovine piccolo che stava amalato nel letto de Pinto" (a small youth, who was ill in Pinto's bed). Subsequently, however, Geronimo puts up little resistance to his interrogators and quickly offers the information that Pinto has buggered him many times, including, most recently, eight or nine days before they were arrested. The first time, however, was about six years earlier when they were both in domestic service, Pinto working as a cook, and the two servants seem to have shared a bed:

> I've been buggered many times by Pinto in this way; that while I was a ser-vant of the treasurer of Segovia and Pinto was his cook, he slept with me, and he buggered me very many times, and most recently it was eight or nine days before we were taken prisoner that he buggered me, and it's six years ago that the said Pinto began to do it to me and he's always gone on doing it to me.

> io son stato piu volte bugiarato da Pinto in questo modo che stando io per servitore con il Tesauriero de Segobia et Pinto era suo coco dormiva con me, et me ha bugiarato assai assai volte, et ultimamente sonno otto o nove di avanti fussemo pigliati prigione che me ha bugiarato et detto Pinto da sei anni fa che lui cominciò a farmelo et ha sempre continuato a farmelo.⁵

The scenario described here is a typical one in early modern Europe. It is worth noting, first, that the two lower-class Iberians find employment in Rome in the household of a Spanish ecclesiastical and financial official, the treasurer of the diocese of Segovia.[6] In this context, the older man can take advantage of his physical proximity to a youth to initiate sexual relations that take place along clearly determined pederastic lines (the former playing an active sexual role, the latter a passive one). In his own interrogation, Pinto will initially deny having had sex with Geronimo ("io non ho bugiarato Hieronimo"), perhaps as much to protect his younger partner as himself. Since the latter has already revealed their relationship, however, this could do little good, and no doubt sensing its futility, Pinto would soon make the following admission: "è la verita che hora me ricordo che io piu volte ho bugiarato piu volte Hieronimo de Pacis carcerato insieme con me et con esso ho fatto piu volte la pugnetta" (in truth, I remember now that many times, I've many times buggered Geronimo, who's in prison with me, and many times I've jerked off with him).

If Pinto introduces the pleasure of mutual masturbation, along with anal sex, we also discover that Geronimo is equally capable of being sexually active since, while he firmly denies being sodomized by anyone other than Pinto, he concedes,

> I think it was a year ago that, while a Frenchman who took care of the mule was staying in the said treasurer's house, I had him come and sleep with me one night; that the Frenchman <u>was called Sticolo</u> and I buggered him once; that then I didn't do it again because he left my master's service.

> credo che sia un anno che stando in casa del detto Tesauriero un francese a governargli la mula io lo feci venire a dormir con me una notte che quello francese se <u>adimandava Sticolo</u> et lo bugiarai una volta che non lo feci poi piu perche se partette dal mio patrone. (underlining in original)[7]

Taking sometimes a passive and at other times an active role appears to have been typical behavior for many youths as they matured and moved increasingly from the former to the latter, eventually abandoning their boyhood passivity altogether. At the same time, not all men made this transition, either completely or in part. In the case of the youthful Geronimo, his penetrative role is presented as an exception to his passivity with Pinto. Geronimo may well be hiding other information, of course. But if that were the case, it is strange that he should volunteer the fact of his sodomizing someone, since this act was considered more incriminating in a youth than passivity, which was often excused as unavoidable and resulting from constraint.

As for the Spanish Francesco Errera, he was certainly one of the San Giovanni "hermits" and is referred to as such by Brother Caviedis: "quello Errera, che va vestito da romito" (the Errera who goes about dressed as a hermit). We remember that Errera also had a tawny-colored garment (*abito*), perhaps the religious habit in which he masqueraded as a hermit, that he asked be returned to the church of San Giacomo degli Spagnoli. Errera knew Caviedis and had taken him to Robles's room in the city.

Is this man the member of the group who cooperated with the court, offering evidence against his friends, the witness we saw brought in by the judge to confront Bernardo Alfaro? As noted earlier, there was also a Portuguese man among the prisoners by the same name, who was not, however, one of those executed. Largely on this basis, Giuseppe Marcocci affirms that it was the Portuguese Errera (whose name he accordingly renders as Ferreira, as opposed to the Spaniard, whom he designates Herrera) who betrayed the others. While this hypothesis is possible, it raises a problem since the Portuguese Errera is said to be barely known to the group. Alfaro affirms, for example, that he had never met him before the day of the arrest and that the others were mistrustful of him. The Portuguese Errera's lack of familiarity with the men might be considered as corroborating the likelihood of his betraying them; by the same token, however, it is difficult to explain how he could have come into possession of the wealth of information he confides to the judge. This concerns not only Valez but also Alfaro and Robles, whom he claims to have seen sleep together many times in the place where Robles first lodged; he also states that Alfaro buggered Agilar and that Robles told him that Alfaro buggered him as well. All this implies a good deal of familiarity, even intimacy, with Robles and the others, hardly compatible with someone the group regarded as suspicious. Furthermore, during the interrogation of Antonio Valez, the judge asks the prisoner if he knows Bernardo Alfaro. This is because Alfaro has revealed information about him and one Cristopharo Ribera, whom we shall meet shortly. The judge next asks him if he knows Francesco Errera the Spaniard, which Valez denies. At this point, then, the judge seems to be asking Valez to comment on his relationships with the people who have given testimony against him. This is the most logical way to understand his evoking in succession the two particular individuals Alfaro and Errera. Without being able to be certain, then, it might seem more likely that it was the Spanish Errera, one of the youths dressed as a hermit, who "cracked" and informed on the others. If this was indeed the case, it did not gain him his life, whereas the Portuguese Errera was not condemned—perhaps he was in fact not closely associated with the group. The two other prisoners who escaped execution on August 13 were Cristopharo Lopez and Battista Caviedis, both of whom we shall meet farther. The release of these men was no doubt related to the stories they told the judge, as well as, in the case of the former, his willingness to inform on the others, and, in the case of the latter, his clerical status and privileges as a priest/religious.

In the interrogation of Marco Pinto, the first person the judge names in order to ask if Pinto has slept with him is Errera. Again, Pinto initially tries to conceal the truth, saying that the youth frequently stayed at his place, sleeping in the same room but on the floor, while Pinto took the bed. After a second denial, the court informs the accused that it knows he is lying. No doubt trying to minimize the guilt of both of them, Pinto then admits, "[L]a verita . . . è che io una volta bugiarai detto Francesco Errera nelle stantie mie che dormissemo assieme nel mio letto et io li messe il cazzo dentro al culo dove feci il fatto mio" (The truth . . . is that, on one occasion, I did bugger the said Francesco Errera in my rooms; that we were sleeping together in my bed and I put my cock in his ass and did what I wanted to do). Pinto's explicit language here might represent a response to a demand for specific details of the sexual act involved, but it might also perhaps express a rare moment of defiance in the extant transcript, a moment when Pinto appropriates his story and, without trying to conceal or mitigate it, puts his desire and his pleasure forthrightly into words. This latter possibility, if it cannot be established with certainty, is nevertheless corroborated by the subsequent exchange with the judge. Not surprisingly, the court is unconvinced by the concession that Pinto has buggered Errera, but only once. Alfaro, for one, has already testified that "lui ha bugiarato molti ragazzi" (he's buggered many boys). As a result, the judge instructs Pinto to list everyone he has slept with (*subagitare* = *subigitare*), whether in his rooms or elsewhere, at which point, the prisoner retorts, "Signore io me deletto di bugiarare et l'o fatto piu volte ma hora io non me ricordo quanti ne habbia bugiarati" (My Lord, my pleasure is to bugger and I've done it many times, but now I don't remember how many I've buggered). This is a striking affirmation since, at one and the same time, Pinto refuses to give any specific details (thus avoiding farther incrimination of himself and any partner he might name), yet does not back down before his judges; he does not try to hide or evade what he does and who he is, but instead defiantly claims his pleasure. The way in which Pinto does this, moreover, recalls similar vocabulary used in the same kind of situation in literary texts of the period. In a novella by Matteo Bandello, for example, a certain Porcellio, believed to be dying, is exhorted repeatedly by a priest to confess his sins against nature. Three times Porcellio denies committing any sin against nature, before exclaiming,

> Ho, ho, Reverend Father, you didn't know how to question me. Amusing myself with boys is more natural to me than eating and drinking is to mankind, and you asked me if I sinned against nature. Get along with you, Sir, for you don't know what a good morsel is.

> Oh, oh, padre reverendo, voi non mi sapeste interrogare. Il trastullarmi con i fanciulli a me è più naturale che non è il mangiar e il ber a l'uomo, e voi mi domandavate se io peccava contra natura. Andate, andate, messere, ché voi non sapete che cosa sia un buon boccone.[8]

If the protagonist here speaks in terms of amusement or play (*trastullarsi*), this echoes the earlier use by the narrator of the noun "delight" (*diletto*), which is the same expression employed by Pinto in verbal form. Porcellio furthermore uses a vocabulary of eating and of taste, to which, as we shall see shortly, Pinto also has recourse.

As with Porcellio (a fictional character apparently drawn after a historical figure), Pinto's sexual pleasure takes shape in pederastic form; it may nonetheless fail to conform to traditional expectations to the extent that his delight in boys does not supplement, but substitutes for and excludes a concomitant delight in women. While we cannot be absolutely certain of his lack of desire for the opposite sex, it is highly likely, given that no relationship with a woman is ever mentioned and that Pinto has surrounded himself at San Giovanni with youthful males.

Pinto's relationships with youths in fact extend beyond the immediate group of men arrested and the "hermits" he brings to the church. Stating that Pinto has buggered many youths, Alfaro continues, "[A]ncora credo che habbia bugiarato alcuni hebrei che praticavano lasu et quanti ne capitavano a san Giovanni dove lui stava tutti cercava di bugiarare" (I also believe that he buggered some Jews who used to go there, and however many of them turned up at San Giovanni, where he lived, he tried to bugger them all) (a statement he subsequently repeats and ratifies). Sexual relations between Christian men and women and those of other religions, notably Jews or Muslims, were, in general, an issue of great concern to the Inquisition and considered a strong indicator of potential heresy. In the present context, the court is no less interested in this question and asks Pinto about the "hebreos inberbes" (young, literally beardless, Jews) who frequented San Giovanni. Pinto denies having had any sexual relations with the Jewish youths, who used to visit, he reveals, on Saturdays (i.e., the Sabbath): "si come io ho detto delli altri che io ho bugiarati cosi direi se havessi bugiarato li hebrei li quali è vero che alle volte il sabbato venivano a san Giovanni ma io non ho bugiarato mai nesuno" (as I've told you about the others I've buggered, so I'd say if I'd buggered the Jews, who, it's true, came sometimes on Saturday to San Giovanni, but I never buggered any of them). When pressed as to whether he at least tried to sleep with them, Pinto persists: "io non ho mai recercato di voler bugiarare nesun hebreo perche io non havevo apetito et io non ne so il nome de nesuno et ce venivano quindici e vinti alla volta ma io non ne so nome de nesuno" (I've never sought to bugger any Jew, because that's not my taste, and I don't know the names of any of them; they came in groups of fifteen or twenty at a time, but I don't know any of their names).

In these few sentences, we have again a rare and precious window that opens briefly onto a hidden corner of life in Renaissance Rome. If the Jewish youths came to Saint John at the Latin Gate on Saturdays, this would indicate that these young people, presumably living in the ghetto, were able to observe the Sabbath as a day of rest and recreation. In Jewish tradition, moreover, the Sabbath eve is considered a particularly favorable time for sexual intercourse, at least within the bounds of the conjugal relationship.[9] It seems highly probable, then, that these youths were also indulging in Sabbath sex, away from the tight confines of the ghetto, with its limited space and prying eyes, under the complicit patronage of Pinto. That Pinto would also have taken part in sexual activities with these young Jews seems not unlikely. To his judges, however, he retorts that they were not his "type," literally, that he had no appetite for them. In this revealing expression, we hear once again an echo of the fictional Porcellio in Bandello's novella, who spoke of his sexual activity in terms of a taste for young goat (or kid) meat and of the choice morsel ("un buon boccone").[10] What Pinto says may have been true, but it is certainly possible to doubt it and to consider that he was again protecting those with whom he had been involved sexually. In fact it is to his credit that, throughout his testimony, Pinto never implicates anyone who is not already in prison with him and whom he knows therefore, in all likelihood, to be doomed. Naming his young Jewish visitors would have exposed them not only to potential prosecution for sodomy; the Inquisition would also have wanted to pursue them for illicit contact with Christians and a Christian religious site, for what we might term religious/ethnic miscegenation.

For, despite the inquisitors' efforts, there were those who found Rome's ethnic diversity sexually stimulating. In a poem by Curzio Marignolli, the speaker, a resident of the "alma città," loves sucking cocks and the more different kinds he can find, the better—those of rich men and poor, of Turks, Persians, and Jews:

> Bountiful city of Rome, where I for so many years
> Sucked so many cocks of so many kinds,
> Vassals to Turks, Persians, and Prester Johns,
> And as far as beyond the frozen Atlas,
> Some willingly and some by means of trickery,
> Some poor, some rich, some rogues;
> I made no distinction between noblemen and commoners,
> I sucked Christians and Jews alike.

> Alma città di Roma, ov'io tanti anni
> tanti cazzi poppai di sorti tante,
> vassali al turco, al persa, al Pretegianni
> et insin di là dall'agghiacciato Atlante,
> qual volontario e qual per via d'inganni,
> qual pover[o], qual ricco e qual furfante;
> non distinsi dal nobile al plebeo,
> tanto poppai il Cristian quanto l'Hebreo.[11]

Here is celebrated a transgressive eroticism of the exotic and the diverse. Sixteenth-century Rome offered something of this racial and ethnic diversity, and while it made religious authorities anxious and vigilant, it evidently fed the desires and imaginations of others. Despite his denial, was Pinto one of these? We cannot be certain, but it is striking that at this sensitive point in his questioning, he is able, once again, to avoid collaborating with his judges, to refuse to incriminate anyone else, and, paradoxically, to affirm his own particular desire and pleasure, to claim his own appetite, precisely in the act of withholding information.

The presence of these young Jews at San Giovanni necessarily reopens the question, raised in relation to the newsletters sent to the Duke of Urbino, of the religious and ethnic origins of the men arrested themselves, of their potential status as converted Jews or so-called New Christians. Were the connections of Pinto and the others with Roman Jews based on a shared, though in the case of the former denied, common religious and ethnic heritage? If so, might they, as a result, have been influenced by other ways of viewing sexual relations between men? In medieval Spain, a rich tradition of Hebrew poetry had evolved, some of it based on and adapting Arabic models, frankly homoerotic in nature.[12] In any event, this is not the last time that Jews will figure in this story. Whatever their own religious history and that of their families, some of these men evidently had close contacts with members of the Jewish community in Rome. At the very least, then, we catch a fleeting glimpse, in this supremely heterotopian site, of a sexual culture cutting across religious divides and of commonality, and even an apparent solidarity, between two marginalized groups—one a minority group within the dominant culture, the other doubly isolated and stigmatized.[13]

Chapter 8

Marriage as Alibi, as Euphemism, as Recruitment

We first encounter Antonio Valez in the testimony of Bernardo Alfaro: "Antonio Valez se era corocciato con Cristopharo perche non li haveva voluto dare da chiavare dicendomi anco che se era confessato et che non voleva più fare questo peccato" (Antonio Valez had become angry with Cristopharo because he didn't want to let him screw him, telling me also that he'd made his confession and that he didn't want to commit that sin any more). The statement, as recorded, is not without a degree of ambiguity, but it seems that Valez did not want to continue a sexual relationship with Cristopharo and that he had told Alfaro this, as well as that he considered what they had done a sin that he wished to avoid in the future. In his final extant interrogation, Alfaro gives further details concerning the former relationship between the two men: "ho inteso dire come ve racontai che Antonio Valez se faceva bugiarare da Cristopharo et che erano venuti insieme di Milano" (I've heard it said, as I told you, that Antonio Valez used to get buggered by Cristopharo and that they had come together from Milan). Here it is clear that the two knew each other before coming to Rome and that Valez was the passive sexual partner.

When the court interrogates Valez himself on July 29, it appears to be for the first time. Accordingly, the judge begins with questions concerning the day of the arrests. Valez states that he was taken prisoner, along with some other Spaniards, whom he knows only by sight, while they were in the tower of the church of San Giovanni. He explains that he had gone there the previous day because he had no money and nowhere to sleep in the city. He thus spent the night on the floor near the church sacristy. This reference to being devoid of any financial resources resonates with what we learned from Valez's will, in which he bequeathed nothing to his parents except a string of debts to various relatives and other creditors. The next morning, Valez affirms, he attended mass, after which two Spaniards arrived with food and all six people present ate together. As the conversation turned to the greatness of the city of Rome, they decided to climb the tower to enjoy the view it affords of the surrounding area. The judge next asks about Pinto, and Valez confirms that the former responded positively to his request to sleep there on Saturday night, but denies that Pinto ever asked him to sleep with him. When asked if he at least ate with Pinto at that point, Valez paints a picture of a convivial but very meager repast:

> My Lord, I will tell you the truth, that a certain big fellow who was staying there at San Giovanni with Pinto, who, I believe, is called Battista, a boatman, who was captured along with us, went into a vineyard where there are snails, which we cooked in Pinto's house. And we ate them there together, Pinto, Battista, myself, and someone else whose name I don't know. And I brought some bread and we drank water; that we had no wine and that is all we ate.

> Signore ve diro la verita che un certo grande che stava li a san Giovanni con Pinto che credo se chiami Batista barcharolo che è stato pigliato insieme con noi ando a una vigna dove sono delle lumache le quali furono cotte in casa de Pinto et ce le magnassemo insieme Pinto, Batista et io e un altro che io non ne so il nome et io portavo del pane et fu bevuto acqua che non ce era vino et altro non fu magnato.

Vineyards outside the city walls, as we saw earlier, were frequently the site of sexual activities, including the abduction and rape of boys by older youths or men. Here, they are presented as a source of precious but limited and basic nourishment. In his descriptions of the two meals he ate at San Giovanni, Valez is thus clearly at pains to convey an image of sober simplicity, as opposed to one of lavish indulgence and drunken excess.

The mention of Battista prompts the judge to ask if the boatman did not try to persuade Valez to sleep with him. When Valez denies this, the judge warns him that it is not credible that neither Battista nor Pinto should have tried to have sex with him and asks for how long he has known them. It is at this point that Valez mentions his friend Cristopharo Ribera, who, he says, took him to San Giovanni for the first time about a month earlier, just before Saint Peter's Day; the two friends slept that night on a table. For reasons we shall discover shortly, Ribera is not among those held in the Corte Savella prison. In the transcript, however, his name is underlined (as earlier with that of the French mule keeper Sticolo), suggesting that the authorities had taken note of it, no doubt with the intention of seeking to apprehend him. When the judge next asks for details of his relationship with Ribera, Valez states that they have known each other for about three years and were soldiers together in Milan. After their time in the army in the north, Valez left for Rome, where he had affairs to deal with, traveling through the Romagna; Ribera followed, making his way through Tuscany, before they met up again in the papal city. What Valez seems to be anxious to establish here, and contrary to the testimony of Alfaro, is that the two men did not come to Rome together, but that each made the journey separately and for different reasons.

The question of marriage comes up in Valez's next statement, in response to the court's telling him to describe what business it was that brought him to Rome:

> I came to Rome because I had made a vow to be a priest and to observe chastity and I wanted to be absolved of it, as indeed I was; that my vow was commuted; that I can get married provided that every day I recite five Our Fathers and five Hail Marys along with a Miserere, and that every month I make my confession and communion, and fast two Fridays each month, and that every year I make my confession and communicate on the Feast of Saint Peter.

> Io son venuto a Roma perche havevo fatto voto di essere prete et servar castita e volevo farmene asolvere si come io ho fatto che il voto mi è stato commutato

che io me posso maritare solamente una volta che ogni di dichi cinque pater-
nostri et cinque ave marie con un miserere et che ogni mese mi confessi et
communichi, et digiuni doi venardi il mese et che ogni anno me confessi
et communichi il di de san Pietro.

In this long and detailed statement, Valez is at pains to impress on the judge
his piety, his good Christian credentials, both in his initial taking of a vow
to remain chaste and become a priest and subsequently in seeking to be freed
from this obligation formally and his acceptance of the penitential exercises
that replaced it. The idea of a desire for chastity serves also, more specifically, to counter suspicions of debauchery and sodomy. And this is also surely
the sense of the reference to marriage. For it seems inconceivable that Valez
would be telling the judge that he would have liked to get married to another man, for example Cristopharo Ribera.[1] To do so would be to incriminate himself inexplicably, whereas his whole strategy up to this point has
been to minimize his friendship with Ribera. On the contrary, and more
logically, in speaking of marriage in the context of his release from his vow
of chastity, Valez again seems to have been seeking to establish his distance
from any form of shameful or illicit sexual activity and the potential of his
contracting an honorable, religious, and legal union with a woman. Marriage, in other words, is adduced here as an alibi.

Following the revelation of his vow, the court asks for details of Valez's
contact with Ribera in Rome. Valez responds that he had eaten with his
friend on two occasions and similarly slept with him twice, once at San
Giovanni (on a table, as he had stated earlier) and once at Cristopharo's house,
in the same bed. Following a series of accusations and denials regarding
whether the two former soldiers had sexual relations, the court questions
Valez specifically about the information it has received from Alfaro, namely
the disagreement said to have arisen between him and Ribera and the latter's departure from the city about two weeks earlier.

Alfaro had presented Valez as being upset with Ribera and not wanting
to have sex with him any more, indeed as repenting of having committed
"that sin." The story envisaged by the judge and proposed to Valez is thus
that he and Ribera had in fact left Rome at the same time with the intention
of traveling together, but that when Valez no longer desired to submit to Ribera's sexual demands, he became angry and returned to Rome by himself.
As the judge expresses it,

In truth when perhaps the accused was no longer willing to consent to that manner of shameful intercourse, he complained about it, and when the two of them had left the city with the intention of traveling together, the prisoner, angry with the same Cristopharo, returned to the city by himself.

verum etiam cum forsan ipse constitutus nollet amplius consentire huius-modi subagitationi de hoc conquestus fuit et cum ambo discessissent ex Urbe animo insimul itinerandi ipse constitutus cum eodem Cristophoro indigna-tus ad Urbem solus redidit.

Valez refutes this story, however, continuing to minimize the significance of his relationship with the other man: "Io son tornato a Roma perche ce havevo da fare et non perche Cristopharo me habbia bugiarato et io non volessi consentir piu et questa è la verita" (I returned to Rome because I had affairs to take care of there and not because Cristopharo buggered me and I didn't want to allow it any more, and that is the truth).

As noted earlier, the judge then asks Valez whether he knows Bernardo Alfaro and Francesco Errera the Spaniard. Since we know that some of the information just presented to Valez comes from Alfaro, it seems plausible to draw a similar conclusion with regard to the Spanish Errera. Following this brief exchange, the judge comes back to the parting of the two friends. Valez states that he saw Ribera for the last time at the Porta del Popolo as the latter left, with two other people he did not know, for Venice. Valez (as he noted earlier) had spent the night with his friend at the house of his master in order to bid him farewell the next morning.[2]

There seems little doubt, then, that Valez and Ribera had had an ongoing affective and sexual relationship, in which Ribera was the active partner, Valez the passive one. Nonetheless, in response to the judge's questions, which are shaped by the testimony he has received from other prisoners, Valez presents himself as merely accompanying his friend, with whom he had been a soldier, to the edge of the city to see him off and as never having had the intention of leaving with him. In this way, he denies any form of sexual relationship—even one he had come to regret, from which he had managed to free himself, and which had ultimately caused him to break off his friendship. On the other hand, Valez tries to show his profound piety, and this is the story he sticks to in his subsequent interrogation on August 3 (with the apparent discrepancy in detail that during the night he spent with

Ribera at San Giovanni, they slept not on a table but on the floor). Accordingly, the judge orders a confrontation with the prisoner Errera, who confirms his earlier denunciation of the two men. Valez continues his denials up to the point at which the fragment of the transcript breaks off.

We first hear the name of Father Battista Caviedis when Alfaro reports of him that he confessed to having been guilty of the same sin as the others, but claimed not to have committed it since the last Holy Year (1575). Soon afterward, the court questioned the priest in person, apparently for the first time as the interrogation begins with the circumstances of his arrest. Caviedis states that he had gone to San Giovanni that Sunday, having first eaten with someone in the city, to meet a Portuguese man with whom he was planning to make a pilgrimage; along with six or seven other Spaniards, he was taken prisoner while they were visiting the church tower in order to admire the view of Rome, which he was happy to be able to do since he was soon to leave. He adds that he had also been to Saint John at the Latin Gate about a week earlier, spending an hour or so viewing the fresco, while making a visit of the Seven Churches.[3]

The judge next questions Caviedis about his relations with Pinto, whom the accused says he has known somewhat ("così per vista") since the Holy Year—that is, for about three years—although he appears not to have been in Rome for the entirety of that time. When he and Pinto met, Caviedis explains, they were neighbors and ate together four or five times, and the priest slept at Pinto's place once or twice; he also slept once at San Giovanni, but by himself on a bench at the foot of an altar in the church. In response to further questioning, Caviedis reiterates that he did not sleep in the same bed or room as Pinto and denies that Pinto ever asked him to sleep with him. Furthermore, he claims not to know the other men arrested with him, given that he had recently journeyed back to Spain to make a pilgrimage to Santiago de Compostela and had only returned to Rome about two weeks previously. Clearly, throughout the early part of his interrogation, Caviedis is trying to understate the extent of his connections with Pinto and the others at San Giovanni, with whom, as will become clear, he is in fact much more familiar than he initially admits. This strategy includes referring to periods of absence from Rome; indeed, for a priest or friar, he appears to be a remarkably free agent, and we never hear of his being attached to any particular order or church. If he arrived at San Giovanni when he states, we can also assume that he did not celebrate the mass that Antonio Valez described attending. This, in turn, points to the presence of at least one other priest at the church that morning, attested also, as we saw in chapter 2, by the *avvisi* sent to the Fugger family on August 2.

Caviedis's relationship with Robles comes under scrutiny at a later point in his interrogation. In response to the judge's questioning, the priest reveals that Errera took him to Robles's house when he lived near San Giacomo degli Spagnoli; there he met, along with Robles, Robles's relative Cristopharo and a woman he did not know. The woman in question is almost certainly Anna Lopez, with whom Robles lodged for a time, and who, according to Battista the boatman, was Robles's aunt. The Cristopharo in question would be Cristopharo Lopez, to whom Pinto later refers as Anna's brother. If both of these pieces of information are accurate, Cristopharo Lopez would have been Robles's uncle, but also younger than his nephew, since Caviedis had referred to him earlier as a *giovine*. It is also Cristopharo Lopez, as we have seen, who has turned informer for the court. In particular, he has recounted two episodes involving the question of marriage that the judge will pursue. Both involve Robles, the first involves also Caviedis. And so, the suspect is asked to describe what the group at Robles's house spoke about that day.

When Battista Caviedis offers a recollection of a conversation about Robles suffering from shoulder pain, the judge says that he is interested in an important matter concerning the priest himself. In response to Caviedis's claim to have no memory of such a matter, the judge asks specifically about an episode, known to the court, when Robles said to Cristopharo, "io te voglio dar qui il patre Batista per moglie et voglio che ve sposate insieme" (I want to give you here Father Battista as your wife, and I want you to get married together). To this Caviedis responds,

> I remember that the said Robles spoke these words, that is, "Cristopharo, I want you to get married here with Father Battista," but I believed and still believe that he was making a joke, and at the time I laughed about it, not knowing what kind of marriage it was, and Cristopharo also laughed about it.

> Io me ricordo che detto Robles disse dette parole cioe Cristophoro voglio che te sposi qui con patre Batista ma io credevo et credo che burlassi, et io al hora me ne risi, non sapendo che sposalitio fusse quello et Cristopharo ancora se ne risi.

Twice, following this declaration, the judge asks what Robles was inferring with these words, and twice Caviedis responds that he does not know: "Io non so quel che se volesse inferire il detto Robles quando diceva di volerme fare sposare con il detto Cristopharo" (I don't know what the said Robles meant when he said he wanted to marry me to the said Cristopharo).

Is this a serious discussion of a marriage project? That hardly seems to be the case. Rather, it is not difficult to believe that Caviedis, while obviously trying to minimize the importance of the moment, is not lying when he says that it was all something of a joke that caused everyone to laugh. The witness is hiding something at this point, but surely not an intention that he and Lopez would solemnize a union. In this respect the adverb *qui* (here), which figures in the words both of the judge and of Caviedis, has a distinct localizing effect—the marriage referred to appears as something immediate, something in the moment and on the spot. It is also striking that in the scene, as recounted, it is not the two parties who take the initiative, but Robles who presses his younger relative to marry Battista, to let Robles give him Battista as his wife. The wording in the latter formulation is undoubtedly significant, implying that the priest will play the role of a woman. All this suggests that what Robles is proposing to Lopez is that, if he wishes, he can have sex with Caviedis and, more precisely, that he can "fuck him." This is what Caviedis would seem to be hiding.

At the end of chapter 3, we saw that the terms *marriage, husband,* and *wife* could signify, in a male–female context, having sexual relations. Likewise, here, marriage seems to function as a euphemism—as something of a code word—for sex, serving to designate in addition in the all-male context, the expected role of each partner. We have noted that, in Italy, as in early modern Europe more generally, boys often began their sex life as the passive partner of an older active youth or adult. After a period of transition during which they might be alternatively passive or active, many or most of these males would ultimately adopt a uniquely active role with other boys and/or women, and ideally with one of the latter in marriage. Cristopharo Lopez, the youth (*giovine*), is likely in this situation. Robles, his older relative, would be indicating to him the availability of the priest as a passive partner. By the same token, Robles infers that the adult Caviedis has not followed the prescribed trajectory of evolving roles. This will be corroborated at the end of Caviedis's interrogation, when the judge inquires about his sexual history.

According to his testimony, Caviedis was first brought to Rome, in 1572 or 1573, as the servant of a nobleman coming from the Spanish court, whom he names as Giovanni Antonio, and who was a guest of Cardinal Justiniano. The prelate in question, Vincenzo Giustiniani, former Superior General of the Order of Preachers (or Dominicans), had close ties with Spain. In 1569–70, he had served as an envoy from Pope Pius V to Philip II, being elevated to the cardinalate in the course of this mission.[4] In 1574, as one of a group of "trustworthy servants of the Catholic King," Giustiniani received a gift of one thousand ducats from the Spanish crown.[5] Both on the journey to Rome and while staying in the cardinal's house, Caviedis states, he was forced to acquiesce to his master's sexual demands:

> I've had dealings with him, that is, he buggered me many times, sometimes in bed, sometimes out of bed, but I don't remember how many times but I remained with him for about three months. And he started doing it to me on the journey and a few times he did it inside—he stuck his cock in my ass and did what he wanted to do—and many times, because I <u>couldn't bear it, he did it between my thighs without putting it</u> inside.

> con lui io ho hauto da fare cioe me ha bugiarato molte volte et qualche volta nel letto et qualche volta fora di letto, ma io non me ricordo quante volte ma con lui io stetti intorno a tre mesi, et mel comincio a fare per viaggio et alcune volte me l'a fatto dentro che me cacciava il cazzo in culo et faceva il fatto suo et molte volte perche io <u>non possevo tenere me lo faceva fra le coscie senza metterlo</u> tentro. (underlining in original)

The scenario described by Caviedis, evidently not particularly pleasurable, was nonetheless quite common. At the same time, we must remember that, in the context of the trial, the suspect has a clear interest in stressing the compulsion and duress under which he was placed. Moreover, even if he might perhaps have remained chaste in recent years, it would seem that being penetrated came to be the sexual activity that Caviedis preferred. So much, as we have seen, is implied by the conversation with Robles regarding Cristopharo Lopez. And if Robles regarded Caviedis in this way, he was not alone. For, while maintaining that he never buggered anyone and that no one other than his master Giovanni Antonio ever buggered him, Caviedis finally admits that, on many occasions, Pinto has tried to do so, as have, no less frequently, "various and diverse people" ("varie et diverse persone").[6] When the court expresses disbelief and presses Caviedis further, the cleric persists in denying any other relationships, then adds, unprompted, "otto giorni avanti che io fussi pigliato prigione passando dalli giudei fu un giudio che io non conosco quale me disse non sei tu delle commare et io li risposi cane perro dove me cognosci tu" (eight days before I was taken prisoner, passing through the ghetto, there was a Jew I don't know who said to me, "Aren't you one of those *commare?*" and I replied, "You dog. What do you know about me?"). The declaration is unexpected, its link with what precedes initially less than clear. What is the sense of this exchange with the Jew? What was the priest doing in the ghetto in the first place? Was the Jew who speaks to Caviedis known to him and vice versa? Perhaps the former was among those of his religion who had visited San Giovanni one Saturday? The priest responds with an insult expressed in both Italian and Spanish (*cane, perro*), suggesting that his interlocutor shared his own national origin or at least that Caviedis believed him to do so.[7] Once again, then, we see evidence both of the association of Jewishness with Spanishness in Renaissance Rome and of specific contacts between the Jewish community of the city and the group of men arrested at the Latin Gate. In the context of the series of exchanges with the judge, however, the supplementary anecdote Caviedis volunteers can only be read as an example of what the prisoner is affirming and the judge doubting: that the priest has frequently resisted many and diverse people who have solicited or tried to have sex with him, to bugger him. The Jew's remark identifying Caviedis as a *commare* would thus not have been intended primarily as an insult, to which the priest responded in kind, but as a pickup line that he angrily refused, proffered by a man who knew—or thought he knew—Caviedis's sexual tastes.

Unfortunately for Caviedis, it becomes quickly apparent that he has repeated verbatim his exchange in the ghetto or relayed it with an eye to authenticity too hastily, without reflecting on the consequences of disclosing all of its details in court. We have seen other prisoners at times reveal more than they intended, and this is certainly the case here with Caviedis. For when the judge asks him to explain what the Jew meant by calling him a *commare*, the priest can only backpedal and pretend not to know, thus abandoning his misjudged defensive strategy. The interrogation of Brother Caviedis ends at this point, and the judge declines to press him further on the meaning of *commare*. In fact, he has no need to do so, since Alfaro has already revealed this information:

> I can't tell you anything about Francesco Errera, the Portuguese man, because I've never seen him except for on the day we were arrested. On the contrary, one of us (I don't remember who) said: "Can we speak openly in this man's presence?" And Errera or Pinto said: "We don't think so; that it's not possible to speak in his presence"; that they said they believed him to be a respectable man, wanting to find out if it was possible to speak openly while we were discussing at times about our buggery, and those who served as women we called a *commare* so that the said Francesco would not suspect our revealing in this way, as we did among ourselves, of what it was we did.

> De Francesco Errera Portugese io non ve posso dir niente perché io non l'o visto mai se non in quel di che fussemo pigliati, anzi uno di nui che non me ricordo chi fusse disse queste parole potemo noi parlare in presentia di costui et Errera o Pinto dissero credemo de no che non si possa parlare in presenza sua che dicevano che lo havevano per homo da bene volendo inferire se si posseva parlare mentre noi ragionavamo alle volte di questi nostri bugiaramenti et quelli che servivano per donne le chiamavamo commare accio che detto Francesco non pigliasse suspetto di questo nostro palesarci così come facevamo tra noi di quel che facevamo.

Immediately following, Alfaro gives a specific example: "<u>Vittorio . . . tra di noi era chiamato per commare perche lui si faceva</u> bugiarare et serviva per donna" (underlining in original) (<u>Vittorio . . . among ourselves was known</u> <u>as a *commare*, because he used to get</u> buggered and served as a woman), information he later repeats in his next and last extant interview.[8]

Among the group of men arrested, then, at least two of them were known or perceived by the others to be a *commare*; that is, adults (as opposed to boys or youths) who chose to take a passive rather than an active role in anal sex. The term was not applied, however, to men who might occasionally take this role; for example, the "versatile" Robles and Alfaro. Nor is Battista the boatman ever referred to in this way, although, according to Alfaro, he too was passive with Robles. Perhaps this is because Battista might on occasion be active also? Perhaps, too, it is because Battista was a burly, masculine individual, and the role of *commare*, serving as a woman, might have implied some degree of perceived effeminacy, making it sit less easily with the combative virility of the boatman.

At this point, then, we can appreciate that the men who met at the Latin Gate had colloquial ways of describing their desire(s), using expressions such as *avere appetito* or *dilettarsi*. To talk about sex, they employed a number of popular expressions, such as *fare la pugnetta* and *chiavare/dare da chiavare*, that were generally current (the last verb remaining so to this day) and employed in opposite- as well as same-sex contexts. The same was true of the verbs *maritare* and *sposare*, though between males these took on a more euphemistic, perhaps even somewhat coded value; this was even more the case with the phrase *dare per moglie*, which alluded not only to a sexual encounter but also indicated a distinction in sexual roles. The most properly coded of the expressions used by the group, however, was the term *commare*; knowledge of its specific meaning was apparently restricted enough that it could be used in the presence of hostile or suspicious individuals. In contrast, it was immediately understood among those who often referred to themselves simply, though with no less self-consciousness, as *us*—"uno di nui," "tra noi," "fra di noi"—and as *friends*—"compagni," "compagni nostri."

The nature and constitution of the group are at issue in the next reference in the transcript of the trial to marriage between two men. The episode evoked again involves Robles and Cristopharo Lopez but now also Marco Pinto.

Immediately following Pinto's affirmation of the pleasure he takes in buggery, the judge asks him if he has had sex with Geronimo, which he denies. Then comes the following question:

Asked whether the accused, having gone to the house of the said Donna Anna, where he found the said Cristopharo, he urged the same to enter the school or society of the prisoner and others, for the purpose of sleeping shamefully with one another, using these or similar words, etc.

Interrogatus an ipse constitutus dum accessit ad domum dicte Donne Anne in qua reperto dicto Christofaro eundem ortatus fuit ut vellet introire in scola seu societate ipsius constituti et aliorum ad effectum se ad invicem subagitandi sub huiusmodi vel similibus verbis etc.

It is unfortunate that the words the judge alleges were used by Pinto are not recorded, but we gain a good sense of what they must have been from Pinto's response:

> [I]t's true that, going on one occasion to the house of Madonna Anna, I found there Robles and Cristopharo and I said to Robles that I would like to marry Cristopharo, and I said to him also that he should get involved with powerful people and not with lowlifes, and I don't remember saying anything else except this.

> è la verita che andando io una volta a casa di madonna Anna dove trovai Robles et Christoforo et dissi a Robles che io me volevo maritare con Christoforo et gli dissi ancora che lui se inpacciasse con persone possente et non con persone basse et non me ricordo che io gli dicessi altro che questo.

Do Pinto's words constitute testimony that he married Cristopharo Lopez, having sought Robles's permission for this as the closest older male relative ("asked for the young man's hand"), and that he likewise advised his friend to "make a good match" by himself marrying someone influential?[9] This does not seem to me to be what the evidence suggests.

Paying attention, once again, to the context of the exchanges in which Pinto's statement is made, the advice to Robles concerning the individuals he should be involved with appears to represent the Portuguese man's response to the accusation of forming a *society* or *school*. Rather than being part of a well-defined coterie, Pinto seems to be saying, he simply advised in general the cultivation of people of influence. In his statement, Pinto does not refer to finding a protector (a so-called husband) in the singular, but to "persone possente" in the plural.[10] It should also be noted that the verb *impacciarsi* (translated as "to get involved with") could have a sexual meaning.[11] It is unlikely that this is the primary sense of Pinto's statement to the judge, but if he did in fact use this particular term in speaking with Robles, it might well have been intended to allow for a sexual sense in his advice to his friend. Cultivating people of influence in the sixteenth century for someone who had little or none of it him- or herself might well have meant being prepared to offer sexual services in return. While perhaps not representing the whole story, then, Pinto's declaration here may well not be untrue; indeed, it fits well with the men's situation. As we have seen, Pinto began his career in

Rome as a cook in the household of the diocesan treasurer of Segovia. Through his association with this influential person or, more likely, with well-placed members of his staff, he seems to have been able to enter into contact with others, notably in the entourage of Cardinal Albani, and to have obtained his post at San Giovanni a Porta Latina. In this way, the Portuguese man was apparently more successful than most of his friends at establishing himself in his adopted environment. By the same token, Pinto may also have been expressing a criticism of Robles's relationship with individuals like the irascible boatman Battista, who, when he was in need of protection, was also able to take advantage, through their mutual friend, of Pinto's connections with the cardinal's household.

It is similarly in reference to initiation into a society that Pinto evokes his conversation with Robles concerning marrying Lopez, since Pinto would have no reason to reveal this were it not in response to the (unrecorded) words of the judge. We know that the latter, in turn, is basing his question on the version of events he has received from an informant, almost certainly Lopez himself. In this way, the young Lopez appears to have divulged two stories to the court concerning the idea of marriage in which he is involved, presenting this second one as relating to a form of initiation—as recruitment. The idea of forming a secret society is one that has long haunted homosexuals and sexual dissidents more generally, often reflecting a double lived experience: that of a group that needs to hide, to remain invisible, and that of the young or uninitiated who explore and learn from encounters with their elders or the less naive. It also reflects a social anxiety, a homophobic paranoid projection ("they're out to get our children"). In fifteenth- and sixteenth-century Italy, the term *school* is encountered in other contexts to designate known groups of sodomites.[12] The cultural scenario informing the framing of the story that passes from Lopez to and through the judge thus corresponds precisely to the one we encountered in a number of the newsletter accounts examined earlier: that of a group of men who attracted, controlled, or abducted boys or youths unable to resist. In the interrogation of Battista, directly preceding that of Pinto, the judge expressed even more clearly the idea of wedding ceremonies as introduction to sexual activity when he asked the prisoner "an saltim audiverit dictum Robles una cum multis aliis hispanis et presertim cum eo captis et carceratis tractare et discurrere super sponsaliis inter eos contractis et contraendis per ipsos ad invicem sodomitan[di]" (whether he had at least heard the said Robles along with many other Spaniards, and in particular those arrested and imprisoned with him, talking of and discussing marriages, contracted among them and to be contracted by them, for the purpose of sodomizing each other).

The judge's vision of marriages as initiation informs his next question to Pinto, when he asks what was meant by that kind of marriage ("huiusmodi maritationem") and with what ceremonies it was celebrated. Pinto's reply is direct and laconic: "questo maritare se faceva così quando una [*sic*] bugiarava l'altro et non ce se faceva altre cerimonie" (this marrying took place like this when one person buggered the other, and no other ceremonies were performed there). According to his own version, then, Pinto recognizes the sexual objective involved, but denies completely that any particular ceremony preceded it. The "marriage" was simply the sex and vice versa. In this way, the Portuguese man would not have been asking his friend Robles for the hand of his young relative; he would have been telling him he would like to fuck his young relative. The adverb *ce* (there) in this passage recalls the *qui* (here) in the story with Caviedis, suggesting the clear localization of the events—that the action designated by the verbal noun, the marrying, could take place there and then, as it were on the spot. In the story he told involving Caviedis, Lopez seems to have accused his relation Robles of inciting him to take advantage of the sexually passive priest. Pinto, in contrast, we know to have had a taste for being sexually active with boys or youths. In this instance, marriage would again be a euphemism or code word for sex, but Lopez was apparently able to tell a plausible story to the court that it also represented an attempt to force him to join a group of which Pinto was one of the mainstays. In this way, he sought—as it would turn out successfully—both to distance himself from the others and to present himself as an innocent victim, of the sort of which sodomy trials were full.

The story told by Pinto—like those of Caviedis and Lopez—probably does not reflect the whole truth, and he too, we must assume, would have sought to minimize his guilt. At the same time, it is possible to consider that his presentation of the events might not represent merely a denial of the facts but might also reflect something of what was going on. For his story does not lack plausibility; indeed for Pinto to tell it to the judge, it must, in his mind at least, have passed this test. That such would, in fact, have been the case is illustrated strikingly by the extent to which the two scenarios presented by Caviedis and Pinto echo many real-life situations that came before the courts in fourteenth- to sixteenth-century Venice, involving vows exchanged as a joke or for immediate sexual gratification.[13] Arising most often among individuals of the lower classes, frequently characterized by one degree or another of marginality or mobility and taking place spontaneously in houses, taverns, along a roadside, or in the street, scenes of this kind might well have been known to Pinto, Caviedis, and the other prisoners, perhaps even have been witnessed by them. They must also have been familiar to Judge Bruno, who, at any event, closes the interrogation of Pinto at this point, declining to press the line of questioning concerning the ceremonies allegedly conducted, which may reflect more his personal train of thought than what Lopez has revealed. Pinto's testimony thus appears a very flimsy basis on which to assert, as does Giuseppe Marcocci, that "di certo, Pinto e López si sposarono" (for certain, Pinto and Lopez got married to each other) and that Lopez was the "marito di Pinto" (Pinto's husband).[14] This is particularly the case, as we have seen, since Lopez is involved in not one but two marriage stories, the other involving himself, Robles, and Caviedis.[15]

As for the judge's "initiation" scenario, Marcocci dismisses it on the grounds that Montaigne affirms the opposite—that the marriages did not give entrance into a confraternity, but that entering the confraternity allowed one to take part in the marriages: "La versione di Montaigne ribalta tale prospettiva.... L'ingresso nella 'strana confraternita' descritta nel *Journal* avrebbe infatti preceduto, e non seguito, i matrimoni" (Montaigne's version reverses this perspective.... Entry into the "strange confraternity" described in the *Journal* is in fact said to have preceded, and not followed, the marriages).[16] While the judge's *scola* or *societas* finds something of an echo in Montaigne's "étrange confrerie" and "belle secte," the two sets of terms are also used very differently. The judge seems to have in mind the idea of a clearly defined association of individuals. Montaigne, in contrast, applies religious terminology playfully and ironically to designate people who are said to have acted in a particularly unexpected way. There is nothing in the essayist's account to suggest the existence of a previously constituted organization that one might formally enter, assenting to its doctrines and rules in order to be able to take part in its rituals. For Montaigne, the Portuguese men do not enter a confraternity in the literal sense; they form a "strange brotherhood" simply by virtue of their actions.[17] Moreover, as we saw earlier, Montaigne's version depicts the marriage ceremonies as being followed immediately by sexual activity, expressed through the common euphemism *habiter*. In this respect then (marriage leads to sex), Montaigne is substantially in agreement with the vision of the judge, as well as with that of Tiepolo and of the informants of the Duke of Urbino and the Fuggers. This is, in fact, one of the few points on which all the early sources examined speak with a single voice.[18] And such a sequence, we must not forget, is typical of how weddings were celebrated in early modern Europe. If marriage was about forming an alliance between individuals and their respective families, about the transfer of goods and the founding of a new household for the raising of children, a wedding was about ratifying the contract on which this was based, a ratification that was completed in the semipublic act of sexual intercourse.

As we shall see in the next chapter, the trial transcript does offer evidence that, on the day of their arrest, the group at the Latin Gate had planned to celebrate a wedding. In relation to the references to marriage examined so far, however, we can appreciate at this point that the men arrested were able to tell a variety of stories, to deploy marriage in different but plausible narrative ways. This is due to the particularities of their individual situations and the strategies they adopt in self-defense. Yet it is also surely the result of other factors. It might perhaps be the case that all these references point to a single scenario and have the same significance. It seems to me more than likely, however, that they do not. Rather, the evidence suggests that *marriage* referred to more than one thing and was used in more than one way by different individuals in different circumstances, that it had multiple meanings. While it is impossible to situate many of the events and episodes referred to in the trial transcript in a precise temporal relationship, they span a period of months and, in some cases, years. Perhaps, then, euphemistic figurative expressions might have encouraged the development of more concrete practices. Maybe, too, not all of the men involved shared exactly the same ideas; maybe there existed among them a diversity or range of opinions and attitudes concerning the events in which they were involved in various ways and to differing degrees. Maybe the ideas of some of them might have evolved in one way or another. At this point, then, let us turn to the particular wedding ceremony about which the transcript does offer information to see what it reveals about the event itself and the group celebrating it.

Chapter 9

MARRIAGE AND COMMUNITY

The first mention of a wedding ceremony celebrated at San Giovanni a Porta Latina comes in the testimony of Geronimo, one of the youths associated with Pinto, probably living under the guise of a hermit. This appears to be his first interrogation and he cracks almost immediately. In response to the judge's second question, concerning the point in time at which he went to the church, Geronimo states that he did so on the day of the arrest, intending, since he was unwell, to continue on to the hospital at Saint John Lateran. He then adds, unprompted,

> My Lord, I want to tell you the truth, which is this, that when it was discussed by Agilar, Robles, and other companions, and Pinto was also involved, to marry Vittorio to Brother Gioseffe who lives at San Giuliano, and Robles promised he would pay for the banquet when the wedding took place, it was agreed that it should take place the following Sunday, which was the one when we were arrested. It's true that the wedding wasn't performed because Br. Gioseffe fell ill and was at the hospital of San Giovanni in Laterano, but

the banquet took place, that is to say, Robles had brought the food for it—
chickens, roosters, meat, cheese, and such like.

Io Signore ve voglio dire la verita la quale è questa che essendose trattato da
Agilar da Robles et da altri compagni che ce intervenne ancora Pinto di fare
sposare il Vittorio con fra Gioseffe che sta a san Giuliano et Robles promese
de voler pagare il banchetto, quando si faceva lo sposalitio ce fu restato
d'acordo che si dovesse fare la Domenica sequente che fu quella quando noi
fussemo presi, è ben vero che lo sposalitio non fu fatto perche fra Gioseffe se
amalo et stava allo hospitale de san Giovanni Laterano ma il banchetto fu
fatto cioe Robles haveva portata la robba per farlo che era gallina pollastro
carne caso et simil cose.

Geronimo proceeds to reveal, as we saw earlier, the nature of his own
relationship with Pinto, which goes back about six years to when they were
both employed in the household of the treasurer of Segovia.

A wedding was planned, then, for the Sunday on which the men were
arrested, July 20, between two adult members of the group, one of whom,
Gasparo Vittorio, is among the prisoners. The other was a certain Brother
Gioseffe, stationed at the church of San Giuliano—that is, Saint Julian the
Hospitaller—on the current Via del Sudario, near the Largo Argentina.
Known today as San Giuliano dei Fiamminghi, the church was attached to
a hospice dedicated to the care of pilgrims from Flanders. As we have seen,
both Robles and Battista had lived for a time in this region, which in 1578
was still part of the Spanish Habsburg Empire, but was involved in a war
for its independence (in which Battista had fought in the army of Philip II).
Given his affiliation with this particular church, it is not surprising to find
Gioseffe associated with Robles and the group of Spaniards who met at the
Latin Gate. In the event, however, the proposed wedding did not go ahead
since Gioseffe was said to have been taken ill, like Geronimo giving the testimony, and to have gone to the Lateran hospital.

If the wedding did not take place, the banquet that was arranged to follow it did. This was apparently a generous affair, especially for men of limited means, involving different kinds of meat, poultry, cheese, and other
foodstuffs. As in the earlier episodes discussed involving marriage, Robles
again plays a key role—Robles, we recall, who was the only member of the
group we know to have been legally married himself—since it is he who is

said to have organized and paid for the feast. What also emerges from this account is that the impetus for the event seems to have come less from the couple than it was a group project. Geronimo recalls a discussion between Robles, Pinto, Brother Agilar, and others concerning the planning of the celebration. While the two intended spouses were presumably in agreement, they are not described explicitly as wanting to marry each other; rather, it is the group that acts like a family or in loco parentis, deciding to *fare sposare* Gioseffe and Vittorio and taking care of the necessary arrangements. It is the group that determines the timing of the event—the following Sunday— even if, as we have seen, Gioseffe would, on the day, be conspicuous by his absence, apparently due to illness—though his good luck must raise the question of whether he might have had prior knowledge of, or even some role in, the group's denunciation to the authorities.

Following this initial major revelation, the court asks Geronimo if he knows of any other marriages of the same sort, to which the prisoner replies, "Io non so veramente che questi sposorii se siano fatti con nesuno se io lo sapessi lo diria" (In truth I do not know of these weddings having been made with anyone else; if I did know, I would tell you). The fact that Geronimo has just blurted out the story of Gioseffe and Vittorio, without any particular pressure being applied by the judge, might lend credibility to his statement of ignorance. On the other hand, given the strong possibility that a wedding ceremony had been performed on more than one occasion, his denial more likely reflects a strategy of self-protection.[1]

The question of the Sunday wedding appears next, briefly, in the final extant testimony of Alfaro, who states, "è anco la verita che il pasto si haveva da fare la domenica la quale fummo pigliati perche fra di noi se era fatta resolutione dello sposalitio che si deveva fare tra Vittorio et Gioseffe si come ho detto" (it's also true that the meal was to take place on the Sunday we were arrested because we had come to a decision among ourselves concerning the wedding that was to happen between Vittorio and Gioseffe, as I told you). As with the testimony of Geronimo, we are struck in particular here by the strongly communal terms in which the decision to perform the wedding is presented.

With Father Battista Caviedis the judge introduces the topic of the marriage celebration differently, asking which of the Spaniards he knew before going to San Giovanni. When the priest names only Pinto, the judge refers specifically to Brother Gioseffe, inquiring whether Caviedis knows him or has at least heard him spoken of. At this point, the prisoner responds,

> I don't know this Brother Gioseffe. It's true that I, the Friday before the Sunday we were arrested, I heard him talked about by the Spaniards who were there at San Giovanni, where they'd had a snack in the afternoon and they just gave me something to drink, but certainly I couldn't tell you for what reason they were talking about the said Br. Gioseffe.

> Io non conosco questo frate Gioseffe è ben vero che io il venardi nanti la Domenica che fussemo pigliati io lo sentii nominare da quelli spagnoli che erano li a san Giovanni dove havevano merendato et a me diedero da bevere solamente, ma certamente non ve saprei dire con che occasione detto fra Gioseffe lo nominassero.

While Caviedis continues to deny that he knows Gioseffe, he acknowledges having heard him discussed when he visited the church two days before the Sunday of the arrests, admitting by the same token that he has been to the Latin Gate more often than he at first revealed. He minimizes his own knowledge of and involvement in events, however, by stating that he did not eat with the others, having only something to drink, and does not know in what connection Gioseffe was discussed. Again, as we shall see, the priest will soon admit to more.

Pressed to name those involved, Caviedis discloses, first, that the discussion took place between Pinto, Robles, Francesco Errera (the one who dresses as a hermit), and the young Cristopharo Lopez ("giovine"). Next Caviedis is warned to tell the truth and informed that the court knows not only that he is familiar with Brother Gioseffe but also that he and the other Spaniards were discussing his imminent marriage with Vittorio. At this point Caviedis concedes, "Io non conosco questo Gioseffe ma è ben vero che quelli spagnoli in quel venardi che io ve ho detto, ragionorno di sposarlo con un altro che io non conosco" (I don't know this Gioseffe, but it is indeed true that the Spaniards, on that Friday I told you about, discussed marrying him to another person whom I don't know). There follows a quite extraordinary moment when the judge asks Caviedis what he had to say about the projected marriage, to which the priest replies simply, "Io non dicevo niente che volete che io ce dicessi" (I didn't say anything about it; what would you have had me say?). When threatened further and reminded of the means of interrogation the court has at its disposal, Caviedis maintains that he has told the truth "e non ve posso dire altramente" (and I can't tell you anything else). At this point, the judge moves on to Caviedis's conversation with Robles and Lopez, discussed earlier, in which the former proposes to give Caviedis to the latter as a wife. Following this, however, the questions return to the marriage of Gioseffe and Gasparo Vittorio, with the priest continuing to maintain that he did not know what it was all about.

From the testimony of Caviedis, then, we gain only limited additional information. First, it appears that any projected ceremony was not to be performed by him. This eventuality is never raised, at any rate, in the judge's questioning, which aligns with evidence from the newsletter sources that identify the officiant as an unnamed hermit. Second, we are struck once more by the fact that the priest speaks of the marriage not as something done *by* the two men involved but as something done *to* them; it appears again, that is, to be very much a group project—the friends decide and plan to marry Gioseffe and Vittorio. These friends include—as we learned earlier from Geronimo—Agilar, Pinto, and Robles. Caviedis adds the names of Errera (the Spaniard) and Lopez. If the latter was able to distance himself from the group and avoid execution, then, it would appear that this was not because he was less implicated in events, but indeed, as we surmised earlier, because of his youth and the story he presented—no doubt of a coerced initiation and participation.

From the interrogations of two other prisoners, we glean a few other details, without these adding significantly to the picture. The judge broaches the subject with Antonio Valez through the question of the banquet and its purpose, of which Valez claims to be ignorant. When asked, he also denies hearing any talk of marriage of any kind. He continues to hold firm, even in the face of the threat of torture, to which he replies, "Io ho detto la verita de tutto quello me havete dimandato et se me volete dar la corda o altri tormenti fate quel che ve piace che io non posso dire altro" (I've told you the truth concerning everything you've asked me about, and if you want to torture me with the rope or by any other means, do whatever you like, because I can't tell you anything else). Valez does admit, however, that he knows Vittorio, indeed that he has done so since before they left Spain—these being the two men who came from the same northeastern region of the Iberian Peninsula under the Crown of Aragon. Given that their friendship goes back some time, it seems safe to assume that it is of a more than passing nature—and therefore that Valez's claim of complete ignorance of his friend's intentions for the Sunday of the arrest is almost certainly false. The closeness of the two men is confirmed by Valez's statement that he was planning to leave Rome, but Vittorio advised him not to do so in the current heat and shared with him the news that he had found someone for whom he could work (a *patrone*). Valez had asked his friend for help in finding a position, and we recall that he stated earlier that he had gone to San Giovanni because he had no money and nowhere to sleep, and that he would leave behind him, in his will, unpaid debts for different kinds of black cloth. If Valez was a good friend of Vittorio, one of the intended spouses, he denies that the two ever slept together. If this is true, the reason likely had to do with what they enjoyed doing in bed, for both men were sexually passive. It is in these terms that Valez's relationship with Cristopharo Ribera is discussed. And Vittorio is one of those known to the group as a *commare*.

Describing his plan to leave Rome, Valez relates that his intention had been to make a pilgrimage for the Madonna degli Angeli and then continue on back to Spain, to Santiago de Compostela. This statement recalls that of Father Caviedis, who claimed to have recently returned from Compostela and to have agreed to meet a Portuguese man to make the same pilgrimage for Our Lady of the Angels on August 1. While there was a church of Our Lady of the Angels newly built at the time in Rome, the two men are undoubtedly speaking of traveling to Assisi and to the famous chapel of the Porziuncola, so central to the life of Saint Francis and the place where he had died. Here, on August 1, preceding the Feast of Our Lady of the Angels on August 2, penitential celebrations were held and the popular Porziuncola indulgence could be gained. In 1578, moreover, work on the new grand basilica, completely enveloping the original chapel, had finally been completed. Given the shared elements of their statements, we might wonder if Valez (although Spanish, not Portuguese) and Caviedis might have been planning on journeying to Assisi together. Or perhaps, more likely, they had simply discussed their stories while in prison and had recourse to a similar alibi.

In the interrogation of Battista the boatman, the question of the marriage of Vittorio and Gioseffe again comes up in connection with the banquet. As we have seen, when asked why he went to San Giovanni, Battista replies that it was to evade the court following his brawl with another ferryman. He then adds that he had not brought the chickens he was plucking when arrested, but that these had come, he believes, from Robles. The judge then suggests that Battista had in fact been sent to the church by Robles for the express purpose of helping to prepare the planned feast. Battista denies this, but admits that Robles sent the chickens and told him he wanted to prepare a meal there. Apart from the fact that Battista is trying to minimize his own role in the organization of the banquet, the detail of the chickens is revealing in two ways. First, we know that Pinto himself owned a sizable flock of poultry. It was not any of these, apparently, that were to be consumed, but others, provided for the occasion by Robles. Second, as the judge would no doubt have appreciated, chickens and other forms of fowl were considered to be particularly appropriate fare at weddings because of their well-established symbolic association with the male sexual organ and their widely credited aphrodisiac properties.[2] In this way, the group's celebration seems to have drawn on customs associated with weddings in the culture of their time. When asked about the people who ate together on the Sunday of the arrests, Battista lists "uno spagnolo vestito da pelligrino che io non ne so nome Pinto, un giovine piccolo che stava amalato nel letto de Pinto che non so chi se sia, Franceso Errera, e un giovine vestito di negro et Robles" (a Spaniard dressed as a pilgrim whose name I don't know, Pinto, a small youth who was ill in Pinto's bed whom I don't know, Francesco Errera, and a youth dressed in black, and Robles). Again then we find Pinto, Robles, and Errera (presumably the Spanish one); the youth who is ill, we recall, is Geronimo. The Spaniard dressed as a pilgrim might have been Caviedis (since he indicates his intention was to leave from there for Assisi). As for the young man dressed in black, it is not possible to be sure, but given his arrival at the church the day before and in light of his will, it is tempting to surmise that Antonio Valez had had his cloth made up into a swish set of clothes. No further information is revealed by Battista. He swears "on his soul" ("in carico del anima mia") that he knows nothing about an intended marriage between Vittorio and Gioseffe. At the conclusion of his testimony, when the judge evokes more generally, as noted earlier, marriages contracted for the purpose of committing sodomy, Battista again pleads complete ignorance of the matter and of "quel che loro se habbiano fatto" (whatever they might have done).

So what kind of marriage might have been planned between Gasparo Vittorio and Brother Gioseffe that Sunday afternoon in late July 1578? A first point to be made is that it seems unlikely that it would have involved living together as a consequence; that is, it would not have involved what was one of the most fundamental aspects of a marriage between a man and a woman, that of setting up a common household. Again, as we have noted, this is not the sense of Montaigne's phrase "puis couchoient et habitoient ensemble." Unless Brother Gioseffe was planning on leaving his order—a complicated process legally and a very risky course of action otherwise—he would have returned in due course to his religious house at San Giuliano. This fundamental consideration makes the situation of the men very different not only from that of a male–female couple but also from that of the early modern women we know about who married each other. As noted in the introduction, Montaigne himself, early on his journey to Rome, recorded a story concerning two such women in eastern France.

Compared to the men in Rome, the women's actions represented in one sense a more individual and less collective desire and course of implementation. They seem to have acted less in collaboration with a group and more for themselves, except to the extent that Mary's initial cross-dressing was inscribed in the context of a shared enterprise of seven or eight young women. What happened to Mary's companions, Montaigne omits to tell us. Most likely, at some point, they abandoned their disguise, though perhaps, by moving far enough away, some might have escaped recognition and arrest. But if Mary, in particular, acted on a more individual basis, her intention, in another sense, was more collective than that of the men in Rome, since her aim was to reintegrate, as a man, her local milieu. If the men's story, especially in Montaigne, focuses on a ceremony, this element is completely absent from the story concerning the women, which is all about living together within a wider community. By changing or hiding her sex, Mary sought to live her marriage openly, to have it known and recognized not by a restricted circle but by the rural society in which she lived. Marriage for her was very much about setting up a household. The degree to which Mary's partner was complicit with her husband is unclear, but it seems unlikely that she can have remained ignorant throughout of his biological sex, even if she might have been so initially. Whatever the case, Mary succeeded brilliantly for four or five months in living not only as a married man with a wife and a trade, integrated into the male structures of community and sociability, but also being generally considered a "fine" young man ("jeune homme bien conditionné").[3] Only when Mary was identified by someone from her past did the life of the married couple come undone.

Nothing suggests that the men in Rome had a similar goal. The only source that mentions cross-dressing is the satirical *Avviso di Parnaso* that, written a full forty years after the events, is the least trustworthy. Moreover, in early modern Europe generally, whereas female cross-dressing intended to be long term or permanent was quite common, such was not the case for male cross-dressing. The latter was generally of limited duration and inscribed in a festive or ludic context. A notable episode of this kind, recounted by Cellini in his memoirs, involves the author taking his sixteen-year-old Spanish model Diego, dressed as a woman, to a dinner hosted by Michelangelo.[4] As we have seen, Aretino's play, *Il Marescalco*, ends with the appearance of a beautiful bride who is in fact a boy. In contrast, I am unaware of any examples from the sixteenth century of men cross-dressing and living publicly as women for an extended period of time. Adopting the life of a woman would have required a male to give up many social advantages. Moreover, whereas it would have been difficult, if not generally impossible, for two unrelated women to live together independently without one of them assuming the role of a man, such was not the case for males, for whom there existed socially acceptable reasons for cohabitation. A tradesman might have one or more apprentices living under his roof, for example. And, as we saw earlier, in these situations a youth might well be considered like a wife to his master.

If the men in Rome did not intend to found a household and live as man and wife, they did, nevertheless, conceive of their sexual roles within the relationship in traditionally masculine and feminine, active and passive, terms. The aspect of their relationship that does not conform to the more accepted early modern paradigm of male–male sexual practices, however, is the fact that the passive partner Gasparo Vittorio, as a *commare*, was not a youth for whom sexual passivity was part of a process of sexual initiation and later transition. Gasparo was old enough to be designated as a man for whom sexual passivity was a choice.

In terms of Gasparo's and Gioseffe's sexual relationship, it also seems unlikely that this would have been an exclusively faithful one. As will by now be evident, the group was characterized by a significant degree of sexual promiscuity, involving multiple contacts between some of its members.[5] Gasparo Vittorio, for example, according to the testimony of Alfaro, had been sodomized by Robles, who, as we have seen, was a principal organizer and funder of the marriage banquet. This detail is revealing since the existence of a (former?) sexual tie between the two men might indicate a closeness that would explain why Robles was so involved in the wedding preparations and, in particular, in covering their financial cost. In addition, according to his own admission to the judge, Gasparo had recently had sex with Brother Agilar, whom he says he had known for no more than two weeks. Agilar, we recall, was also named by Geronimo as one of those involved in discussions of the organization of the wedding. Gasparo describes their encounter as follows: "la verita è che io non ho bugiarato il detto Agilaro ne lui me, è ben vero che in quella notte che dormissemo insieme facessemo assieme la pugnetta cioe se menassemo il cazzo a mano" (the truth is that I didn't bugger the said Agilar or he me; it is true that the night we slept together we jerked off together, that is, we fondled each other's dick with our hands). In the manuscript, the words *pugnetta* and *cazzo* are written in particularly large characters, in a way that draws attention to them immediately. The expression *fare la pugnetta* would be used subsequently by Alfaro (with reference to himself and Robles) and by Pinto (with reference to himself and Geronimo). The way it was transcribed in this instance and the fact that it is followed by an explanation—perhaps asked for by the court— suggest that this may have been the first time it was used in the course of the proceedings.

When the judge expresses doubt that their sexual contact was as limited as Vittorio claims, the latter elaborates:

> My Lord, I told you the truth that I didn't bugger Agilar nor he me, and you can find out more about this from Robles, because, the next morning, Agilar told him that he'd slept with me and that I hadn't buggered him or spoken about it, and that I'd have served better as a woman than as a man.

> Signore io ve ho detto la verita che io non ho bugiarato il detto Agilar ne lui me et di questo ve ne possete informare da Robles perche Agilar la matina seguente li disse che lui haveva dormito con me et che io non lo havevo bugiarato ne detto niente, et che io seria servito meglio per donna che per homo.

Vittorio's words here have a ring of truth in their colloquial familiarity, particularly in his paraphrasing of Agilar's playful teasing the next morning. They also represent a moment in which the man interrogated, as we saw earlier with Marco Pinto, claims his own desire. Vittorio, the *commare*, did not penetrate Agilar because he did not want to; what he desires is to be penetrated, to "serve as a woman." Perhaps, before this moment, Agilar did not appreciate the full extent to which this was true of his new friend. Agilar, by contrast, is a youth and, as such, though perhaps again also out of preference, is usually sexually passive. Errera tells the judge that Agilar was buggered by Alfaro, and Alfaro himself admits that he did this twice. Perhaps it is with hindsight also that Vittorio first described Agilar as follows: "Signor si che io conosco questo Agilaro il quale è un frate giovine sbarbato et per dir la verita per quanto io creda se fa bugiarare" (My Lord, yes, I know Agilar; he's a young friar, still without his beard, and to tell the truth, as far as I know, he gets buggered). To view the encounter between Vittorio and Agilar as a hookup between two bottoms would involve a degree of anachronism, since this terminology fails to take account of the youthfulness of one of the parties, which was a major factor determining Renaissance sexual expectations. What is undoubtedly described, however, is an encounter between two passives. If, in this situation, neither party desires to penetrate the other, this does not mean that other pleasures are not available to them, such as mutual masturbation. In the same way, we have seen that other forms of pleasure might be enjoyed by two men who were usually or always active.

An additional factor to be taken into account in considering the significance of a wedding between Gasparo Vittorio and Gioseffe is that the latter was a friar and thus subject to religious vows, including the vow of chastity. Under canon law, then, Gioseffe would have been ineligible to enter into matrimony, and any marriage he did contract would have been considered by the Church to be null and void. At the same time, ecclesiastical strictures did not prevent some priests and religious, under varying circumstances, from forming a union with a woman.[6] Indeed, some of the surviving records of the Roman Inquisition from the sixteenth century detail a number of such cases—that of a Dominican friar from Verona in 1580, for example, who was said to lack any "vero sentimento del celibato" (true sense of celibacy) or that of an Olivetan monk who took the habit at eighteen, made his solemn profession twelve months later, and then, after fourteen years, abandoned his order. When he ultimately repented and denounced himself to the Inquisition, he had been living with a wife for twenty-five years.[7] Such clerics were often—or suspected of being—heretics, influenced by the ideas of Luther and other Reformers. This was the case in 1580 with a professed monk from Bergamo, who had married and had children, and was said to believe that "monacum professum posse uxorem ducere" (a professed monk could take a wife). He was forced to leave the woman he considered his spouse, return to his order, and perform "salutary penances."[8] As we saw earlier, the Church's right to control marriage was also frequently challenged or resisted by laypeople, who continued to marry, especially in Italy, late in the sixteenth century without recourse to the ministrations of a priest.

The difference between the cases of these clerics and that of the men at the Latin Gate is that those tried by the Inquisition did in fact abandon their religious houses and habits in order to live as married laymen. While we cannot know for sure, we have no indication that Gioseffe intended to do this or that he and Gasparo had plans to live together. Their situation, then, seems closer to that of the friars involved in the academy of the Abate Volpino, except that the wife in this case was not a young boy but a *commare*, even if youths were involved in the life of the group. These various considerations—along with the high level of sexual promiscuity among the participants, the fact that all the early sources agree that the wedding was to culminate in the act of sexual consummation, and finally the presence in Italy at the time of play around marriage in both courtesan and clerical culture—must necessarily raise the question of what kind of wedding ceremony the men intended to perform at San Giovanni a Porta Latina and whether it was exclusively serious in nature or, in part or in whole, parodic or ludic.

Advocating strongly that the men performed a straightforward marriage ceremony, Giuseppe Marcocci has sought to identify traces of the ritual celebration in the trial documents. Notably, Marcocci presents a priest's garment ("chamisa da prete"), in the possession of Geronimo, as being worn by the spouses ("[la] camicia di lino indossata dagli sposi").[9] Nowhere is this stated in the transcript, however, and one wonders why a clerical garment—a shirt or perhaps a surplice—would be worn by the spouses as opposed to the officiant, and indeed by which one of the two. It is the case that the judge asks Geronimo about the shirt directly after his revelations concerning the marriage planned between Gasparo and Gioseffe and his own sexual relationship with Pinto going back to their time in the household of the treasurer of Segovia. Following these admissions, the judge first asks if there were other such marriages, of which, as we noted earlier, Geronimo says he has no knowledge. The judge then moves on to ask about a linen shirt:

> Asked and warned to prepare himself to tell the whole truth and to beware
> of lying, and to say whether anything was ever given to him by anyone, and
> by whom, and specifically a certain linen shirt, on the occasion when he was
> sodomized.

> Interrogatus et monitus ut bene se disponat ad dicendam integram veritatem
> et caveat a mendaciis et dicat an unquam ipsi constituto fuerit aliquod da-
> tum ab aliquo et a quo et signanter quandam camisam linei occasione qua
> fuerit sodomitatus.

It is apparent, then, that the court introduces the question of a linen shirt in
relation to Geronimo being sodomized, rather than in the context of the
marriage. While, as we have seen, the two issues are not entirely separate in
the judge's mind, the primary idea here seems to be that of a gift given by
someone in exchange for sex. It was, in fact, an extremely common practice
for a passive youth to receive or at least to expect gifts—clothes, food and
drink, money—or other favors in return for his willingness to satisfy an
older partner's desires.[10] We can discern the shadow of this assumption at
several points in the trial transcript, as when, for example, Caviedis admits
to having eaten four or five times with Pinto but insists that Pinto never invited him and that he always supplied the provisions himself, or when Battista
claims to have given money to Robles, whereas, for Alfaro, it was Robles
who "kept" Battista. To the judge's suggestion that he has accepted a linen
shirt in this way, Geronimo replies that "a me non me è stata data mai
camisa da nesuno per quanto conto è ben vero que io havevo una chamisa
da prete che me haveva lassata com altre robbe il detto tesauriere de Segobia
la quale poi io ho impegnato per quattro julii al portinaro di porta Latina"
(to me a shirt was never given me by anyone on any account; it's true that I
had a priest's smock which the said treasurer of Segovia had left me with
some other things, and which afterwards I pawned for four giuli with the
doorkeeper at the Latin Gate). The treasurer of Segovia would be a credible
source from whom someone like Geronimo might obtain a clerical garment,
perhaps when the former left Rome or when Geronimo left his employment.
Might it suggest that the treasurer was also rewarding his young servant for
more personal services? If so, Geronimo never discloses this. In response, the
judge repeats his question as to whether the young prisoner has been sodomized by anyone other than Pinto. Geronimo denies this but admits, as

discussed earlier, to sodomizing, again in the treasurer's house, a French mule keeper. The link between this linen garment and any other events at San Giovanni is thus wholly speculative.[11]

For Marcocci, since the men at the Latin Gate believed in the real (spiritual, magical) power of the sacrament to make their same-sex unions acceptable, they consciously and deliberately committed a sacrilege, making use of it in a way they knew to be abusive.[12] As we have seen, this is the interpretation presented in the later *Avviso di Parnaso*. It also echoes one of the two possible literal ways of reading the account of Montaigne, if the commentary of the Roman wits is taken at face value. A significant problem with this view and with the hypothesis of a completely "straight," mimetic performance of a wedding, destined to efface the sinfulness of illicit sexual acts, is the men's sexual promiscuity and the unlikelihood that their intention was to be faithful to a single person for the rest of their days. For unless the intended spouses were to renounce all sexual activity except with each other, they would have gained little or nothing in terms of avoiding sin. Of this the men at the Latin Gate cannot have been unaware. It is true, of course, that many men married women without intending to limit their sexual relations to their wife. The difference is that for them marriage was an expected development, not an act by which they risked suspicion of heresy and sacrilege and the forfeiting of their life if discovered. Moreover, husbands' marital infidelities were widely viewed with indulgence. What these considerations raise, in turn, is the question of the extent to which the men who met at the Latin Gate did in fact consider sodomy to be a grave sin. Perhaps they, or some of them, might have viewed it in the same way that many men and women viewed fornication and adultery—i.e., as much less serious than the theologians would have liked to have them believe. Perhaps some of them did not consider it a sin at all: Pinto, for example, and perhaps Vittorio, who asserted their desires in front of the judge. Others, however, to one degree or another, may well have done so: Valez, said to have repented and broken with Ribera who was continually soliciting him, or Caviedis, who had reportedly turned over a new leaf in the Holy Year and for the last three years remained chaste. It would seem likely that on the question of sodomy there would have been among the group a range of opinions—as there might well have been also on the question of marriage itself. We never hear the voices of the men involved on these issues directly and without constraints; in all likelihood, then, we will never know what was in their minds with absolute certainty.

The evidence examined here, however, seems to me to suggest the not simply straightforward or single nature of the San Giovanni wedding(s) (planned) between two males. Nor should similarities between the group meeting at the Latin Gate, the academy in Naples, and other situations involving pastiche of marriages be ignored. It is the case that the element of play or parody is less evident in the documents associated with the Roman group and that the setting for their activities was a church complex.[13] Yet we should not allow ourselves to be misled by an anachronistic idea of church buildings, which, in the early modern period were far less pristine than might be imagined today, a situation the Counter-Reformation Church worked strenuously to change. People regularly spent the night in churches, for example—like Caviedis, who in all innocence told the judge that he slept in San Giovanni on a bench at the foot of an altar. They might also eat there, bring in and tether animals, meet with business associates to carry out transactions or with friends for conversation, or arrange trysts with a lover. Churches, with their dimly lit and secluded corners, afforded a particularly favorable setting for covert or illicit sexual activities, between both same-sex and opposite-sex couples.[14] Churches, in short, were accessible and public places that simultaneously offered spaces with a degree of seclusion in an urban environment in which privacy was in short supply. As we have seen, San Giovanni, in particular, was in an isolated and marginal location even before Marco Pinto arrived there, so that, with little difficulty, he was able to run it as a house for sex ("lui teneva quel loco per bugiarare").

In both the Rome and Naples groups, the presence of priests and religious was marked. The Naples weddings took place in a carnivalesque atmosphere and were clearly not intended to effect a union in reality. Nonetheless, parody can have a serious, polemical character, and two modern historians stress that, while the weddings enacted by the Naples academy were of a ludic nature, they were accompanied by the formulation of claims of the legitimacy of marriage between men.[15] If the performance itself was not intended to enact a same-sex union, it did convey a provocative criticism of the Church and the assertion that such marriages should be possible. Moreover, whereas Montaigne and other sources speak of weddings conducted at the Latin Gate (thereby offering striking testimony that the idea of marriage between people of the same sex was "thinkable" for many sixteenth-century Europeans), Tiepolo's reference to "certain ceremonies" or "some ceremonies of theirs" that defile the name of matrimony would not be inconsistent with something involving a ludic or parodic element.

In addition to the issue of sexual promiscuity, then, the importance accorded to the festive banquet also suggests something other than a simple desire to legitimate otherwise sinful sexual acts. For in terms of this objective, the feast and the presence of so many people were wholly superfluous, indeed counterproductive, for they could serve only to make the group more visible, to attract attention, and to increase exponentially the risk of detection. Why not conduct a simple marriage ceremony at the church discreetly, if this was the only or principal motivation? It was rather the preparation of the feast, the collective celebration, that was the focus of the men's discussions and activities in the days preceding their arrest. And at San Giovanni, as in Naples and as was frequently the case for a husband and wife in consummation of their union, the banquet was to be the occasion for sexual activity. Given what we know about the group of men and the generous, celebratory repast that had been prepared, it is difficult to imagine that it would have been the context for intercourse between the couple alone, and not also for the expression of a more general sexual license and exuberance. It would seem likely, in other words, that if Gioseffe and Gasparo were to have sex with each other, then Pinto, Robles, or others might equally have taken advantage of the occasion to enjoy the pleasures of the flesh. We remember that it is in precisely these terms that the very earliest testimony, that of the informant of the Duke of Urbino, presented the events. Indeed, this account emphasizes this element of the narrative to such an extent that it is said to precede and in part explain the rest: the men eat and drink to excess, to the point of inebriation, then marry and go to bed together. Even if this explanation of events is almost certainly inaccurate—overly determined, as we have seen, by a different, familiar, and thus expected cultural scenario—the importance of the collective feasting accompanied by sexual activities is beyond doubt. The banquet at the Latin Gate may thus have shared aspects not only with the celebrations of the Naples academy but also with the courtesan's "solemn nuptials."

At the same time, a parodic or ludic dimension does not necessarily signal the absence of polemical intent or effect. Neither does it mean that the celebration might not have had the effect of recognizing and sanctioning a relationship between the two parties involved—Gasparo and Gioseffe— both in their eyes and that of the wider group. This, indeed, seems very probable. In this way, in differing degrees, conformity and dissent might both have been present in the men's actions. The wedding celebration might have been characterized by multiple dimensions—serious, parodic, and polemic—between which it would be a mistake to try to distinguish too clearly. If this was the case—as I believe the evidence suggests—then it would represent a striking form of polyvalent—*queer*—appropriation.

The aspect of the events planned and prepared at Saint John at the Latin Gate that appears the most clearly in the trial transcripts is their communal nature. If the men marrying did not do so to found a household and to have and raise offspring, then the modern observer might have supposed that they did so for more private reasons—out of love. Strikingly, this sentiment is never mentioned at all, either in the trial transcript or in any of the other documents.[16] In the context of the trial, to be sure, this absence is perhaps not wholly surprising, nor can it be taken to indicate that there was no shared affection between Gioseffe and Gasparo; again, on the contrary, this would seem likely. Nevertheless, what characterizes the way the projected marriage is described is the role and agency of the wider collective. In his rich study of Renaissance identity, John Jeffries Martin analyses inquisitorial trials in order to argue that different forms of selfhood coexisted in the period and that these might be variously layered in different subjects.[17] One of the cases examined by Martin involves three journeymen from Abruzzo, immigrants in the city of Venice in 1582. The men attract attention and are denounced for performing pastiches of religious ceremonies:

> In the room were an altar and six candles, two large and four smaller ones, which they would light during the service. But the most peculiar part of the ceremony was the fact that they dressed up in clerical vestments. They put on white frocks. Two of them wore red cardinal's hats while the third dressed as the pope, wearing a paper mitre. . . . So dressed, they sang vespers. They followed the office from a book opened on the altar. On one occasion at least, Evangelista had preached a sermon on the Good Samaritan. They also had a censer and three chandeliers, one of which they placed up high and the two others below. Those who wore the cardinals' hats kissed the feet of the one who played the pope, and they censed him, and he gave them the benediction, making the sign of the cross with his hand.[18]

As Martin's study demonstrates, the mimicking of religious rituals and practices in early modern Italy was a not uncommon practice.[19] The four inquisitors who examined the Abruzzesi rendered conflicting judgments, one finding the men slightly suspect of heresy, one deeming them strongly suspect, while two found them guilty of actual heresy. If the Inquisition had examined the men in Rome four years earlier, its experts might likewise have come to differing conclusions. Martin sees the journeymen's ceremonies, performed repeatedly, as being inspired both by religious rites and by carnival parodies of these rites associated with the Feast of Fools. Playfully inventive *and* serious, mocking *and* devout, they were, in a context of alienation from existing civic rituals, "deliberative performances, . . . efforts by particular individuals in a particular social location to make sense of their identities and to forge a sense of community."[20]

Guido Ruggiero has also emphasized that a sense of identity in the Renaissance, while not necessarily devoid of interiority, was more externally and socially defined by "consensus realities": "Family, friends, neighbors, fellow citizens, and other social solidarities such as guilds and confraternities each constructed in dialogue with a person a socially recognized personal identity for that individual." When it came to sexual identity, Ruggiero points out, one of the most important social spaces where this was "assayed and confirmed was the marital bed."[21] The escorting of the couple publicly to bed, the noise and ruckus, the exhibition of the blood-stained sheets—all this served to establish the reality of a marriage, a husband's potency, and a bride's virginity and honor.

In the light of the fundamental importance of both ritual and marriage to sexual identity, to social identity, and to community, the actions of the marginalized men at the Latin Gate, whatever their precise nature, no longer appear so strange.

Female couples in Montier-en-Der and elsewhere sought to reproduce the lived reality of marriage in a local community, the cross-dressing and cross-gendering of one of them being the necessary condition that opened the rare possibility of cohabitation for two unrelated women. If men were able to cohabit more easily, they might do so in a way that communities correlated to man and wife most readily in pederastic configuration. In Renaissance Rome, a group of mostly foreign immigrants appropriated the social and religious rituals of marriage in the context of their own self-defined community, one that allowed both for the expression of a traditionally gendered vision of sexual activity and for more fluid attitudes and practices.

PART III

Histories

Chapter 10

Looking Forward / Looking Back

The History of Sexuality

A century and a half later in another European capital, that of Montaigne's France, men having sex with other men regularly found themselves in front of officers of the king's justice.[1] Eighteenth-century Paris, like London, is generally considered by historians as having had a well-developed subculture in which men attracted to other men could find each other, socialize, or go cruising for sex; referred to as *gens de la manchette* (or mollies in London), these men also lived under constant surveillance by the police, ever ready to move in to make an arrest.[2] In the transcriptions of the resulting interrogations, conserved in the archives of the Bastille, the question of marriage appears a number of times. In most instances, this is not in the context of a description of a stable couple.[3] One exception is the case of a man named Gobert, who says he has lived in a house in the suburbs with a young man for four years and refers to another "good-looking boy" with whom he had lived "like man and wife."[4] Strikingly, this relationship appears to conform to the traditional pederastic model that, as we have seen, might equally be characterized in the sixteenth century in terms of *husband* and *wife*.

In the 1730s and 40s, a number of cases offer evidence of men using marriage in a metaphorically euphemistic way, also similar to what we observed earlier in relation to the sixteenth century. A narrative from 1735 concerning Jacques Baron comes from a police informer (*mouche*), who goes to see the suspect several times with a friend. Baron gives them drink, makes passes at them, exposes himself, and asks them for sex. During a particular visit on Saint Marcel's Day, when five men were present, Baron, wearing a woman's headdress, put pompoms in everyone's hair, "disant qu'il estoit la mariée . . . , et pendant le diné il fust parlé de miles infamies et Baron disoit qu'il vouloit estre la mariée, et ils fesoient voir à travers leur culotte qu'ils en estoient en humeur, et Baron vouloit qu'on consommat l'action avec luy" (saying that he was the bride . . . , and during the dinner there was talk of a thousand shameful things and Baron said he wanted to be the bride and it was obvious from their breeches that they were in the mood, and Baron wanted them to do it with him).[5] Here, then, marriage refers to sex, but also, through the sexual differentiation of the spouses, expresses expected or desired sexual roles—like the bride at a wedding banquet, the sexually passive Baron hopes, in the context of their supper party, to be taken by a "man."

A little more than a decade later, in 1748, a certain Pierre Pinson describes the gatherings of the *gens de la manchette* taking place in different taverns and typically involving between eight and fifteen or so people, saying

> that in these assemblies the talk is almost always about that taste; that some of them put napkins on their heads and imitate women, making affected gestures and curtsying as they do; that when some new young man comes along, they call him the bride and, when this happens, he becomes the object of everyone's attentions; that they pair off in these assemblies to feel each other up and perform shameful acts; that sometimes this happens also after they leave the tavern.

> que dans ces assemblées la conversation est presque toujours sur ce gout-là, qu'il y en a qui mettent des serviettes sur leurs testes, contrefont les femmes, faisant des minauderies et des reverences comm'elles, que quand il s'y trouve quelque nouveau jeune homme on l'appelle la mariée et, dans ce cas, il devient l'objet des complaisances d'un chacun; qu'on se choisit dans ces assemblées pour se toucher et faire des infamies, que quelquesfoys aussi cela arrive apres etre sortis du cabaret.[6]

Here marriage once again has a sexual connotation, but now the primary aspect of the situation of the bride that is activated metaphorically is that of the deflowering or initiation of the sexually inexperienced virgin, the role played by the newcomer, the young man introduced to the milieu for the first time. The youth in question naturally becomes the focus of attention, indeed of everyone's "attentions," as the *habitués* press around, perhaps even pounce on, the new blood.

In the same year, two men describe a notable example of this kind of event, the locksmith's wedding ("mariage du serrurier"). In his indictment of a certain Louis Rousseau, a police informer states that "ceux de cette assemblée ont fait des infamies les uns avec les autres soit dans le cabaret soit en s'en retournant chez eux; comme aussy qu'on y fit le même jour le mariage d'un jeune garçon serrurier, c'est-à-dire qu'on le debaucha à faire des infamies pour la premiere foys" (those present at this assembly did shameful things with each other, either in the tavern or on the way home; as well as that, on the same day, they celebrated the marriage of a young locksmith, that is to say that they corrupted him into doing shameful things for the first time).[7] Here again it is the reception by the group of a new youth that is indicated by the marriage metaphor evoking the idea of sexual initiation. Whether or not it is the first time this young locksmith has had a sexual encounter, it is impossible to know, but certainly it is the first time one has occurred in the context of the subculture. The contact between the young locksmith and another man present at the same gathering, Nicolas Harault, is described as follows:

> [T]his past summer he went seven or eight times to assemblies that were held in different taverns of la Courtille and notably three or four times to the Horse Shoe Tavern; that at the said assemblies there were some who mimicked women's manners; that nonetheless, he, the deponent, did not commit any shameful acts; that it's true that a young locksmith was brought to one of the said assemblies, and this assembly was called the locksmith's wedding; that he, the deponent, and the [? indecipherable], when they left the assembly took the young locksmith with them and, along the way, he, the deponent, jerked off with the said young locksmith.

> [C]et été dernier il s'est trouvé sept ou huit foys dans les assemblées qui se sont tenues dans differents cabarets de la Courtille et notamment trois ou quatre

foys au cabaret du fer à cheval; que dans lesdites assemblées il s'y en est trouvé qui ont contrefait les manieres des femmes, que cependant lui, deposant, n'y a point fait d'infamies; qu'il est bien vray que dans une des dites assemblées on y amena un jeune garçon serrurier, et cette assemblée s'est appellée le mariage du serrurier; que lui, deposant, et les [? indecipherable], en sortant de ladite assemblée ont emmené le jeune serrurier et dans le chemin lui deposant s'est manualisé avec ledit garçon serrurier.[8]

It is in the first decade of the eighteenth century, however, that by far the longest exchange concerning marriage occurs between Marc René d'Argenson, *lieutenant de police*, and two men who were arrested: Simon Langlois, aged twenty-nine and a half, and Emmanuel Bertault, known as La Brie, aged thirty-four, both lackeys.[9] Here, in addition to the alleged actual performance of a marriage, it is the issue of a ceremony of initiation or (re)affirmation of fidelity to a quasi-chivalric or religious order that preoccupies the authorities. These two concerns appear at once in the case summary, recorded on the uppermost folio, which indicates that the men are accused of holding assemblies "sous un espese d'ordre où ils recevoient tous les jeunes garçons qui voulaient y entrer et prenoient des noms de femme, faisoient des mariages ensembles" (in the form of a sort of order, into which they received all the young men who wanted to enter it, and they took women's names and got married together). The description of the charges concludes as follows: "Ils faisoient certaines ceremonies pour la receptions [*sic*] des prozelytes et leurs faisoient prêter serment de fidelité à l'ordre" (They performed certain ceremonies for the reception of new converts and had them swear an oath of fidelity to the order). The extent to which the idea of a secret "order" is coming from the police is evident in the fact that the two specific terms "prozelytes" and "à l'ordre" have been written over two much simpler expressions, which were used first and then crossed out: "nouveaux venus" (newcomers) and "pour entrer dans leur société" (to enter their society). As for the term "certaines ceremonies," it echoes strikingly Antonio Tiepolo's "alcune lor cerimonie." In the first interrogation of Langlois, the questions turn quickly to the issue of an order, into which people were received and referred to as knights. While he initially denies everything, Langlois eventually admits that they used women's names. From this point on, D'Argenson abandons his use of the term "order" with Langlois and speaks instead of a society, *societé*. This description Langlois does not contest.[10] The *lieutenant de police* returns to using the word *ordre* in his interrogation of Bertault, who also rejects this description. What Langlois himself calls their gatherings is "parties de plaisir" or "parties de cabaret"—gatherings for fun or at the tavern.

In relation to the use of women's names, specifically that of Mme de St Antoine, Langlois says that it was given to Bertault/La Brie by the women of the Faubourg Saint-Antoine the previous year during carnival ("les jours gras"), when he and Langlois, dressed as women, were selling cooked apples. Bertault both lived and worked in the Rue Saint-Antoine, so this name is appropriate, although, at the end of his own interrogation, he later gives a different account, according to which he was given the name by a shopkeeper's assistant on the Rue Saint-Honoré. He also associates the women's names not specifically with the carnival but with the festive occasion of a ball, when "chacun s'habilla differament et prirent des noms convenables à leurs habits de masque" (everyone dressed differently and took names that suited their costume).[11] Langlois, in his first interrogation, corroborates this when he also affirms that some of the names were given on the occasion of a ball.

A major concern of the police in these interrogations is an alleged ceremony of the renewal of vows in the order, whose existence they suspect. When Langlois first denies this, they ask more specifically about a candle used for the ritual. The lackey's story involves him leaving the *cabaret* to accompany his mistress home and buying a stub of candle to put in a lantern to light a staircase. When he returned to the *assemblée*, a certain Jean-Baptiste Lebel snatched the candle from his hands and lit it, before giving it back to him. When asked if he did not have Lebel kneel down, Langlois admits that "en riant il fit mettre ledit Lebel à genouil luy disant de demander pardon de ce qu'il avoit arraché la bougie des mains du repondant" (as a joke, he had the said Lebel kneel down, telling him to ask for forgiveness for having snatched the candle from his hand). He denies, however, having Lebel swear an oath of fidelity to their society. In his second interview, by contrast, when D'Argenson returns to the same question, Langlois admits that this was the case and that he asked Lebel "s'il ne vouloit pas renouveller ses voeux, et garder fidelité à la societé" (if he wouldn't renew his vows and remain faithful to the society). This Lebel did, holding the candle, after which the other ten or eleven present "vinrent à luy, luy osterent des mains la bougie qu'il tenoit et se mirent à boire" (came up to him, took the candle he was holding from his hands, and began drinking).[12] When asked what this renewal of vows signified, Langlois replies that "Le Bel continueroit d'estre de leur societé," an expression that might indicate remaining in their society or simply continuing to keep their company. As the interview continues, Langlois is asked if he recited a set prayer ("une formulle de priere"), made the sign of the cross over Lebel, and had him kiss a diamond cross. Langlois denies the aping of religious ritual, but admits to having had Lebel kiss two roses made of fake diamonds, which he was going to put in his hat for the ball.

It seems clear that the police have become aware of some kind of initiatory rite or rite of welcome or association taking place in the context of the gatherings organized by Langlois, since, as Bertault states, it was Langlois who came by where he lived to inform him when and where an *assemblée* was to take place. The central role played by Langlois is suggested moreover by his nicknames: "Mme la Générale" or "Mr le Grand-Maître." Clearly seeking to uncover a hierarchical organization in the group, D'Argenson returned to this detail later when he asked if Bertault and a certain Alexandre were not the henchmen ("suppots") of his so-called generalship ("pretendu Generalat"); this Langlois denies, but Bertault admits.[13] D'Argenson would return to the same idea yet again, asking Bertault if Langlois was not the leader ("chef") of the gathering, to which the prisoner replies that he "s'estoit rendu comme maistre de cette assemblee par son obstination, et parce qu'on le craignoit" (had made himself as it were the master of this assembly by his tenacity and because he was feared).

If there was some kind of ludic, stylized, or ritualized welcome of Lebel, the latter was, nonetheless, anything but a young innocent. Langlois states that he has known him for more than ten years, having known also his father and mother, and that he is "adonné à la sodomie" (addicted to sodomy). He is also aware of Lebel's arrest four years ago for sodomy, of which Lebel himself had informed him.[14] In the scene investigated by the police, then, Lebel, following his release from prison, seems to have reestablished contact with other *gens de la manchette*, to have (re)connected with the group around Langlois, and in this context to have been playfully required by Mme la Générale to "renew his vows." The ludic performance was not unique, however, for Langlois admits that he had embraced a number of other newcomers, putting his hands on their shoulders, having them kiss the two roses made of diamonds as if they were kissing a cross, and giving them a female nickname.[15] Once more, then, the evidence points to an inventive and playful community-building gesture, a perhaps brief but stylized performance that serves both to mark the arrival of and to affiliate a new member and to affirm the identity of the group as a whole. It is both serious in its context and a parody of more mainstream religious and social rituals, drawing both on these rituals themselves and on the ways in which they might be regularly parodied in the wider society during carnival. They include rites such as taking vows (as when entering a religious order to become a monk or nun) and perhaps the sacrament of confirmation (representing a renewal of baptismal vows), both of which also involve the acquiring of a new name.

The social rituals on which the *gens de la manchette* were drawing also likely included those associated with trade organizations, such as guilds, confraternities, and, most notably, *compagnonnage*.[16] The last of these, which originated in the fifteenth and sixteenth centuries and became widespread from around 1650, was constituted by (semi-)clandestine and illegal associations promoting the interests of but also affording a sense of community and solidarity to an itinerant and dependent category of workers—mostly young, unmarried journeymen.[17] Their collective rituals mimicked and transformed (as did those of the formal guilds) much Christian symbolism and the rites of the Catholic liturgy, notably baptism and the Eucharist, but also the taking of vows to enter a religious order. The appropriation was serious in intent, while not excluding the possibility of parody, levity, and even, on occasion, considerable vulgarity.[18] In the eighteenth century, indeed, *compagnonnage* itself became an object of parody by its members, who founded purely ludic associations.[19] On entering a trade brotherhood, a new member would go through a ceremony of initiation, originally called a reception or baptism, at which he would receive a nickname by which he would thenceforth be known, and would swear loyalty to the group, secrecy, and obedience to its officers and statutes. These receptions involved rituals more or less closely resembling Catholic rites: for example, the giving of a new name might be accompanied by the pouring of water, and perhaps wine, over the initiate's head; an altar might even be set up, at which the presider, dressed in priest's vestments, might imitate the consecration of bread and wine at mass. The brotherhoods were also organized hierarchically, with a *premier chef* or *capitaine*, a *lieutenant*, and so on. In addition to receptions of members, they held regular *assemblées* in taverns or *cabarets*, where they also lodged, and ceremonies of welcome (*bienvenue*) and separation (*conduite*), when a member arrived from or departed for another town, often followed, like receptions, by communal drinking and feasting.

Many of the *gens de la manchette* came from the social milieu of *compagnonnage*: in addition to lackeys, there were also apprentices, journeymen, and some master tradesmen. It is not unlikely, then, that they would have imbibed these forms of clandestine association and sociability. The same cultural horizon also shaped the questioning of the police, moreover. In the seventeenth century, the authorities tracking down and seeking to eradicate *compagnonnage* associations referred to them as *sociétés*, perceiving as threatening their secrecy, their swearing of oaths, their illicit hierarchy, and their sacrilegious counterfeiting of sacred ritual; they also associated them with debauchery. In the eighteenth century, according to Cynthia Truant, the police were less interested in the nature of the *compagnons'* rituals, which had, in any case, become somewhat simplified. By contrast, exactly the same preoccupations and assumptions concerning clandestine association can be seen in their questioning of the *gens de la manchette*. In this case, however, the sacrament said to be performed that interests the police is not baptism or the Eucharist, but matrimony.

Immediately following the series of questions concerning the alleged "renewal of vows," D'Argenson asks Langlois if they did not also perform marriages. Langlois responds

> that he never performed any marriage; that it's true that on mid-Lent Sunday last year, when about fifteen of them had got together at the Cauldron Tavern [in the Rue Saint-Antoine], several of those at the assembly put posies in the suspect's wig, saying that they should have a wedding between him and the individual named Labrie (known in their society as Madame de Saint-Antoine), and straightaway they led the suspect (known in the society as Madame la Générale) and the said Labrie into a room next to the one in which they were gathered, telling them that they should go and consummate the marriage in this room, where they closed them in. And they made noise outside the door, saying it was the charivari.

> qu'il n'a fait aucun mariage; qu'il est vray que le jour de la My-Caresme de l'année derniere, s'estans assemblez au nombre de quinze dans le cabaret du Chaudron, plusieurs de l'assemblée mirent des bouquets dans la perruque du respondant disant qu'il falloit faire un mariage de luy avec le nommé Labrie (surnommé dans leur societé Madame de St Antoine) et aussitost conduisirent le repondant (surnommé dans cette societé Mad^e Lageneralle) et ledit Labrie

dans une chambre a costé de celle où ils estoient assemblez, leur disant qu'il falloit aller consommer le mariage dans cette chambre dans laquelle ils les enfermerent. Et firent du bruit à la porte disant que c'estoit le Charivary.

Here, we are once more in a festive context, the fourth Sunday of Lent, the moment when, at the midpoint of the penitential season, carnival suddenly and briefly resurges. Whether Langlois is fully cross-dressed, as he said he was during carnival, is unclear, but at the least he is wearing a wig in which the others place flowers. Unlike the vows scene, this one is not initiated by Langlois or La Brie/Bertault. As with the group at Rome's Latin Gate in the sixteenth century, it is the assembled company as a whole that is presented as deciding that a marriage must be held. Rather than being planned in advance along with a projected feast, however, the group's actions are described as being spontaneous, improvised in the context of a prearranged gathering. As in the case of a male–female couple, the "spouses" are led to a room nearby (said to be closed or locked behind them) to consummate the "marriage" immediately, while the rest of those present make a raucous noise to celebrate and to encourage, but also to put pressure on the "newlyweds." In response to D'Argenson's further questioning, Langlois denies that they performed any other kind of ceremony and maintains that they remained in the room only briefly, the door being reopened almost at once, and that not so much as any touching took place between them, let alone the act of sodomy. In the face of D'Argenson's skepticism, Langlois admits that he and La Brie felt each other up ("se toucherent l'un l'autre") on another occasion, when the former visited the latter and found him in bed having taken medicine.

The version of the story given by Bertault during his interrogation, while similar, differs in important details. When asked if last mid-Lent he and Langlois took each other as husband and wife, he states that Langlois told him that he should marry him, which he perceived as a form of mockery or teasing. Here, then, it is Langlois himself who is remembered as having been the primary instigator; if it was in fact the case that the others were not involved, then Langlois, in his earlier testimony, would clearly have been seeking to understate the extent of his role in events. When asked if they were taken into a room in order for them to consummate their marriage, La Brie replies that those who were at the assembly pushed him, along with the said Langlois, into a room, where they all entered and which the suspect left immediately, telling the said Langlois that he'd be both husband and wife together, and he doesn't remember anyone at the assembly telling him he should consummate the marriage.

ceux qui estoient de l'assemblée le pousserent luy et ledit Langlois dans une chambre en laquelle ils entrerent tous, et d'où le repondant sortit dans l'instant, disant audit Langlois qu'il feroit le mary et la femme ensemble et ne se souvient pas qu'aucun de l'assemblée luy ait dit qu'il falloit consommer le mariage.

At this point, in his turn, no doubt minimizing his own involvement, Bertault describes himself as being jostled, along with the others, into a room from which he immediately exits. Rather than the couple being inside and the rest outside making a ruckus, here everyone is in the room except Bertault, who turns the joke back on Langlois, saying that he will have to be both husband and wife himself.[20] When pressed further, Bertault affirms that Langlois remained afterward in the room alone, of which the door was never locked, and that while some of the group made a noise, he does not know why. He similarly denies that Langlois ever visited him when he was ill in bed. Since Bertault here is clearly seeking to deny as much of the episode as possible, it seems safe to assume that Langlois's version of events is closer to the truth, whereas the latter, in contrast, might have sought to deflect the initial responsibility for the scene onto the group in general. It also seems likely, despite the denials of both men, that some form of sexual activity took place between them. It is to this subject that D'Argenson moves next with Langlois, in reference to another episode, in which he and others are said to have had sex involving some kind of rope tackle ("une suspente"), perhaps a hoist above the door of the bedroom and that, it seems to be suggested, might have functioned like a sling. In general, however, Langlois and Bertault will admit to no more than mutual touching: the former states that "lors qu'ils estoient à table ils se faisoient les uns aux autres des attouchemens qui ne paroissoient que tres peu parce qu'ils passoient leurs mains par dessous les serviettes" (while they were at table they would fondle each other, which was not very noticeable, because they slipped their hands under their napkins); according to the latter, they would "se mettre la main dans la culotte des uns des autres et . . . dire des sottises" (put their hands in each other's breeches and . . . talk nonsense).[21]

This flash-forward from Renaissance Rome to Enlightenment Paris has taken us from the century that stands at the beginning of the period termed "early modern" to the century that marks its temporal limit, ushering in "modernity." Its purpose is to gain a vantage point from which to analyze and compare sexual practices and forms of sexual culture in relation to gender and sexual identities as they evolved in western Europe over this period and beyond.

The Parisian subculture of the *gens de la manchette* needed to be both hidden and able to be found by potential future members, those who might be interested in becoming part of it. As a result, it became a profile on the horizon and an object of surveillance for those policing society's norms. The records of that process of enforcement point strikingly to a number of elements that were already of concern to observers and officers of the criminal justice system in Renaissance Rome; these elements reflect, at one and the same time, something of a group's strategies for survival in constrained circumstances and a hostile society's paranoias: the performance of particular rituals—ceremonies associated with initiation—or "recruitment"—into a secret society (order, school, confraternity) and/or with marriage and sex.

For the *gens de la manchette*, marriage functioned both as a discursive euphemism and as the ground for performative play alluding to or incorporating sex, the figure of the bride being associated variously with sexual passivity and the arrival/welcome of a newcomer. In the context of their *assemblées*, these men improvised inventively on the rituals of contemporary social and religious life, as well as on the mainstream parodying of these rituals during carnival, in order to create their own ludic forms of behavior, both playful and derisory, and serving to affirm and solidify community and identity. These creative appropriations of normative social institutions themselves often took place during carnival (*jours gras* or mid-Lent). Carnival thus offered a form of cover, a context in which excess, inversion, and license could be indulged in without attracting hostile attention, since they were temporarily the norm. Carnival, later, also offered the men arrested an alibi, a story they could tell to present their activities as less threatening, less abnormal. This situation also reveals, however, that their activities, their way of life, were not only subcultural; in certain ways and to a certain degree, they remained part of traditional urban and popular culture, part of the culture of carnival, of charivari, of *compagnonnage*.

This realization is important since, for many historians, the emergence of subcultures in eighteenth-century Paris and other large European cities goes along with the formation of a distinct homosexual identity, understood in terms of an exclusive or strongly primary and enduring attraction to people of the same sex: homosexual men are those who are not sexually attracted to women; rather than sexual role (penetrating/being penetrated), the sex of the object of desire is the fundamental defining characteristic in this schema. By contrast, it has often been argued that before the eighteenth century there were no such things as a homosexual identity or a homosexual subculture. Certain forms of same-sex activity existed as a general feature of premodern cultures, according to a universalizing paradigm.[22] As a corollary, relationships between males conformed essentially to a pederastic (age/rank-differentiated) model and might be engaged in potentially by any male, as long as the older man played a penetrative sexual role with a still youthful partner. The late seventeenth and eighteenth centuries saw the isolation of homosexuality through the disappearance of this universalizing paradigm and a focus on desire and the sex of the object of desire rather than on sexual role. Concomitant with this development was that of a new conception of the sexes based on a radical, physiological dimorphism. Whereas earlier ideas of the division of the sexes had been balanced by models that viewed masculinity and femininity as situated along a sexual continuum, the "one-sex model" also disappeared at this time.[23]

Bringing into dialogue the two male collectives in sixteenth-century Rome and eighteenth-century Paris enables us to see, first of all, that the subculture constituted by the latter was also part of and not detached from the wider culture of the time. Moreover, in this context, aspects of older models of sexual life also remained current, such as the pederastic attraction of the adult male for the youth, assumed to be passive.

No less compellingly, the group of mostly Spanish men in Rome in 1578 calls for a reevaluation of the earlier period. As we saw in chapter 7 in relation to a novella by Bandello, sixteenth-century literary texts offer evidence of people with an attraction toward those of their own sex that they considered to be exclusive and permanent and that they had various means of conceptualizing: in particular, the idea of an inborn, natural taste. We also find scattered references to adult male sexual passivity or versatility, as in Aretino's *Ragionamenti*, discussed in chapter 3.[24] Similarly, historians have un-covered examples of pairs involved in relationships maintained over some length of time.[25] They have also been able to identify occasional exceptions to prevailing cultural paradigms and practices, such as older men who con-tinue to enjoy being penetrated or individuals who engage in active and pas-sive sexual roles. Such evidence has remained sparse, however. As Michael Rocke notes in his analysis of fifteenth-century Florentine judicial records, "Reciprocal or role-trading sexual relations were rare and limited almost entirely to adolescents, while it was rarer still for adult males to take the sexu-ally receptive role."[26] Studies of Venice and other locations have come to simi-lar conclusions.[27] It is in this light that the evidence relating to the group meeting at the Latin Gate is so rich and so significant.

On the one hand, then, the trial documents offer examples of homosex-ual behavior that conforms to a pederastic model. Marco Pinto, for instance, seems to have been mostly attracted to youths; one of those with whom he had sex, Geronimo, was someone he had known for six years, from the time they were servants together in the same household. The priest Battista Ca-viedis also recounts that his sexual initiation was due to the master with whom he came to Italy, a Spanish nobleman who sodomized him repeatedly while they lodged in the house of a cardinal. Cristopharo Lopez almost cer-tainly explained his involvement with the group in these terms, doing so to the apparent satisfaction of the judge. It was in the same way, finally, that a number of outside commentators on the group perceived the dynamic oper-ating within it, as they portrayed the sexual exploitation of boys "used" by adults (the *avvisi* to Urbino and the Fuggers, Castellani's *Avviso di Parnaso*). An additional piece of evidence, significant in this regard, is contained in the last newsletter report sent to the Fugger family on August 23. This refers to the arrest not only of several more men but also of seven boys who have been whipped: "sendo anco stati frustati 7 putti per queste effette."[28] This identi-fication of a precise number of boys and the more lenient punishment im-posed on them would seem to offer corroboration of indications that at least some of the group's activities involved a pederastic element, raising again the question of whether certain youngsters may in fact have acted under a de-gree of compulsion or at least in the absence of much choice. Like most of those who found themselves implicated in sodomy trials, moreover, with one exception the mature men arrested at the Latin Gate did not have a wife. While marriage with a woman was a state to which they might not generally have aspired, it was also one that for many in their position—(im)migrants with severely limited resources, living in an overwhelmingly male city—remained impossible to attain.

On the other hand, if some of the behavior associated with the group fits a pederastic paradigm, it does not in all respects fit a universalizing one. We know nothing more about Caviedis's Spanish master, but Pinto seems to have been characterized by an enduring and exclusive same-sex desire. The same was likely true of other of the friends, including Caviedis, who, in addition, was perceived as preferring a receptive to a penetrative sexual role. Not all the mature men, moreover, have sex only (or at all?) with youths or boys; most of those arrested and executed had sex with other adults, sometimes in the context of a relationship lasting for a period of time, like those between Robles and Battista and between Valez and Ribera. Some of the men like passive sex—Valez, for example, as well as Vittorio and Caviedis, both of whom were thought of and may well have thought of themselves in feminine terms as a *commare*, but also the virile Battista, for whom this was not the case. No less significantly, there were men who were alternatively active and passive, and there is even an example of a sexual relationship between adults involving reciprocal penetration, that of Alfaro and Robles, who in modern terms were versatile. Couples also attest to engaging in sexual activities for pleasure that do not involve penetration, especially mutual masturbation. The wealth of evidence regarding the San Giovanni group thus offers a precious window onto a historical reality that we rarely have the possibility of observing—one involving a multiplicity and flexibility of sexual practices sometimes claimed by historians to be "modern" phenomena that only came into existence two centuries later.[29] Should we then think of these men as having a "homosexual identity"?

Much of the evidence we have examined, I believe, supports this view. At the same time, it is critical to remember that in different historical periods identities have been formed in different ways. In Renaissance Europe, as was discussed in the previous chapter, they were strongly grounded in social practices and in community, whereas the techniques of interiority that constitute what Michel Foucault terms the "hermeneutics of the self" were not yet fully developed. It was this consideration that famously led the philosopher–historian to maintain that not only homosexuality, but more generally sexuality itself, was a product of the nineteenth century.[30] Ascribing a homosexual identity to the men who met at the Latin Gate would thus require that we not construe it in restrictively modern terms. Furthermore, while we recognize significant commonalities between the groups of men from the sixteenth and the eighteenth centuries, and between the latter or both and homosexuals, especially gay men, today, it is equally important to remain attentive to differences. In particular, we must not overlook the ways in which aspects of the behaviors of the San Giovanni group are bound up with and reflect universalizing structures of desire and sexual activity typical of the sixteenth century—the ways in which, that is, they are necessarily implicated in the structures and habits of their particular culture, from which it would be a mistake to seek to extricate or abstract them.

These considerations notwithstanding, in a society in which universalizing structures were prevalent, the friends meeting at the Latin Gate manifest their difference. Given the abundance of "exceptional" practices associated with them and the fact that they represented a small part of a considerably more extended network, their example might suggest, moreover, that such practices were more widespread than previously available evidence has allowed us to suspect. For at least some of the men, it is clear that a permanent homosexual desire was a defining characteristic not only of their sexual life but also of their life more generally. Indeed, no doubt drawing momentum from some particularly strong personalities (Pinto, Robles), they had created a form of subculture—less developed and more fragile than that of the *gens de la manchette* to be sure, but involving a network of people, with their own places for meeting, a shared coded language for talking about their sexual desires and practices, and particular forms of sociability, including the collective appropriation of the central social institution of marriage.[31] Consequently, if a pederastic universalizing paradigm of same-sex relationship had to be eclipsed to found a strict division of male from female and hetero from homo, the same paradigm, earlier, did not preclude the existence of minoritizing forms of same-sex desire and practice. These were not invented only from around the late seventeenth or eighteenth century onward; in numerous ways they characterize the men who met at the Latin Gate. In medieval and early modern Europe same-sex desire and practices might thus be *both* universalizing *and* minoritizing, *both* part of the general culture *and* associated in particular ways with marginalized individuals or groups.[32]

Despite the one hundred and fifty years that separate them, the San Giovanni companions and the *gens de la manchette* are related: the former anticipate and look forward to the latter as the latter not only look forward to the future but also echo and look back toward the past. Both are implicated in different socio-sexual models. Together, then, they might remind us—if such a reminder were necessary—to beware of assuming a unified homosexuality in the present, of naturalizing a self-evident homosexuality—and heterosexuality "as we know them today."[33] In varying sets of circumstances, men and women in the twenty-first century also have multiple and diverse ways of understanding themselves as gendered and sexual subjects. They may be more or less invested in the conviction that their (homo)sexuality is innate, exclusive, or permanent; in a privileging of the significance of desire and the sex of the object of desire over acts and roles; in the sense of belonging (or not) to a given community or (sub)culture; and so on. Finally, the men in sixteenth-century Rome and eighteenth-century Paris challenge us to explore their and our place in a historical trajectory, without seeking to trace this in overly smooth or selectively polished terms, allowing for the co-existence and overlapping of different paradigms rather than their necessarily discrete supersession. They invite us neither to seek in the past mirror images of ourselves nor to construct a breach between "us" and the rest of history.

Chapter 11

Ghost Stories

Queer History

This book has introduced a group of men from the sixteenth century with whom we have been able to become quite familiar. For some of them, we know not only their names and places of origin but also numerous details about their lives: where they lived, how they were employed, who their friends were, and so on. In many cases, we have also learned intimate information concerning their sex lives—what they liked to do and with whom— of considerable importance for the history of sexuality. For me personally, having set out to discover what lay behind the story I first read in Montaigne's *Journal de voyage*, the process of searching has been a lengthy one, involving moments not only of breakthrough and insight but also of frustration and disappointment. And so the history it has been possible to recover has many holes, including, most fundamentally, more detailed evidence concerning what exactly those present at the Latin Gate would have done that Sunday morning in July 1578 had Brother Gioseffe turned up as expected. Like the histories of colonized peoples, this history is one of both oppression and erasure—of bodies reduced to ashes scattered to the wind, of records destroyed. Responding to similar challenges, Saidiya Hartman undertook the writing of a memoir reflecting on a personal journey along the former transatlantic slave route. A crucial moment in her encounters with places— as bearers of both the presences and absences of the men and women condemned to exile and slavery—occurred for Hartman in the dungeon of Cape Coast Castle in Ghana. The room was empty, but its very floor, she realized, was made in part of the "feces, blood, and exfoliated skin" of those imprisoned there before being shipped off to the Americas.[1] While conducting research in Rome, I made two visits to the church of Saint John at the Latin Gate, which provoked strong and contrasting emotions: profound sadness and melancholy, but also anger, a sense of identification, and pride.

What the visitor to the Latin Gate encounters today is not a swamp but an architectural jewel, nestled in a part of Rome that is verdant and tranquil. The basilica stands just inside the Aurelian Walls in what is still one of the most remote and least developed parts of the city, surrounded by parks and villas. Founded in the late fifth century, restored in the eighth and then again in the twelfth, San Giovanni offers the vision of a predominantly Romanesque building incorporating much older elements. The beautiful courtyard through which one approaches the church, with its eighth-century well, is dominated by a majestic cedar. Above its portico of reused ancient columns rises a distinctive bell tower—the one from the top of which some of Pinto's and Robles's companions had been drawn to admire the view when they were arrested. Inside, a pre-twelfth-century mosaic pavement in the sanctuary also contains an abundance of ancient pieces. An extraordinary cycle of Romanesque frescoes decorating the walls of the nave, covered over in the seventeenth or eighteenth century, was restored in the twentieth. "Trust the gays to find the most beautiful place to get married," I found myself thinking anachronistically—and before discovering that, for centuries, it had stood in inhospitable marshland. The beauty of the edifice and its setting no doubt account for the fact that the church has become—to borrow an expression from a friend who is a priest—a wedding factory. In early summer, a multiplicity of notices contained instructions and information for engaged couples, including the hours of the week when marriages were celebrated (Wednesday, Thursday, and Friday, 4 p.m. to 7 p.m., and Saturday, 10 a.m. to 12:30 p.m. and 4 p.m. to 7 p.m.!). The church itself was decorated in constant readiness for a wedding.

Decorated for a wedding, but, when I visited, empty. Except for my part-ner and me. Waiting. As I, too, waited, in limbo between future and past, for those to whose wedding I had, belatedly, invited myself. The stones, seem-ingly redolent with memories, were silent. The ghosts who filled my thoughts, unknown to most of those who came here, would they stir? Would they offer some sign? Slowly, I became aware of the presence of other specters in this edifice constructed from so much ancient stone. Stone from pagan buildings, built by those whose tombs line the Via Appia Antica, so close by. In the facade itself, a piece of *spolia*, a fragment of some monument—a tomb? pre-Christian?—inscribed "TITIENIA" and underneath "UXSOR VIRO," apparently dedicated by a wife to her husband, seemed to reinforce the marital hege-mony. And yet these remnants from an ancient, classical past whispered also of an other culture, one a new order would strive to make them disavow, a culture that celebrated in thought, in song, and in art the love of men for handsome youths, in which Hadrian might deify Antinous and Nero take Pythagoras as husband and Sporus as wife.

How, then, to be haunted by these ghosts? Carla Freccero has called for "a more ethical relation to the past and the future" through a practice of writing history that "would neither 'forget the dead' nor 'successfully' mourn them."[2] The work of the Confraternity of San Giovanni Decollato was to prevent precisely this: to bring those executed to accept their fate, and thus to assuage the guilt always inherent in taking a human life—even in accor-dance with the law—to reassure the living that those executed would not return in anger to haunt them.[3] San Giovanni's ghosts would seem to require first of all a much more general acknowledgment of the fact that marriage has a history: a history that both excludes and includes same-sex couples, a history into which sexual dissidents have invited themselves, gate-crashing the party of their straight neighbors and cousins, exuberantly, embarrassingly— to take part or to mock—even if they knew they would be ejected by force. Marriage is not an unchanging and universal phenomenon. Even in the West, its history is that of a complex, evolving, and contested institution—one that authorities have striven to control as a means of controlling people, one, too, that individuals have sought to engage with while maintaining different forms of autonomy.

Same-sex couples and same-sex groups, in particular, have appropriated marriage in their own ways. What remains questionable, however, is the ex-tent to which it was possible in early modern Europe to conceive of a marriage between two "masculinities" or two "femininities." From the evidence presented here, Montaigne's conception of "male to male" marriages appears to have been unusual. Rather the marital model would seem to have been more readily assimilated by/to gender-differentiated couples: that is, where one partner took on the role of the other sex or at least was thought of and thought of him- or herself sexually in terms of adopting the role of the other sex. At the same time, of course, this does not mean that such couples necessarily adopted all the other customary male–female hierarchical positions in their relationship with each other. It is also the case that various degrees and forms of self-affirmed or perceived gender differentiation may characterize same-sex couples in the twenty-first century. This differentiation is no longer a determining or even a significant factor, however, in relation to the desire to marry on the part of gay and lesbian couples. For contemporary same-sex couples, as for opposite-sex ones, marriage is a vehicle for the expression of love and the validation of a personal relationship based on choice. At the same time, as Michael Warner has noted, marriage is a "package," a whole series of rights that are bundled together and granted by the state under the umbrella of the single institution.[4] Over the course of the last century, western nations came increasingly to extend these legal rights equally to both partners, no longer disadvantaging one—the woman—in relation to the other, as was the case in the past. As George Chauncey has argued, then, it is the fundamental evolution that marriage has undergone that explains why access to the personal, social, and legal advantages it confers has been the main goal of gay and lesbian politics in recent decades.[5] As discussed at the beginning of this book, the campaign for "marriage equality" has achieved considerable successes in Europe, North America, and elsewhere, but it has also provoked much hostile reaction and preemptive outlawing. Opposition to legalizing same-sex marriage is frequently formulated by reactionary forces in the terms of outright rejection. By those who wish to appear more moderate, it may also be expressed in terms of a "not yet": "Now is not the right time." This second, "stagist" argument recalls starkly that of some of the colonial powers toward subjected nations' demands for independence, trenchantly analyzed by Dipesh Chakrabarty in relation to India and the British Empire.[6]

Yet questioning of and indeed opposition to a political focus on marriage equality have come not only from homophobic quarters but also from queer political activists. Warner, in particular, has been critical of a certain gay temporal and evolutive paradigm, one designed to respond in part to stagist arguments of deferral. According to Warner, marriage-equality activists like Andrew Sullivan and William Eskridge have portrayed the "bad" behavior of some gays as a kind of "adolescent" rebellion, a form of acting out due to not having been allowed to form firm bonds: on the one hand, however, the majority of gays do not in fact behave in this way and, on the other hand, those who do so will "grow up" and accept their "adult" responsibilities given access to the corresponding rights. For his part, Warner takes aim at the normalizing hegemony of the institutionalization of the spousal couple, em-phasizing that marriage is not simply a choice among others; by endorsing some kinds of relationship, the state necessarily excludes and devalues others. Warner, therefore, wishes to celebrate the many different kinds of alterna-tive relationships queer individuals have forged and asks why it should not be possible to formalize arrangements irrespective not only of the sex of the partners involved but also of their number.[7] Alternative queer temporalities, especially that of a "prolonged adolescence," have also been powerfully cel-ebrated and advocated by queer critics such as Judith Halberstam.[8]

An awareness of the appropriation of marriage by sexual dissidents in the past might seem to be most obviously usable—that is, able to be mobilized politically—in support of gay and lesbian marriage rights ("same-sex couples have always striven for this"). Some of the examples discussed in this book certainly lend themselves readily to this project. Others, like the group at the Latin Gate, may do so as well, but in a less straightforward way. For these men, with their exuberant sexual promiscuity, also resist the hegemony of the single couple. They were not simply "good gays" before their time, ready to settle down (happy to be dragooned) into "adult" responsibilities and com-panionate marriage; they lived, after all, at a time when the institution of marriage was about anything but equality. They claimed marriage on their own terms. They also claimed a festive irresponsibility, an "adolescent" way-wardness. In their refusal to choose, their "wanting it all," their example becomes doubly usable—for both gay–lesbian and for queer political ends. At one and the same time, the men themselves and the stories and histories they generate appear ready to stand for the right to marry and to question the normative institution of marriage.

The ghosts of Saint John at the Latin Gate do not—cannot, perhaps will not?—tell their whole story. The voices of the men involved, having been constrained to speak, were cut off. Thus, while this study preserves and works to understand what was said by and written around them, it also seeks to allow their silences to become oppositional, to point to the elisions and erasures—the fictionality—of the ideological discourse invested in underpinning and maintaining the hegemony of a certain form and idea of marriage.[9] There is, first, the stubborn, poignant silence, before his death, of Gasparo Vittorio. We hear the intended spouse briefly in the earliest trial fragment, telling of his sexual encounter with the young Brother Agilar, who said of him afterward that he took more the role of a woman than of a man. Gasparo appears to have been considerably less cooperative than were his friends with his coercive comforters from San Giovanni Decollato. He is the only one who is not said to have received communion with great devotion or even with any devotion at all; his entry in the confraternity registers contains merely the terse affirmation that he was given communion: "il detto fu comunicato." No less summarily, Gasparo's testament describes him as saying and bequeathing nothing to anyone: "non volse lassar memoria alcuna" (he wished to leave no memory/no remembrance).[10] Does this turning away from the future perhaps reveal Gasparo's awareness of the impossibility, now, of leaving behind any authentic trace? His silence, in any case, bespeaks his resistance, no less than his courage.

There is the silence also of the other intended spouse, Brother Gioseffe, whom some of the men claim not to know (Caviedis, Valez), and who, reportedly having fallen ill and gone to hospital, avoided arrest with the others. Was this man lucky, better informed, or perhaps treacherous? Did he remain at San Giuliano? Was he also interrogated? And what of the "evil hermit" said to have performed other weddings? Was he apprehended, as we know a number of individuals were, including a hermit and a university graduate, following the execution of the eight friends?[11] Whether arrested or evading capture, these men were also silenced, as were a good number of others who escaped. This point is made by several early sources, including the informant of the Duke of Urbino; with relative precision, Tiepolo records the number of twenty-seven men or more, who met on repeated occasions. The men arrested and punished, then, represented the tip of an iceberg. The stories of the others, while related to those we have, might also be different in ways unknown. Is it possible to wonder if some of them might have lived, if not happily ever after, at least with some happiness for a time? Those who got away—who got away with it—also escape us. The limits of our history of a criminalized sexuality thus coincide not only with repressions but also with survivals, perhaps freedoms of the past.

These alternative histories could only be because they were and are hidden from History.[12] The members of the San Giovanni group thus offer us, finally, the queer possibility of standing at a moment in the past and suspending teleological knowledge in order to envision other (still future?) possibilities, apart from the history that we know will be.[13] Once again, in a postcolonial context, Édouard Glissant drew on Deleuze and Guattari's concept of the rhizome to advocate a turning away from an impossible search for African origins, from the "single root," in favor of a lateral exploration of present Caribbean creolity or mixity.[14] But perhaps it might be possible to think of history itself, or at least of certain of its subjects, in rhizomatic or even stoloniferous terms: as not characterized at all points by a linear evolution, nor even by any readily apparent link, but as having the possibility to strike out underground, to sprout up not only in other places and conditions but also in other times. New growth thus produced would be related to the old, yet tangentially, opaquely, or organically so. Since history is always written from a present that is a future, a point necessarily transitory and relative, past events might come to relate to others in a more distant future in ways not yet appreciable. With those outside History, we might then dream of other histories, histories perhaps in the making, histories that might yet still be . . .

NOTES

Introduction

1. As is discussed later, the French *pacs* (Pacte Civil de Solidarité), which was instituted in 1999, is distinctive in that it offers restricted legal benefits to two cohabiting
adults of either sex, excluding close relatives. In addition to gay and lesbian couples,
therefore, two distant relations, two friends, or a heterosexual couple are able to enter
into a *pacs*.

2. The two cases were, respectively, *US v. Windsor* and *Obergefell v. Hodges*.

3. See, for example, François de La Mothe Le Vayer, *Le Banquet Sceptique*, in [Ora-
sius Tubero, pseud.], *Quatre Dialogues faits à l'imitation des Anciens* (Frankfurt: Jean
Sarius, 1604 [France, c. 1630]), 132; or Jean-Baptiste Thiers, *Traité des superstitions*, 4 vols.
(Paris: Compagnie des Libraires, 1741), 4:550. Cf. Gary Ferguson, *Queer (Re)Readings in
the French Renaissance: Homosexuality, Gender, Culture* (Aldershot, UK: Ashgate, 2008),
234 and 238.

4. [Artus Thomas?], *L'Isle des Hermaphrodites*, ed. Claude-Gilbert Dubois (Geneva:
Droz, 1996), 75.

5. Pierre de L'Estoile, *Registre-Journal du règne de Henri III*, ed. Madeleine Lazard
and Gilbert Schrenck, 6 vols. (Geneva: Droz, 1992–2003), 3:170–80, esp. 171–72. On
Henry III, see, notably, Ferguson, *Queer (Re)Readings*, chaps. 3 and 6; Guy Poirier,

L'Homosexualité dans l'imaginaire de la Renaissance (Paris: Champion, 1996); idem, *Henri III de France en mascarades imaginaires: Mœurs, humeurs et comportements d'un roi de la Renaissance* (Quebec City: Presses de l'Université Laval, 2010); and Nicolas Le Roux, *La Faveur du roi: Mignons et courtisans au temps des derniers Valois (vers 1547–vers 1589)* (Seyssel: Champ Vallon, 2000).

6. Ovid, *Metamorphoses*, Book 9, vv. 666–797.

7. See Thomas Laqueur, *Making Sex: Body and Gender from the Greeks to Freud* (Cambridge, MA: Harvard University Press, 1990); cf. Sylvie Steinberg, *La Confusion des sexes: Le Travestissement de la Renaissance à la Révolution* (Paris: Fayard, 2001). For a comprehensive discussion of the criticism of Laqueur's work, see Helen King, *The One-Sex Body on Trial: The Classical and Early Modern Evidence* (Farnham, UK: Ashgate, 2013); cf. Ferguson, *Queer (Re)Readings*, 25–28.

8. Isaac de Benserade, *Iphis et Iante*, ed. Anne Verdier, with Christian Biet and Lise Leibacher-Ouvrard (Vijon: Lampsaque, 2000). For a discussion, see David M. Robinson, *Closeted Writing and Lesbian and Gay Literature: Classical, Early Modern, Eighteenth-Century* (Aldershot, UK: Ashgate, 2006), esp. 224–37. The French thirteenth-century epic *Chanson d'Yde et Olive* and a cluster of subsequent reworkings recount a story that also involves cross-dressing, marriage between two women, and sex change. For a reading that argues for a source in *The Thousand and One Nights*, see Sahar Amer, "Cross-Dressing and Female Same-Sex Marriage in Medieval French and Arabic Literatures," in *Islamicate Sexualities: Translations Across Temporal Geographies of Desire*, ed. Kathryn Babayan and Afsaneh Najmabadi (Cambridge, MA: Harvard Center for Middle Eastern Studies, 2008), 72–113; cf. the critique of this essay by Brad Epps in the same volume, "Comparison, Competition, and Cross-Dressing: Cross-Cultural Analysis in a Contested World," 114–60.

9. Quoted from Laurie Shannon, "Nature's Bias: Renaissance Homonormativity and Elizabethan Comic Likeness," *Modern Philology* 98, no. 2 (2000–2001): 183–210. The passage, from a letter addressed by the ambassador to Philip II, dated June 27, 1564, is found on p. 195. Shannon illuminates Elizabeth's "thought experiment" by setting it in relation to sixteenth-century ideals of likeness that constitute what she terms "Renaissance homonormativity" (pp. 195–96).

10. Henri Estienne, *Apologie pour Hérodote*, ed. P. Ristelhuber, 2 vols. (Geneva: Slatkine, 1969; first pub. Paris, 1879), 1:178. Cf. Ferguson, *Queer (Re)Readings*, 270–72.

11. Michel de Montaigne, *Journal de voyage*, ed. François Rigolot (Paris: Presses universitaires de France, 1992), 6; translation from Michel de Montaigne, *The Complete Works: Essays, Travel Journal, Letters*, trans. Donald M. Frame (New York: Alfred A. Knopf, 2003), 1059. For further discussion, see Gary Ferguson, "Early Modern Transitions: From Montaigne to Choisy," in "Transgender France," ed. Todd W. Reeser, *L'Esprit Créateur* 53, no. 1 (2013): 145–57.

12. Rudolf M. Dekker and Lotte C. van de Pol, *The Tradition of Female Transvestism in Early Modern Europe* (New York: St Martin's Press, 1989), 58–63 and throughout.

13. See, notably, Israel Burshatin, "Written on the Body: Slave or Hermaphrodite in Sixteenth-Century Spain," in *Queer Iberia: Sexualities, Cultures, and Crossings from the Middle Ages to the Renaissance*, ed. Josiah Blackmore and Gregory S. Hutcheson (Dur-

ham, NC: Duke University Press, 1999), 420–56. See also, especially on the role of the doctors involved, François Soyer, *Ambiguous Gender in Early Modern Spain and Portugal: Inquisitors, Doctors and the Transgression of Gender Norms* (Leiden: Brill, 2012), 57–67.

14. Ruth Mazzo Karras, *Unmarriages: Women, Men, and Sexual Unions in the Middle Ages* (Philadelphia: University of Pennsylvania Press, 2012), 2.

15. Ibid. Cecilia Cristellon paints a similar picture with regard to Venice prior to the Council of Trent:

> [M]arital matters were managed according to a variety of legal systems that intertwined, interacted, and often collided. . . . Marriage was a bond without clearly defined boundaries, whose value and nature were interpreted differently in the ecclesiastical courts, in the eyes of the community, and by people from different social classes and geographical origins. . . . In the mid-sixteenth century, such fundamental principles of Catholic marriage as marital indissolubility and the primacy of consent in forming the marriage bond— principles established in the twelfth century—were still far from being accepted by the laity and often by the secular clergy who shared lay attitudes.

"Marriage and Consent in Pre-Tridentine Venice: Between Lay Conception and Ecclesiastical Conception, 1420–1545," *Sixteenth Century Journal* 39, no. 2 (2008): 389–418 (p. 416).

16. Karras, *Unmarriages*, 8.

17. The fullest discussions of the group and its activities until recently were Giuseppe Marcocci, "Matrimoni omosessuali nella Roma del tardo Cinquecento: Su un passo del 'Journal' di Montaigne," *Quaderni storici* 133 (2010): 107–37; and Gary Ferguson, "(Same-Sex) Marriage and the Making of Europe: Renaissance Rome Revisited," in *What's Queer About Europe? Productive Encounters and Re-Enchanting Paradigms*, ed. Mireille Rosello and Sudeep Dasgupta (New York: Fordham University Press, 2014), 27–47 and 190–95. As the manuscript of this book was in the process of revision, Giuseppe Marcocci shared with me, several weeks in advance of its publication, the text of his article "Is This Love? Same-Sex Marriages in Renaissance Rome," *Historical Reflections* 41, no. 2 (2015): 37–52. Without making fundamental changes, I have thus been able to take account of the author's most recent arguments, as well as of new source material he presents (in particular a series of newsletters or *avvisi* written for the German banking family, the Fuggers), though in a less detailed way than the other contemporary documents discussed. A short essay by Giovanni Dall'Orto also appeared at the same time in *Tutta un'altra storia: L'omosessualità dall'antichità al secondo dopoguerra* (Milan: il Saggiatore, 2015), 315–24. Dall'Orto follows Marcocci's first article closely while also signaling a number of points of comparison that will be developed here.

18. Carlo Ginzburg, *The Cheese and the Worms: The Cosmos of a Sixteenth-Century Miller*, trans. John and Anne Tedeschi (Baltimore: Johns Hopkins University Press, 1980), xxvi; Natalie Zemon Davis, *The Return of Martin Guerre* (Cambridge, MA: Harvard University Press, 1983).

19. See, for example, the memoir of Saidiya V. Hartman, *Lose Your Mother: A Journey Along the Atlantic Slave Route* (New York: Farrar, Straus and Giroux, 2007). On

oppositional silence as revelatory of colonial history's elisions and fictionality, see Beat-riz Pastor, "Silence and Writing: The History of the Conquest," trans. Jason Wood, in *1492–1992: Re/Discovering Colonial Writing*, ed. René Jara and Nicholas Spadaccini (Minneapolis, MN: Prisma Institute, 1989; repr. University of Minnesota Press, 1991), 121–63. On the fictional nature of all historical narratives, see the earlier essays by Hayden White collected in *Tropics of Discourse: Essays in Cultural Criticism* (Baltimore: Johns Hopkins University Press, 1978), esp. "The Historical Text as Literary Artifact," 81–100. Among other influential contributions, see Jonathan Goldberg, "The History that Will Be," in *Premodern Sexualities*, ed. Louise Fradenburg and Carla Freccero, with Kathy Lavezzo (New York: Routledge, 1996), 3–21; Scott Bravmann, *Queer Fic-tions of the Past: History, Culture, and Difference* (Cambridge: Cambridge University Press, 1997); Carolyn Dinshaw, *Getting Medieval: Sexualities and Communities, Pre- and Postmodern* (Durham, NC: Duke University Press, 1999); Carla Freccero, *Queer/Early/Modern* (Durham, NC: Duke University Press, 2006); Heather Love, *Feeling Backward: Loss and the Politics of Queer History* (Cambridge, MA: Harvard University Press, 2007); Elizabeth Freeman, ed., "Queer Temporalities," a special issue of *GLQ: A Journal of Lesbian and Gay Studies* 13, nos. 2–3 (2007). In relation to Italy, see Gary P. Cestaro, ed., *Queer Italia: Same-Sex Desire in Italian Literature and Film* (New York: Palgrave Macmillan, 2004).

20. Walter Benjamin, "Theses on the Philosophy of History," in *Reading the Past: Lit-erature and History*, ed. Tamsin Spargo (Basingstoke: Palgrave, 2000), 118–26 (p. 126).

21. The question of teleology is central to current debates between early modern queer critics with differing primary engagements—that of tracing the development of sexual phenomena or of queerness over time and that of queering notions of temporal-ity through the promotion of "unhistoricism." See, notably, Valerie Traub's engagement with recent work of Jonathan Goldberg, Madhavi Menon, and Carla Freccero (an ex-change in part growing out of and prolonging that between David Halperin and Eve Sedgwick, cf. chap. 10, note 30 in this volume): Jonathan Goldberg and Madhavi Me-non, "Queering History," *PMLA* 120, no. 5 (2005): 1608–17; Valerie Traub, "The New Unhistoricism in Queer Studies," *PMLA* 128, no. 1 (2013): 21–39; "Historicism and Un-historicism in Queer Studies," letters to the editor from Carla Freccero, Madhavi Me-non, and Valerie Traub, *PMLA* 128, no. 3 (2013): 781–86. The present study draws on the work of historicists and nonhistoricists. Reflecting the belief that historical writing need not be confined to "straight" narratives of necessary outcomes and of progress toward a self-evident and self-identical present, it seeks to contribute both to the history of sexuality and to a number of queer political and historical lines of inquiry.

22. Chimamanda Ngozi Adichie, "The Danger of a Single Story," TED talk, re-corded July 2009, http://www.ted.com/talks/chimamanda_adichie_the_danger_of_a _single_story. Again in a postcolonial context, Édouard Glissant earlier set a plurality of histories in opposition to History: " 'Là où se joignent les histoires des peuples, hier réputés sans histoire, finit l'Histoire.' . . . Se battre contre l'un de l'Histoire, pour la Re-lation des histoires, c'est peut-être à la fois retrouver son temps vrai et son identité" ('His-tory ends where the histories of peoples, only yesterday deemed devoid of history, come together.' . . . To fight against the one of History, for the Interrelation of histories, is per-

haps at the same time to discover one's true time and one's identity), *Le discours antillais* (Paris: Gallimard, 1997), 227 and 276; cf., in general, 219–79.

1. A French Writer Visits

1. For a notable expression of such sentiments, see the French poet Joachim Du Bellay, *Les Antiquitez de Rome* and *Les Regrets.*

2. On the complexity of the enunciative situation, especially in the first part of the text, see *Journal de voyage,* ed. Rigolot, introduction, xii–xix.

3. For a brief account, see ibid., v–vi; cf. xxiii.

4. "La Copie Leydet du *'Journal de Voyage'* présentée et annotée par François Moureau," in *Autour du Journal de Voyage de Montaigne, 1580–1980,* Actes des Journées Montaigne, Mulhouse, Bâle, October 1980, ed. François Moureau and René Bernoulli (Geneva: Slatkine, 1982), 107–85 (esp. 146).

5. *Journal de voyage de Michel de Montaigne en Italie . . . Avec des notes par M. de Querlon,* 1 vol. in 4° (À Rome, et se trouve à Paris, chez Le Jay, 1774), 156.

6. *Complete Works,* trans. Frame, 1164–65, modified.

7. *Journal,* ed. Rigolot, 118. Rigolot takes as his base text Querlon's 1774, 3 vol. in 12° edition, incorporating corrections from Leydet, as well as from Lautrey (see note 17), where these resolve an obviously faulty reading. All corrections are signaled in the footnotes. Rigolot also modifies the spelling to reflect sixteenth-century rather than eighteenth-century norms (cf. pp. xxxiv–xxxvi). The text of the passage given here differs from the Querlon edition, referred to in note 5, pp. 156–57, only in spelling and punctuation.

8. As will be discussed later, this is the interpretation advanced by Marcocci, "Matrimoni omosessuali."

9. "Des cannibales," *Essais,* I, 31, in *Œuvres complètes,* ed. Albert Thibaudet and Maurice Rat, Bibliothèque de la Pléiade (Paris: Gallimard, 1962), 202.

10. Federico Barbierato, *The Inquisitor in the Hat Shop: Inquisition, Forbidden Books and Unbelief in Early Modern Venice* (Farnham, UK: Ashgate, 2012), 176 and 181.

11. Ibid., 182 and 185. On Ginzburg's study of Menocchio, see "Engagement."

12. In her study of prostitution in Rome from 1566 to 1656, Tessa Storey also refers to early seventeenth-century *libertini,* who "refuted Christian ethics on sexual matters, stressing the importance of the power of nature and accepting the essential naturalness of sexual desire"; *Carnal Commerce in Counter-Reformation Rome* (Cambridge: Cambridge University Press, 2008), 222–23.

13. One of the sexual liberties claimed by an individual discussed by Barbierato was precisely the freedom from marriage (*The Inquisitor,* 181).

14. See Todd W. Reeser, "Re-Reading Platonic Sexuality Sceptically in Montaigne's *'Apologie de Raimond Sebond,'* " in *Masculinities in Sixteenth-Century France: Proceedings of the Eighth Cambridge French Renaissance Colloquium, 5–7 July 2003,* ed. Philip Ford and Paul White (Cambridge: Cambridge French Colloquia, 2006), 103–26. Cf. Ferguson, *Queer (Re)Readings,* 239–43.

15. William John Beck, "Montaigne face à la [*sic*] homosexualité," *Bulletin de la Société des Amis de Montaigne*, 6th ser., 9–10 (1982): 41–50; cf. idem, "The Obscure Montaigne: The Quotation, the Addition, and the Footnote," *College Language Association Journal* 34, no. 2 (1990): 228–52. John Boswell, *Same-Sex Unions in Premodern Europe* (New York: Villard Books, 1994), 264–65.

16. Meusnier de Querlon, ed. cit., 156.

17. Michel de Montaigne, *Journal de voyage*, ed. Louis Lautrey (Paris: Hachette, 1906), 248. The amended reading is followed in the edition of the *Journal* by Charles Dédéyan (Paris: Belles Lettres, 1946), 231. It is signaled in the Thibaudet/Rat edition as a variant, p. 1698, note 1 to p. 1228.

18. "Roman experts said that since sex between male and female could be legitimate only within marriage, it had seemed equally fair [*juste*] to them to authorize [these] ceremonies and mysteries of the church" (Boswell, *Same-Sex Unions*, 265; author's italics and square brackets).

19. On this anthropological vision, at once curious and skeptical, see Frédéric Tinguely, *Le voyageur aux mille tours: Les ruses de l'écriture du monde à la Renaissance* (Paris: Honoré Champion, 2014), chap. 8, "Montaigne et les curiosités de l'Église romaine," 125–39.

20. See *Journal*, ed. Rigolot, 123–24; *Complete Works*, 1170–71.

21. See Thomas James Dandelet, *Spanish Rome, 1500–1700* (New Haven, CT: Yale University Press, 2001). In relation to Philip II and Gregory XIII, however, Ludwig von Pastor emphasizes the differences between the two men's interests and policies and, in particular, what he terms the king's "Caesaro-Papism"; see Ludwig Freiherr von Pastor (Ludovico Barone von Pastor), *Storia dei Papi dalla fine del Medio Evo*, vol. 9, *Gregorio XIII (1572–1585)*, trans. Pio Cenci (Rome: Desclée & Ci, 1955), esp. 232–69; trans. from *Geschichte der Päpste seit dem Ausgang des Mittelalters*, 16 vols. (Freiburg im Breisgau: Herder, 1886–1933).

22. Dandelet, *Spanish Rome*, 9. Michael J. Levin, in contrast, emphasizes that Spanish control in Italy was less hegemonic and absolute than has been argued by some historians; see *Agents of Empire: Spanish Ambassadors in Sixteenth-Century Italy* (Ithaca, NY: Cornell University Press, 2005).

23. In yet another twist of irony, Henry inherited the Portuguese crown unexpectedly when King Sebastian died in an ill-fated campaign against Muslims in Morocco, supported by forces that Pope Gregory had provided for a rebellion from Ireland against the Protestant Queen Elizabeth I of England. Sebastian's death occurred on August 4, 1578, a few days after the men at the Latin Gate had been arrested and while their trial was underway.

24. The details of the reception of the ambassador come from a contemporary description by the papal master of ceremonies, reproduced in the edition of the *Journal de voyage* by Alessandro D'Ancona, *L'Italia alla fine del secolo XVI. Giornale del viaggio di Michele de Montaigne in Italia nel 1580 e 1581* (Città di Castello: S. Lapi, 1889), 289–92.

25. Philippe Desan, "L'appel de Rome, ou comment Montaigne ne devint jamais ambassadeur," in *Chemins de l'exil, havres de paix: migrations d'hommes et d'idées au XVIe siècle*, ed. Jean Balsamo and Chiara Lastraioli (Paris: Champion, 2010), 229–59; Warren Boutcher, "'Le moyen de voir ce Senecque escrit à la main': Montaigne's *Journal de voy-*

age and the Politics of *Science* and *Faveur* in the Vatican Library," in "(Ré)interprétations: Études sur le Seizième Siècle," ed. John O'Brien, *Michigan Romance Studies* 15 (1995): 177–214.

26. Mail between Paris and Rome generally took around seventeen and, at the very least, ten to twelve days. On March 13, Montaigne did, however, receive letters conferring on him Roman citizenship.

27. Timothy Hampton, *Fictions of Embassy: Literature and Diplomacy in Early Modern Europe* (Ithaca, NY: Cornell University Press, 2009), 41.

28. Ibid., 21–24.

29. *Lettres de Henri III, roi de France*, vol. 4 (11 mai 1578–7 avril 1580), ed. Pierre Champion and Michel François, with Bernard Barbiche and Henri Zuber (Paris: Klincksieck, 1984), 208–9, no. 3389, June 8, 1579; 223, no. 3412, June 22; 248, no. 3454, July 20; 256–57, no. 3475, August 18; 260, no. 3486, August 31; 273–74, no. 3515, September 29; 299, no. 3578, November 25. King Henry also refers to Philip's readying of troops for an invasion, which he sees clearly will be of Portugal. Throughout 1580 and the first months of 1581, a number of the king's letters to La Roche-Posay, to his ambassador in Spain, Jean de Vivonne de Saint-Gouard, and to others refer to the evolving situation as Philip imposed his claim against those of Don Antonio and the Duchess of Braganza. Cf. *Lettres de Henri III, roi de France*, vol. 5 (8 avril 1580–31 décembre 1582), ed. Pierre Champion, Michel François, and Jacqueline Boucher, with Henri Zuber (Paris: Honoré Champion, 2000), nos. 3764, 3904, 4109, 4121, 4142, 4169, 4171, 4178, and 4179.

30. Montaigne himself attended the station mass on February 16 and again on March 1. On the second occasion, the pope was present.

2. "Our Marriages"?

1. Venice, Archivio di Stato, Senato, Dispacci ambasciatori, Roma, filza 13, fols. 120v–121r; reproduced, with minor differences, in Fabio Mutinelli, *Storia arcana ed aneddotica d'Italia raccontata dai veneti ambasciatori*, 4 vols. (Venice: Pietro Naratovich, 1855), 1:121.

2. Tiepolo composed an account of this journey. See *Due ambasciatori veneziani nella Spagna di fine Cinquecento. I diari dei viaggi di Antonio Tiepolo (1571–1572) e Francesco Vendramin (1592–1593)*, ed. Luigi Monga (Moncalieri: Centro Interuniversitario di Ricerche sul "Viaggio in Italia," 2000). For details of the author's biography, see pp. 15–17. Cf. *Relazioni degli ambasciatori veneti al Senato*, ed. Eugenio Albèri, 15 vols. (1839–63), vol. 10/series 2, vol. 4 (Florence: Società editrice fiorentina, 1857), 243–44.

3. On this difficult moment in Roman–Venetian relations and Paolo Tiepolo's role in it, see Ludwig von Pastor, *Storia dei Papi*, 9:238–45.

4. See Valter Boggione and Giovanni Casalegno, *Dizionario storico del lessico erotico italiano: Metafore, eufemismi, oscenità, doppi sensi, parole dotte e parole basse in otto secoli di letteratura italiana* (Milan: Longanesi, 1996), 60–61. Cf. Claudio Fraccari, "Addendum. La chiave nella toppa: Repertorio lessicale e mappa per aree semantiche dei *Cicalamenti* del Grappa," in *El più soave et dolce et dilectevole et gratioso bochone: Amore e*

sesso al tempo dei Gonzaga, ed. Costantino Cipolla and Giancarlo Malacarne (Milan: FrancoAngeli, 2006), 327–40 (esp. 331).

5. See Claudio Fraccari, "Le parole per dirlo. Glossario," in *El più soave et dolce et dilectevole et gratioso bochone*, 341–54 (esp. 345); cf. by the same author in the same volume, "Per amor di metafora: Linguaggio erotico e travestimenti dell'osceno nella corrispondenza gonzaghesca," 265–89 (esp. 273).

6. *Le Decameron de Messire Jehan Bocace*, trans. Antoine Le Maçon (Paris: Estienne Roffet, 1545), 139r.

7. On this novella in general, see Ferguson, *Queer (Re)Readings*, chap. 1, 55–91, and on the expression *habiter*, p. 84, note 80. For examples of *cohabiter* used with a sexual meaning, see ibid., 212 (in a translation of Plutarch) and 278–80 (in a translation of Lucian). According to Boggione and Casalegno, the Italian *abitare* can have the same sense; see *Dizionario storico del lessico erotico italiano*, 83.

8. As the bibliography on the history of marriage is vast, the following is necessarily a restricted selection. For a good general introduction, see Stephanie Coontz, *Marriage, a History: How Love Conquered Marriage* (New York: Penguin, 2005). For the Middle Ages and early modern period, see Karras, *Unmarriages*, and Philip L. Reynolds and John Witte Jr., eds., *To Have and to Hold: Marrying and Its Documentation in Western Christendom, 400–1600* (Cambridge: Cambridge University Press, 2007). On Italy, see Trevor Dean and K. J. P. Lowe, eds., *Marriage in Italy, 1300–1600* (Cambridge: Cambridge University Press, 1998); several chapters in Christiane Klapisch-Zuber, *Women, Family, and Ritual in Renaissance Italy*, trans. Lydia G. Cochrane (Chicago: University of Chicago Press, 1985); Michela de Giorgio and Christiane Klapisch-Zuber, eds., *Storia del matrimonio* (Bari: Laterza, 1996); Daniela Lombardi, *Matrimoni di antico regime* (Bologna: Il Mulino, 2001); Jacqueline Murray, ed., *Marriage in Premodern Europe: Italy and Beyond* (Toronto: Centre for Reformation and Renaissance Studies, 2012); and the series of volumes edited by Silvana Seidel Menchi and Diego Quaglioni: *Coniugi nemici: La separazione in Italia dal XII al XVIII secolo* (2000), *Matrimoni in dubbio: Unioni controverse e nozze clandestine in Italia dal XIV al XVIII secolo* (2001), *Trasgressioni: Seduzione, concubinato, adulterio, bigamia (XIV–XVIII secolo)* (2004), and *I tribunali del matrimonio (secoli XV–XVIII)* (2006) (Bologna: Il Mulino). On ideas and social practices prior to the Council of Trent, see also Cristellon, "Marriage and Consent," and idem, "Public Display of Affection: The Making of Marriage in the Venetian Courts Before the Council of Trent (1420–1545)," in *Erotic Cultures of Renaissance Italy*, ed. Sara F. Matthews-Grieco (Farnham, UK: Ashgate, 2010), 173–97.

9. Dean and Lowe, *Marriage in Italy*, 2–4.

10. See especially *Essais*, III, 5, "Sur des vers de Virgile," and I, 28, "De l'amitié." For a discussion of the complicated contours of Montaigne's exploration of friendship, marriage, and sex, see Ferguson, *Queer (Re)Readings*, chap. 4, 191–243.

11. For a helpful summary, see Philip L. Reynolds, "Marrying and Its Documentation in Pre-Modern Europe: Consent, Celebration, and Property," in *To Have and to Hold*, chap. 1, 1–42.

12. Matteo Bandello, *Le novelle*, ed. Delmo Maestri, 4 vols. (Alessandria: Edizioni dell'Orso, 1992–96), 1:389–98; Pierre Boaistuau, *Histoires tragiques*, ed. Richard A. Carr

(Paris: Honoré Champion, 1977), 139–67, quotation on p. 146. For a comparative analysis of the two versions of the story, see Bénédicte Boudou, "Le Mariage clandestin et la rupture du mariage dans la nouvelle de Violente et Didaco, chez Bandello et Boaistuau," *Cahiers de recherches médiévales et humanistes* 21 (2011): 343–58. On the representation of the contracting of marriage by Bandello, see Reinier Leushuis, "'Col publicamento del matrimonio sgannar ciascuno': Marriage and Betrothal in Bandello's *Novelle*," in *Marriage in Premodern Europe: Italy and Beyond*, ed. Jacqueline Murray (Toronto: Centre for Reformation and Renaissance Studies, 2012), 307–31.

13. Marguerite de Navarre, *L'Heptaméron*, nouvelles 21 and 40.

14. See Marian Rothstein, *Reading in the Renaissance: "Amadis de Gaule" and the Lessons of Memory* (Newark: University of Delaware Press, 1999), 125–38.

15. Similar issues return in the second volume of *Don Quixote*, published ten years later, in chaps. 20–21 (the story of Quiteria, Basilio, and Camacho) and chaps. 38–39.

16. Natalie Zemon Davis suggests, for example, that Bertrande de Rols and Arnaud du Tilh, masquerading as Martin Guerre, were probably encouraged in their actions by a popular peasant tradition of manipulating marriage law and practices to one's own advantage. They may also have been aware of new Protestant ideas. See *The Return of Martin Guerre*, 46–50.

17. Ginzburg, *The Cheese and the Worms*, 10.

18. On Italian civil laws, see Trevor Dean, "Fathers and Daughters: Marriage Laws and Marriage Disputes in Bologna and Italy, 1200–1500," in *Marriage in Italy*, 85–106. For the age of consent following the Tridentine reform, see *Rituale Romanum. Editio Princpes (1614)*, ed. Manlio Sodi and Juan Javier Flores Arcas (Vatican City: Libreria Editrice Vaticana, 2004), 144.

19. On the decisions of the churchmen at Trent and the details of the discussions that led up to them, see Charlotte Christensen-Nugues, "Parental Authority and Freedom of Choice: The Debate on Clandestinity and Parental Consent at the Council of Trent," *Sixteenth Century Journal* 45 (2014): 51–72. Joanne M. Ferraro examines Church regulation of marriage and its breakup in Venice in the century following the Council of Trent in *Marriage Wars in Late Renaissance Venice* (Oxford: Oxford University Press, 2001). On the adjudication of questions regarding the new Tridentine rules, which in certain cases might also be manipulated by litigants to their advantage, see Cecilia Cristellon, "Does the Priest Have to Be There? Contested Marriages Before Roman Tribunals: Italy, Sixteenth to Eighteenth Centuries," *Österreichische Zeitschrift für Geschichtswissenschaften* 20, no. 3 (2009): 10–30.

20. Vienna, Österreichische Nationalbibliothek, Cod. 8951 Han, *Novellae Fuggerianae* (1578), fol. 508r. A digital version can be consulted online through the library's website, scan 1024: http://data.onb.ac.at/rec/AL00169821. The presence of a hermit, said to have officiated, is also attested by a newsletter dated the same day sent to the Grand Duke of Tuscany. See Marcocci, "Is This Love?," 42 and 48.

21. The 1612 *Vocabolario degli accademici della Crusca* defines *tirare/trarre* as "Condurre, o fare accostare a se con violenza, strascinare" (to lead or to pull to oneself with violence, to drag), http://www.lessicografia.it/Controller?lemma=TIRARE_e_TRARRE_ed1&rewrite=1.

3. Marriage—Rites, Analogues, Meanings

1. See Allan A. Tulchin, "Same-Sex Couples Creating Households in Old Regime France: The Uses of the *Affrèrement*," *Journal of Modern History* 79 (2007): 613–47; and R. Aubenas, "Le Contrat d'"affrairamentum' dans le droit provençal du moyen âge," *Revue historique de droit français et étranger*, 4th ser., 12 (1933): 478–524.

2. An *affrèrement* was also sometimes entered into by a husband and wife in order to modify the financial basis of their marriage; see Tulchin, "Same-Sex Couples," 632–33.

3. Boswell, *Same-Sex Unions*.

4. See Alan Bray, *The Friend* (Chicago: University of Chicago Press, 2003), 13–41, 126–33, and elsewhere.

5. Ferguson, *Queer (Re)Readings*, 229–36.

6. Jean Gerson, *Considérations sur saint Joseph*, in *Œuvres complètes*, ed. P. Glorieux, 10 vols. in 11 (Paris: Desclée, 1961–73), vol. 7, bk. 1 (1966), 82.

7. This remains the case under current canon law, according to which "antecedent and perpetual impotence to have intercourse" nullifies a marriage but sterility does not: Canon 1084.1–3, http://www.vatican.va/archive/ENG1104/__P3Y.HTM.

8. Reynolds, "Marrying and Its Documentation," 9. According to current canon law, it would constitute grounds for an annulment (i.e., a declaration that the marriage had never validly existed). Canon 1096.1 describes marriage as being "ordered to the procreation of offspring by means of some sexual cooperation." According to Canon 1101.2, "[i]f, however, either or both of the parties by a positive act of the will exclude marriage itself, some essential element of marriage, or some essential property of marriage, the party contracts invalidly." See http://www.vatican.va/archive/ENG1104/__P3Z.HTM.

9. As I have noted elsewhere, "the differential element crucial for marriage according to Gerson is not fundamentally that of the sex of the partners, but that of their sexual roles and the hierarchical values attached to them. The functioning of sex difference as a determining factor, that is, is dependent on a vision of the essential inequality of the sexes, founded on their ontological identification with a particular role" (Ferguson, *Queer (Re)Readings*, 235–36). On Gerson's views on the status of women and on marriage in general, see D. Catherine Brown, *Pastor and Laity in the Theology of Jean Gerson* (Cambridge: Cambridge University Press, 1987), chap. 7, 209–38.

10. This is the view of Karras, *Unmarriages*, 9.

11. See *Rituale romanum*, 136–40. The preliminary instructions occupy three pages, the rite less than two pages.

12. *Pastorale, canones et ritus ecclesiasticos, qui ad sacramentorum administrationem aliaque pastoralia officia rite obeunda pertinent, complectens* (Antwerp: ex officina Christophori Plantini, 1589). The rites for betrothal and marriage are found on pp. 121–36. Legally independent, Malines was located within the territory of the Duchy of Brabant, adjacent to the County of Flanders. Both were part of the Burgundian, then Spanish/Habsburg Netherlands.

13. Subject to various constraints, the current Roman Catholic liturgy allows a choice of Scripture readings. Matthew 19:3–6 remains a possible gospel passage.

14. Michael J. Rocke, *Forbidden Friendships: Homosexuality and Male Culture in Renaissance Florence* (Oxford: Oxford University Press, 1996), 149; cf. esp. 148–91. Rocke

estimates that "many, if not most, Florentine males engaged in homosexual activity at some point in their lives" (p. 150) and that, by age forty, two out of every three men had been implicated in formal sodomy charges to the Office of the Night (pp. 114–15). See also Michael J. Rocke, "Sodomites in Fifteenth-Century Tuscany: The Views of Bernardino of Siena," in *The Pursuit of Sodomy: Male Homosexuality in Renaissance and Enlightenment Europe*, ed. Kent Gerard and Gert Hekma (New York: Harrington Park/ Haworth Press, 1989), 7–31 (esp. 11), published simultaneously as the *Journal of Homosexuality* 16, nos. 1–2 (1988). On Venice, see Guido Ruggiero, *The Boundaries of Eros: Sex Crime and Sexuality in Renaissance Venice* (Oxford: Oxford University Press, 1985), 109–45; on Rome, Marina Baldassari, *Bande giovanili e "vizio nefando": Violenza e sessualità nella Roma barocca* (Rome: Viella, 2005); on Spain, Cristian Berco, *Sexual Hierarchies, Public Status: Men, Sodomy, and Society in Spain's Golden Age* (Toronto: University of Toronto Press, 2007); on England, Alan Bray, *Homosexuality in Renaissance England* (London: Gay Men's Press, 1982); on France, and for a general overview, see Ferguson, *Queer (Re)Readings*, 1–49.

15. Eve Kosofsky Sedgwick, *Epistemology of the Closet* (Berkeley: University of California Press, 1990), esp. 1–2 and 47. For a discussion, see Ferguson, *Queer (Re)Readings*, esp. 1–16.

16. Ferguson, *Queer (Re)Readings*, 18; cf., in general, 16–37.

17. See Rocke, *Forbidden Friendships*, 88–89.

18. Ibid., 170; cf., 108–9 and 170–72.

19. See Margaret A. Gallucci, "Cellini's Trial for Sodomy: Power and Patronage at the Court of Cosimo I," in *The Cultural Politics of Duke Cosimo I de' Medici*, ed. Konrad Eisenbichler (Aldershot, UK: Ashgate, 2001), 37–46 (esp. 37, author's translation); cf. idem, "ACTing UP in the Renaissance: The Case of Benvenuto Cellini," in *Queer Italia: Same-Sex Desire in Italian Literature and Film*, ed. Gary P. Cestaro (New York: Palgrave Macmillan, 2004), 71–82. In addition to other informal accusations, Cellini had already been convicted on charges of sodomy in 1523. On the artist more generally and on the pederastic subject of a number of sculptures from the second half of the 1540s, see James M. Saslow, *Ganymede in the Renaissance: Homosexuality in Art and Society* (New Haven, CT: Yale University Press, 1986), 142–74.

20. Quoted in Berco, *Sexual Hierarchies*, 154, note 32; cf. 30–31, 52, and 149, note 20.

21. Ibid., 30.

22. Rocke, *Forbidden Friendships*, 172.

23. See Giovanni Romeo, *Amori proibiti: I concubini tra Chiesa e Inquisizione. Napoli 1563–1656* (Bari: Editori Laterza, 2008), 107–9; Pierroberto Scaramella, "Sodomia," in *Dizionario storico dell'Inquisizione*, ed. Adriano Prosperi, with Vincenzo Lavenia and John Tedeschi, 4 vols. (Pisa: Edizioni della Normale, 2010), 3:1445–50 (esp. 1449); and Marcocci, "Matrimoni omosessuali," who draws on both, pp. 122–24. On the potential association of academies in other contexts with games and ludic pastimes of an anti-clerical, irreligious, or even blasphemous character, see George McClure, "Heresy at Play: Academies and the Literary Underground in Counter-Reformation Siena," *Renaissance Quarterly* 63 (2010): 1151–1207.

24. *Zia* is not listed in Boggione and Casalegno, *Dizionario storico del lessico erotico italiano*. It is signaled, however, with the sense of "[p]ersona di sesso maschile di tendenze

omosessuali" (male person with homosexual tendencies), in the *Grande Dizionario della lingua italiana*, ed. Salvatore Battaglia, 21 vols. plus index and supplement (Turin: Unione Tipografico-Editrice Torinese, 1961–2009), sv. Unfortunately, no information on the history of the usage is given. The same meaning attaches to the French *tante*. *Zio* (uncle) was likely coined in contrast, reflecting the particular gendered contours of sixteenth-century sexual attitudes.

25. Archivio Storico Diocesano di Napoli, Sant'Ufficio, 856, c. 52; quoted from Marcocci, "Matrimoni omosessuali," 124.

26. Scaramella, "Sodomia," 1149.

27. Romeo, *Amori proibiti*, 107. Later the pastiche vice-regal document is described as being presented to the young boys as "un'iniziativa che mirava, malgrado i suoi contenuti, ben diversi, a condannare i matrimoni con le donne e a legalizzare i rapporti omosessuali maschili ('non volevano meglio moglie che li figlioli')" (an initiative aimed, despite its quite different content, at condemning marriages with women and at legalizing male homosexual relations ['they desired no better wives than the boys']) (p. 109). Like many other scholars, I would not apply without qualification the terms *homosexual* and *gay* to early modern pederastic relationships between men and boys, given the generally different social configurations involved. For a discussion, see Ferguson, *Queer (Re)Readings*, esp. introduction and chap. 1.

28. The case dates to 1680–81. See Barbierato, *The Inquisitor*, 140–44 (esp. 142). No further details are given in relation to the question of same-sex marriages.

29. Giovanni Battista Petrucci, *Poema Latino Anepigrafo su S. Giacomo della Marca*, ed. and trans. Luigi de Luca and Girolamo Mascia (Naples: S. Francesco al Vomero, 1975), 116–18. Cf. Rocke, *Forbidden Friendships*, 171. Giovanni Dall'Orto refers to a late fifteenth-century sermon by Michele Carcano that gives a slightly different version of the story, supposedly told to the preacher by the friar himself. According to this account, although the growth of the boy's hand had made it impossible to remove the ring, the friar was able to do so easily. See *Tutta un'altra storia*, 317.

30. The discussion here is based on the excellent study of Laura Giannetti, *Lelia's Kiss: Imagining Gender, Sex, and Marriage in Italian Renaissance Comedy* (Toronto: University of Toronto Press, 2009).

31. Ibid., 166–68 and 227–28; quotation on p. 166.

32. Niccolò Machiavelli, *Teatro. Andria, Mandragola, Clizia*, ed. Guido Davico Bonino (Turin: Einaudi, 2001), 194 (act 5, scene 2) and 200 (act 5, scene 7).

33. See Giannetti, *Lelia's Kiss*, 185–88 and 228–29; quotation on pp. 228–29. Cf. Guido Ruggiero, *Machiavelli in Love: Sex, Self, and Society in the Italian Renaissance* (Baltimore: Johns Hopkins University Press, 2007), 19–40; and Michael Sherberg, "Il potere e il piacere: la sodomia del *Marescalco*," in *La Rappresentazione dell'altro nei testi del Rinascimento*, ed. Sergio Zatti (Lucca: Maria Pacini Fazzi Editore, 1998), 96–110. The text of the play is included in *Pietro Aretino*, ed. Carlo Serafini and Luciana Zampolli, intro. Giulio Ferroni, Cento Libri per Mille Anni (Rome: Istituto Poligrafico e Zecca dello Stato, 2002), 899–990; English translation in *Five Comedies from the Italian Renaissance*, ed. and trans. Laura Giannetti and Guido Ruggiero (Baltimore: Johns Hopkins University Press, 2003), 117–204.

34. Characters negotiating a similarly problematic desire, although having married women, are found in contemporary short stories; for example, Pietro di Vinciolo in Giovanni Boccaccio's *Decameron*, V, 10, and Porcellio in Matteo Bandello's *Novelle*, I, 6. See Ferguson, *Queer (Re)Readings*, chap. 1, 55–91.

35. Pietro Aretino, *Ragionamenti*, ed. Giovanni Aquilecchia, with French translation by Paul Larivaille, 2 vols. (Paris: Belles Lettres, 1998–99), 2:84.

36. Pietro Aretino, *Sonetti sopra i "XVI modi,"* ed. Giovanni Aquilecchia (Rome: Salerno Editrice, 1992), 31.

37. See Tessa Storey, "Courtesan Culture: Manhood, Honour and Sociability," in *Erotic Cultures of Renaissance Italy*, ed. Sara Matthews-Grieco (Aldershot, UK: Ashgate, 2010), 247–73.

38. Quoted from ibid., 271, note 79.

39. Ibid., 260.

40. Ibid., 272, note 97, and 262; translation from Storey, slightly modified.

41. Ibid., 272, note 98, and 262; translation from Storey.

42. Giorgio Masi, " 'Gente scapigliatissima e bizzarra': La poesia libertina di Curzio Marignolli," in *Extravagances amoureuses: L'Amour au-delà de la norme à la Renaissance / Stravaganze amorose: L'Amore oltre la norma nel Rinascimento*, Actes du Colloque international du groupe de recherche *Cinquecento plurale*, Tours, 18–20 September 2008, ed. Élise Boillet and Chiara Lastraioli (Paris: Honoré Champion, 2010), 341–414 (esp. 377). From a manuscript dated 1611. Barbierato discusses the case of a Franciscan friar in the 1720s, still using the term *marriage* in the same way to designate simply sexual relations (*The Inquisitor*, 211).

4. Other Witnesses, Other Stories

1. Vatican City, Biblioteca Apostolica Vaticana, MS Urbinati Latini, 1046, *Avvisi di Venezia con notizie anche da varie località d'Italia e d'Europa inviate da Girolamo Cortese e da altri raccoglitori al duca d'Urbino Francesco Maria II Della Rovere*, fols. 299r, 317v, and 324r–v. A microfilm copy of the manuscript can be consulted at the Pius XII Memorial Library of Saint Louis University, Knights of Columbus Vatican Film Library, Roll 1401. On the practice and the "genre" of both manuscript and printed *avvisi*, including the series prepared for the Duke of Urbino (BAV, MS Urb. Lat., 1043–1101), see Johann Petitjean, *L'Intelligence des choses: Une histoire de l'information entre Italie et Méditerranée (XVIe-XVIIe siècles)* (Rome: École française de Rome, 2013), esp. 81–125.

2. Rocke, *Forbidden Friendships*, 189.

3. Baldassari, *Bande giovanili*, esp. 14, 55, 63–65, and 121. Baldassari focuses on fifty-five trials over the period 1600–1666. Vineyards and gardens also afforded places in which prostitutes might meet their clients, see Storey, *Carnal Commerce*, 108–10.

4. The *avvisi* sent to the Fuggers on August 9 also portray the pope as intervening at this point to bring the interrogations and the trial to a close and the prisoners to swift punishment. See Vienna, Österreichische Nationalbibliothek, Cod. 8951 Han, fol. 512r/ scan 1032; cf. Marcocci, "Is This Love?," 48.

5. For a brief but helpful overview of the place of Jews in the city, see Laurie Nussdorfer, "The Politics of Space in Early Modern Rome," *Memoirs of the American Academy in Rome* 42 (1997): 161–86 (esp. 171–75).

6. For a survey of the historical situation in late medieval and early modern Spain of Jews and Muslims, as well as of converts from Judaism and Islam and their descendants (grouped together under the term "New Christians"), see James S. Amelang, *Parallel Histories: Muslims and Jews in Inquisitorial Spain* (Baton Rouge: Louisiana State University Press, 2013).

7. See *Grande Dizionario*, ed. Battaglia, sv: "Religione che non riconosce il vero Dio (in contrapposizione alla religione ebraica, poi alla cristiana).—In senso generico: paganesimo, idolatria; civiltà, arte, cultura inspirata dal paganesimo" (Religion that does not recognize the true God [in contrast to Judaism then Christianity].—In a general sense: paganism, idolatry; the civilization, arts, and culture inspired by paganism). An example is given from Tasso: "Ora il mondo è in istato che non dee temer ragionevolmente d'ammorbarsi per alcuna gentilità o idolatria" (At present the world is in such a state that no one has reason to fear corrupting himself with any paganism or idolatry).

8. Cf. the example given in *Grande Dizionario* from Carlo Borromeo: "Gustano solamente libri profani e lascivi; dilettansi delle gentilità e dei spassi che già erano del paganesimo; renovano i nomi, le memorie e i costumi delle genti che non conoscevano Dio" (They enjoy only profane and lascivious books; they take pleasure in things pagan and in the entertainments belonging formerly to paganism; they renew the names, memories, and customs of the peoples ignorant of God).

9. Benvenuto Cellini, *La Vita*, ed. Lorenzo Bellotto (Parma: Fondazione Pietro Bembo/Ugo Guanda Editore, 1996), 83–84 and 339.

10. This is the position of Marccoci, who qualifies the report as unreliable and sensationalist ("Is This Love?," 39–40).

11. Amelang, *Parallel Histories*, 80–91 (esp. 85–86).

12. Although focused on the early seventeenth century, a comprehensive introduction to the institution and workings of the Roman Inquisition, founded (or refounded) in 1542, and distinct from the Spanish and Portuguese Inquisitions, is offered by Thomas F. Mayer, *The Roman Inquisition: A Papal Bureaucracy and Its Laws in the Age of Galileo* (Philadelphia: University of Pennsylvania Press, 2013), and idem, *The Roman Inquisition on the Stage of Italy, c. 1590–1640* (Philadelphia: University of Pennsylvania Press, 2014). See also the article "Inquisizione romana," by Adriano Prosperi, in *Dizionario storico dell'Inquisizione*, ed. Adriano Prosperi, with Vincenzo Lavenia and John Tedeschi, 4 vols. (Pisa: Edizioni della Normale, 2010), 2:815–27, and Prosperi's earlier work, *L'Inquisizione romana: Letture e ricerche* (Rome: Edizioni di storia e letteratura, 2003).

13. The story of the removal of Inquisition records from Rome is a fascinating one, with most of the few that survived the process being held today by the library of Trinity College Dublin (19 ms. vols. spanning the years 1564–1660, cataloged under the call numbers TCD 1224–1242). See John Tedeschi, *La dispersione degli archivi della Inquisizione Romana* (Florence: Leo Olschki, 1973), and idem, "A 'Queer Story': The Inquisitorial Manuscripts," in *Treasures of the Library, Trinity College Dublin*, ed. Peter Fox (Dublin: Royal Irish Academy for the Library of Trinity College Dublin, 1986), 67–74. The Trinity manuscripts contain no reference to the Roman marriage case.

14. There is at least no reference that I was able to identify: Vatican City, Archivio della Congregazione per la dottrina della Fede, S. O. (Sanctum Officium), Decreta 1577–78 and S. O., Decreta 1578–79. According to Mayer, the meetings of the Congregation regularly included a secret part, during which particularly sensitive and potentially embarrassing matters, such as clerical misdemeanors, would be discussed. The *decreta* in general, moreover, reveal numerous omissions and errors. See Mayer, *The Roman Inquisition: A Papal Bureaucracy*, 20–37.

15. In his history of the papacy from the end of the Middle Ages, Ludwig Freihher von Pastor (1854–1928) describes Gregory XIII's measures against apostate Jews in Rome and the Italian peninsula. As evidence of these he refers to the second and third of the reports recorded in the *Avvisi*. Since Pastor also draws extensively on Montaigne's *Journal de voyage* but fails to make the connection between the information contained in the two sources, Giuseppe Marcocci presents the earlier historian as deliberately covering up the story of same-sex marriages. It should be noted that Pastor derived the information regarding seven "Portughesi et Marrani" from the *Avvisi*, as well as the fact that they were being questioned by the Inquisition regarding the faith; he may also have been unaware of the account of Tiepolo. On the other hand, Pastor did choose not to refer to the story from Montaigne. Moreover, he uses the *Avvisi* selectively, omitting to signal the first account of July 30—which he must surely have known—the one referring specifically to same-sex marriage. He also suppresses information regarding the crime of sodomy in the second report. See Ludwig von Pastor, *Storia dei Papi*, 9:220–21. Cf. Marcocci, "Matrimoni omosessuali," 109–10; cf. idem, "Is This Love?," 39.

16. See Luigi Firpo, "La satira politica in forma di ragguaglio di Parnaso. I—Dal 1614 al 1620," *Atti della Accademia delle scienze di Torino*, Series 2, Classe di scienze morali, storiche e filologiche 87 (1952–53), 197–247 (esp. 221–32). Cf. the information given in the online catalog of the Bibliothèque nationale de France and, in general, Petitjean, *L'Intelligence des choses*. Marcocci first discussed this work, "Matrimoni omosessuali," 125–26.

17. Giacomo Castellani, *Avviso di Parnaso nel quale si racconta la povertà e miseria dove è giunta la Republica di Venetia et il Duca di Savoia. Scritto da un curioso novellista spagnuolo. Con alcune annotationi molto importanti sopra le cose che in esso si contengono. Per Valerio Fulvio, Savoiano* ("In Antopoli: Stamperia Regia," 1619; first published 1618), 53.

18. Marcocci, "Matrimoni omosessuali," 125, and "Is This Love?," 38. On this genre of painting, see Gherardo Ortalli, *La pittura infamante nei secoli XIII–XVI* (Rome: Società Editoriale Jouvence, 1979); and Samuel Y. Edgerton Jr., *Pictures and Punishment: Art and Criminal Prosecution during the Florentine Renaissance* (Ithaca, NY: Cornell University Press, 1985). The following discussion is based on the work of these two scholars.

19. Ortalli mentions only one example in Rome, directed against Muzio Attendolo Sforza, a traitor to the pontifical army in 1412 (*La pittura infamante*, 80). The reference to John XXIII, however, is erroneous; the pope in 1412 was Gregory XII.

20. On this case, see also William J. Connell and Giles Constable, *Sacrilege and Redemption in Renaissance Florence: The Case of Antonio Rinaldeschi* (Toronto: Centre for Reformation and Renaissance Studies, 2005). Given the particular circumstances of its creation, the authors argue that the painting, attributed to Filippo di Lorenzo Dolciati,

"needs to be understood not in the tradition of *pitture infamanti* . . . but . . . as the record of a *cause célèbre* which gave rise to a popular devotion" (p. 21). Commenting on the severity of Antonio's punishment, they conclude, "The popular devotion and miracles that appeared during the ten days between Rinaldeschi's offense and his trial may to this extent have been decisive in determining his execution. To have spared him at that point would have put into question both the honour and the power of the Virgin and the legitimacy of the devotion to her image" (p. 71).

21. On the career of Juan de Zúñiga, Philip II's ambassador to the papal court from 1568 to 1579, and on diplomatic relations between the Spanish monarch and the papacy in general, see Levin, *Agents of Empire*, esp. 83–112. Cf. Dandelet, *Spanish Rome*.

22. *Archivo General de Simancas, Catalogo XIV, Secretaría de Estado, Negociación de Roma. Primera Parte, Años 1381 a 1700* (Valladolid: Imprenta Allén, 1936), 71.

23. Archivo de la Embajada de España cerca de la Santa Sede, Archivo General del Ministerio de Asuntos Exteriores y de Cooperación. The archive's contents are described in *Archivo de la Embajada de España cerca de la Santa Sede*, 4 vols., Vol. 1, *Indice Analítico de los documentos del siglo XVI* (Rome: Palacio de España, 1915).

5. Final Hours

1. Among the extensive historical literature on these confraternities, see Vincenzo Paglia, *La Morte confortata: Riti della paura e mentalità religiosa a Roma nell'età moderna* (Rome: Edizioni di Storia e Letteratura, 1982); Nicholas Terpstra, ed., *The Art of Executing Well: Rituals of Execution in Renaissance Italy* (Kirksville, MO: Truman State University Press, 2008), which offers six essays, including two on the devotional songs and paintings used by the brothers, and a translation of the Bolognese *Comforters' Manual*; Christopher Black and Pamela Gravestock, eds., *Early Modern Confraternities in Europe and the Americas: International and Interdisciplinary Perspectives* (Aldershot, UK: Ashgate, 2006), esp. the essay by Gravestock, "Comforting the Condemned and the Role of the *Laude* in Early Modern Italy," 129–50; Samuel Edgerton, *Pictures and Punishment*, esp. 126–64, "Images of Public Execution," and 165–221, "Pictures of Redemption," which discusses the Confraternity of San Giovanni and its use of painted *tavolette*. Irene Fosi offers a sociological analysis of the confraternity and its membership in relation to the Florentine community in Rome, "Pietà, devozione e politica: due confraternite fiorentine nella Roma del Rinascimento," *Archivio storico italiano* 149, no. 1 (1991): 119–61; cf. idem, *Papal Justice: Subjects and Courts in the Papal State, 1500–1750*, trans. Thomas V. Cohen (Washington, DC: Catholic University of America Press, 2011), 57–59. For a history of the particular Roman church of San Giovanni Decollato and its confraternity, see Vittorio Moschini, *S. Giovanni Decollato*, Le Chiese di Roma illustrate 26 (Rome: Danesi, [1926/1930?]). More generally, see Christopher Black, *Italian Confraternities in the Sixteenth Century* (Cambridge: Cambridge University Press, 1989), the work of Nicholas Terpstra on Bologna, and the two partially overlapping volumes edited by Stefania Pastore, Adriano Prosperi, and Nicholas Terpstra, *Brotherhood and Boundaries. Fraternità e barriere* (Pisa: Edizioni della Normale, 2011) and *Faith's Boundaries: Laity and Clergy in Early Modern Confraternities* (Turnhout: Brepols, 2012).

2. See Domenico Orano, *Liberi pensatori bruciati in Roma dal XVI al XVIII secolo* (Rome, 1904; Livorno: U. Bastogi Editore, 1971), 13 and 88–89. On the different techniques of "comforting" used, see esp. Paglia, *La Morte confortata*, 115–22.

3. Rome, Archivio di Stato, Fondo della Confraternita di S. Giovanni Decollato, *Giornale*, busta 5, vol. 10, fols. 174r–176v; *Testamenti*, busta 16, vol. 34, fols. 52r–54v. The *Testamenti* series was published by Orano, *Liberi pensatori*, 55–61, nos. 53–60. For an introduction to the confraternity archive, see Michele Di Sivo, "Il fondo della *Confraternita di S. Giovanni decollato* nell'Archivio di Stato di Roma (1497–1870). Inventario," *Rivista storica del Lazio* 12 (2000): 181–225.

4. Dandelet documents how in Rome, especially from the 1580s onward, Iberians from different regions tended to be seen and to see themselves as sharing a common Spanish identity: "Rome provided . . . a context, where the monarchs and their primary subjects generally succeeded in achieving the 'Union in Name' that was often so elusive in Iberia itself. In Rome, at least, regional 'national' identities, although they did not disappear, took second place to the larger Spanish nation" (*Spanish Rome*, 119).

5. See Stephan Karl Sander-Faes, *Urban Elites of Zadar: Dalmatia and the Venetian Commonwealth (1540–1569)* (Rome: Viella, 2013), 29 and 31; cf., in general, 15–61.

6. See Orano, *Liberi pensatori*, 73–74.

7. Allie Terry, "The Craft of Torture: Bronze Sculptures and the Punishment of Sexual Offense," in *Sex Acts in Early Modern Italy: Practice, Performance, Perversion, Punishment*, ed. Allison Levy (Farnham, UK: Ashgate, 2010), 209–23 (esp. 219; cf. p. 213).

8. After extensive alterations in the nineteenth century, this became Nostra Signora del Sacro Cuore on the Piazza Navona. On the church and its history, see Francesco Russo, *Nostra Signora del Sacro Cuore (Già S. Giacomo degli Spagnoli)*, Le Chiese di Roma illustrate 105 (Rome: Marietti, 1969).

9. See Laurie Nussdorfer, "Men at Home in Baroque Rome," in "Gender in Early Modern Rome," ed. Julia L. Hairston, *I Tatti Studies in the Italian Renaissance* 17, no. 1 (2014): 103–29 (esp. 128). The details that follow are drawn from this article and from that of Eleonora Canepari in the same volume, "Cohabitations, Household Structures, and Gender Identities in Seventeenth-Century Rome," 131–54.

10. Nussdorfer, "Men at Home," 110–11; cf. Canepari, "Cohabitations," 136.

11. Such households might be close to 95 percent male; see Nussdorfer, "Men at Home," 125.

12. See Baldassari, *Bande giovanili*, 13–16, 83–88, and 121–22. In the sample of cases analyzed by Baldassari, 40 percent of those investigated were not native Romans.

13. The principal coins in use in the papal city and their relative values were as follows: 1 scudo = 10 giuli = 100 baiocchi = 500 quattrini. In *Liberi pensatori*, Orano's transcription gives the much more valuable *scudi* here, rather than *baiocchi*. The word, crossed out in the *Testamenti* manuscript and supplied by the editor, is, however, clearly legible in the *Giornale*.

14. As will be seen later, Rogles is a deformation of the name Robles.

15. Beds and bedding were items frequently bequeathed in wills. See Canepari, "Cohabitations," 137.

16. This is according to the text of the *Testamenti*, which refers to one chest. The *Giornale*, which speaks of three chests, states twenty chickens, seventy cockerels, and six

pairs of doves. Coincidentally, as a common noun in Portuguese, *pinto* designates a baby chicken as well as, euphemistically, a penis.

17. The text of the *Giornale* includes "un giubbone di tela" (a cloth jacket) that the redactor of the *Testamenti* transforms into a more mysterious "celone da tavola."

18. Michel Foucault, "Lives of Infamous Men," in *The Essential Foucault: Selections from The Essential Works of Foucault, 1954–1984,* ed. Paul Rabinow and Nikolas Rose (New York: New Press, 2003), 279–93 (esp. 280–81). For a luminous discussion, see Love, *Feeling Backward,* 47–52. See also Dinshaw, *Getting Medieval,* 46–47, on Barthes and Michelet.

19. Foucault, "Infamous Men," 282–83.

20. On the concept of the reality effect, see Roland Barthes, "L'effet de réel," *Communications* 11 (1968): 84–89.

6. Voices on Trial

1. Rome, Archivio di Stato, Tribunale Criminale del Governatore, *Processi,* busta 168, n. 2; cf. Marcocci, "Matrimoni omosessuali." In quoting from the trial proceedings, I add only occasional apostrophes and add or remove some accents, for example to distinguish between *è* and *e.*

2. Vienna, Österreichische Nationalbibliothek, Cod. 8951 Han, fol. 516v/scan 1041. See Marcocci, "Matrimoni omosessuali," 110–12, and "Is This Love?," 39.

3. The *avvisi* sent to the Fuggers on August 2 and 23 also confirm these two figures.

4. On the Roman judicial system and its multiple courts, see Fosi, *Papal Justice*; on the prosecution of sodomy, see esp. 52–53 and 149–54, and, on polygamy, 142–46. The cases examined by Baldassari were also tried by the *tribunale del Governatore.* According to Baldassari, this court's jurisdiction became increasingly extensive. It applied the inquisitorial practices of secrecy, presumption of guilt, and the transcription of proceedings by a notary, as well as the *processus informativus*: the interrogation and confrontation of witnesses, depositions by police and surgeons, and the possible use of torture. See Baldassari, *Bande giovanili,* 15–17; cf. 118–21 and 129–38. See also Thomas V. Cohen and Elizabeth S. Cohen, *Words and Deeds in Renaissance Rome: Trials Before the Papal Magistrates* (Toronto: University of Toronto Press, 1993).

5. Marcocci, "Matrimoni omosessuali," 126–29.

6. "The accused's hands were tied behind the back, attached to a rope which was thrown over a beam in the ceiling, and hauled into the air, there to hang for a period of time, then let down, then raised again. Sometimes weights were attached to the feet of the accused, therefore increasing the strain on the arm and back muscles once the process was begun," Edward Peters, *Torture,* rev. ed. (Philadelphia: University of Pennsylvania Press, 1996; first pub. 1985), 68. Cf. Baldassari, *Bande giovanili,* 138–40.

7. See Canepari, "Cohabitations," 142–48.

8. See Storey, *Carnal Commerce,* 95. Saint Augustine's was just to the south of the *luoghi,* the area allocated to prostitutes in the early 1590s (p. 80).

9. On the status of certain religious institutions, noble and episcopal houses, and ambassadors' residences beyond the reach of the police, see Fosi, *Papal Justice,* 73.

10. This is the view of Marcocci, who describes them as forming "una coppia stabile" (a stable couple); the corresponding supposition that the sexual relations Robles is said to have had with Alfaro and other members of the group were *earlier* ("prima") seems to me unfounded, especially since Robles has known Battista the longest ("Matrimoni omosessuali," 115–16; cf. "Is This Love?," 45).

7. Saint John at the Latin Gate

1. On the history of the church, see G. Matthiae, A. Missori, et al., *S. Giovanni a Porta Latina e L'Oratorio di S. Giovanni in Oleo*, Le Chiese di Roma illustrate 51 (Rome: Marietti, [1960?]); and Giovanni Mario Crescimbeni, *L'Istoria della Chiesa di S. Giovanni avanti Porta Latina* (Rome: Antonio de' Rossi, 1716).

2. "Dura e difficile è sempre stata la vita delle Congregazioni religiose, che si sono alternate a S. Giovanni di Porta Latina. Il pieno isolamento della chiesa, sperduta nell'aperta campagna, su una strada poco frequentata e completamente interrotta quando la Porta veniva chiusa, e la [*sic*] molte ristrettezze derivate dal fatto che il Capitolo lateranense beneficiava per intero dei suoi beni, hanno causato più volte il suo completo abbandono" (For the religious congregations that succeeded one another at Saint John at the Latin Gate, life was always hard and difficult. The complete isolation of the church, lost in the open countryside on a quiet road, that would be completely blocked whenever the Gate was closed, and the many shortages due to the fact that the Lateran Chapter received the entirety of the revenues from its possessions, caused, on more than one occasion, its complete abandonment), Matthiae, Missori, et al., *S. Giovanni*, 22–23.

3. Interestingly in this regard, Storey notes that courtesans sometimes disguised themselves as nuns (*Carnal Commerce*, 105).

4. Cf. Alfaro's earlier statement: "Quanto a Pinto . . . lui teneva quel loco per bugiarare."

5. Later Alfaro will also affirm, "Et è similmente vero che Hieronimo se faceva bugiarare da Pinto per quanto ho inteso dire dalli altri compagni nostri" (And it's also true that Geronimo used to get buggered by Pinto, as far as I've heard said by the rest of our companions).

6. Later we will encounter a similar situation described by the cleric Battista Caviedis.

7. The underlining of the Frenchman's name in the transcript and the fact that it is written out in the adjacent margin suggest that the court has taken note of it, no doubt with a view to a possible future arrest. The same procedure will be observed later in relation to one Cristopharo Ribera.

8. Bandello, *Le novelle*, ed. Maestri, Part I, nov. 6, 1:66–72 (p. 71). For a discussion of the story, see Ferguson, *Queer (Re)Readings*, 82–88.

9. See Roni Weinstein, *Juvenile Sexuality, Kabbalah, and Catholic Reformation in Italy: Tiferet Bahurim by Pinhas Barukh ben Pelatiyah Monselice* (Leiden: Brill, 2009), 280. The treatise introduced and edited is a late seventeenth-century guide to sex and marriage by a Ferrarese sage addressed to young Italian Jewish men.

10. See Ferguson, *Queer (Re)Readings*, 80–82, and, more generally on the deployment of the concepts of taste and nature, 37–49; cf. Gary Ferguson, "Avant-goûts:

(Homo)sexualités comparées au seuil de la modernité," in *Littérature et identités sexuelles*, ed. Anne Tomiche and Pierre Zoberman, Collection *Poétiques Comparatistes* (Paris: Société Française de Littérature Générale et Comparée, 2007), 105–22.

11. Giorgio Masi, "'Gente scapigliatissima e bizzarra,'" in *Extravagances amoureuses*, 341–414 (esp. 373); cf. 390.

12. See Peter Cole, trans. and ed., *The Dream of the Poem: Hebrew Poetry from Muslim and Christian Spain, 950–1492* (Princeton, NJ: Princeton University Press, 2007). The discussions of poems of desire and the image of the gazelle offer a brief presentation and references to some of the relevant homoerotic pieces (pp. 530–34).

13. For Michel Foucault's development of the concept of heterotopia, see principally "Of Other Spaces," *Diacritics* 16, no. 1 (1986): 22–27. For its application in a historical context, see Kevin Hetherington, *The Badlands of Modernity: Heterotopia and Social Ordering* (London: Routledge, 1997), 8–9, 12–13, and elsewhere.

8. Marriage as Alibi, as Euphemism, as Recruitment

1. While admitting that it is not possible to know if Valez wanted to marry Ribera, Marcocci nevertheless presents him as renouncing his vow of chastity as a consequence of their meeting ("Matrimoni omosessuali," 120).

2. The scenario put forward by Marcocci, different again, supposes that Ribera's departure was painful for Valez and imagines that he spoke "bitterly" in court of the two people he did not know. No description of Valez's attitude figures in the transcript, however. Moreover, Valez's account of his separation from Ribera seems wholly consistent with his general strategy of minimizing the importance of the relationship. As earlier (cf. the previous note), Marcocci also assumes a relation of cause and effect, not evident in the documents, by supposing that Valez's repenting of and confessing his sin came *after* and represented a frustrated *reaction to* Ribera's departure ("Matrimoni omosessuali," 120). This is not specified; in fact, as we have seen, this hypothesis contradicts the temporal sequence presumed by the judge, on the basis of information received from other prisoners, for whom Valez's repentance *precedes and causes* his own voluntary decision to separate from his friend.

3. The Seven Churches were (and are) Rome's principal pilgrimage churches. Saint John at the Latin Gate is not one of them, but it does lie between Saint Sebastian's on the Via Appia (removed from the official list in 2000) and Saint John Lateran.

4. Giustiniani's mission is discussed by Ludwig von Pastor, *Storia dei Papi dalla fine del Medio Evo*, vol. 8, *Pio V (1566–1572)*, trans. Angelo Mercati (Rome: Desclée & Ci, 1951), 306–8.

5. See Dandelet, *Spanish Rome*, 135–36.

6. In his own interrogation, Pinto will reveal that he has heard that "Patre Batista era bugiarone" (Father Battista was a bugger). If this expression might suggest that he took a penetrative sexual role, Caviedis always speaks of Pinto as trying to bugger him.

7. On the long history of the Christian vilification of Jews as dogs, an insult involving a reading of Matthew 15:26 and (Jewish) dogs consuming (Christian, Eucharistic) bread, extended in the twelfth and thirteenth centuries to accusations of the murder of

(martyred, Eucharistic) Christian children, see Kenneth Stow, *Jewish Dogs: An Image and Its Interpreters. Continuity in the Catholic–Jewish Encounter* (Stanford, CA: Stanford University Press, 2006). The accusation was also associated at times with the idea of sexual promiscuity.

8. The term *commare*—or in its more usual spelling *comare*, plural *comari*—had several standard meanings in the sixteenth century, but denoted properly a godmother. By extension, it also designated a close female friend or neighbor and, pejoratively, a gossip. Suggestively, the same nexus of meanings is found in other languages: in the French *commère*, for example, but also in English since *gossip* derives from the Old English *godsibb*, godparent. In a number of contexts, gossip is also associated with sexual deviance and especially with male homosexuality. See Nicholas Hammond, *Gossip, Sexuality and Scandal in France (1610–1715)* (Oxford: Peter Lang, 2011); cf. idem, "Bavards et bardaches: Relectures du XVIIᵉ siècle," in *Queer: Écritures de la différence?*, ed. Pierre Zoberman, 2 vols. (Paris: L'Harmattan, 2008), 1:133–41, and idem, "Bavardages et masculinités," in "L'Homme en tous genres: Masculinités, textes et contextes," ed. Gary Ferguson, *Itinéraires. Littérature, textes, cultures* (2008/2009): 91–105. In Italian, *comare* also designated a midwife and in this context might again carry sexual overtones, as in Pietro Aretino's *Ragionamenti*, where the *comare* is a procuress; see Giannetti, *Lelia's Kiss*, 90–91. The sense attributed to the term by the San Giovanni group is not signaled in any of the dictionaries, glossaries, or sources I have consulted, including the *Grande Dizionario*, ed. Battaglia; Boggione and Casalegno, *Dizionario storico del lessico erotico italiano*; or, by the same editors, *Dizionario letterario del lessico amoroso: Metafore, eufemismi, trivialismi* (Turin: Unione Tipografico-Editrice Torinese, 2000).

9. This is Marcocci's argument, "Matrimoni omosessuali," 123–24; cf. 129.

10. Marcocci takes these words as a "raccomandazione di convolare a nozze con un uomo rispettabile e altolocato" (a recommendation to tie the knot with a respectable and high-placed man), ibid., 124.

11. See Boggione and Casalegno, *Dizionario storico del lessico erotico italiano*, sv. In the *Bibbia volgare*, for example, Exodus 22:19 is rendered as "Chi si impaccerà con le bestie inonestamente di morte morra" (Whoever lies with [Vulgate: *coeo cum*] an animal shall be put to death) (New Revised Standard Version). Further examples are given from Piccolomini and Campanella, among others.

12. Ruggiero notes references in the *Diaries* of Marino Sanuto to "scuole sodomiti," which he suggests may reflect the association of sodomy with schools of music, gymnastics, abacus, and fencing in Venice (*Boundaries of Eros*, 138 and 195, note 125). N. S. Davidson describes a case in the same city of sodomy involving female prostitutes, the brothel where they worked being qualified as "a school of sodomy for men with women," "Sodomy in Early Modern Venice," in *Sodomy in Early Modern Europe*, ed. Tom Betteridge (Manchester: Manchester University Press, 2002), 65–81 (esp. 68–69). More generally, the expression inevitably carries connotations of ancient pedagogical pederasty and its Renaissance equivalents, as portrayed, for example, in Antonio Rocco's *L'Alcibiade fanciullo a scola* (written c. 1631). The same word also designated a Jewish synagogue. Rocke notes in Florence an occurrence of the term *sect*, a word in that city carrying political connotations (*Forbidden Friendships*, 189), that also recalls Montaigne's expression "belle secte."

13. See Ermanno Orlando, "Il matrimonio delle beffe: Unioni finte, simulate, per gioco. Padova e Venezia, fine secolo XIV–inizi secolo XVI," in *Trasgressioni: Seduzione, concubinato, adulterio, bigamia (XIV–XVIII secolo)*, ed. Silvana Seidel Menchi and Diego Quaglioni (Bologna: Il Mulino, 2004), 231–67.

14. Marcocci, "Matrimoni omosessuali," 123 and 129.

15. From everything we know of Pinto's sex life, we would expect him to be the "husband" in any relationship, not the "wife." A "wifely" role may also have been resisted by Lopez; in any event, it contrasts with the active role Robles proposed for him in relation to Caviedis.

16. Marcocci, "Matrimoni omosessuali," 124.

17. In this respect, Marcocci may have been influenced by the Italian translation of the *Journal* that he cites. This renders "certains Portugais . . . *estoient entrés en* une estrange confrerie" as "certi portoghesi *avevano fondato* . . . una strana confraternita" (ibid., 107, my italics).

18. Marcocci seems to me to understate greatly the sexual elements present in these accounts, claiming, for instance, that only one source, the Urbino *avvisi*, expresses this link between marriage and consummation ("Is This Love?," 43). For the reasons presented earlier, this is also strongly suggested by Tiepolo. As for Montaigne, while Marcocci concedes that the link is also found in the *Journal de voyage*, he states that the writer nevertheless affirms the strength of the bond in that the men "went to bed and lived together." As I have shown, this interpretation is based on a misunderstanding of the meaning of the verb *habiter* in this context. Finally, and again as has been noted previously, the first newsletter sent to the Fuggers describes young boys being sodomized in a way that resonates with what is stated in the Urbino *avvisi*.

9. Marriage and Community

1. Both the accounts of Tiepolo and Montaigne suggest that more than one celebration was held. The Fugger *avvisi* refer to similar practices in various places over a period of twelve years: "Et hanno confessato haver esercitato una tanta scelleragine per 12 anni continui in parecchi luoghi d'Italia, et lasciati lì complici" (And they have confessed to having practiced such a great wickedness over a period of twelve years in several places in Italy, where they have left accomplices) (August 2), Vienna, Österreichische Nationalbibliothek, Cod. 8951 Han, fol. 508r/scan 1024. According to the 1612 *Vocabolario degli accademici della Crusca, parecchi* signifies a "numero indeterminato, ma di piccola quantità" (indeterminate number, but of small quantity), http://www.lessicografia .it/Controller?lemma=PARECCHI_e_PARECCHIE_ed1&rewrite=1.

2. See Allen J. Grieco, "From Roosters to Cocks: Italian Renaissance Fowl and Sexuality," in *Erotic Cultures of Renaissance Italy*, ed. Sara F. Matthews-Grieco (Farnham, UK: Ashgate, 2010), 89–140 (esp. 116). On metaphorical and euphemistic expressions designating sexual acts and organs in general, see Paul Larivaille, "Entre hédonisme et hermétisme: Notes sur l'équivoque érotique dans la littérature italienne de la Renaissance," in *Figures et langages de la marginalité aux XVIᵉ et XVIIᵉ siècles*, ed. Maria Teresa Ricci (Paris: Champion, 2013), 21–41; Allison Levy, ed., *Sex Acts in Early Modern Italy:*

Practice, Performance, Perversion, Punishment (Farnham, UK: Ashgate, 2010), especially the essays by Paolo Fasoli, Will Fisher, and Sergius Kodera; and Claudio Fraccari, "Per amor di metafora" and, by the same author also in *El più soave et dolce et dilectevole et gratioso bochone*, the two glossaries, pp. 327–54.

3. *Journal de voyage*, ed. Rigolot, 6.

4. Benvenuto Cellini, *La Vita*, book 1, chap. 30.

5. Rocke similarly notes the promiscuity of the adolescents arrested for sodomy in Florence (*Forbidden Friendships*, 164–65).

6. On marriages and other forms of relationship entered into by medieval and early modern clerics, see Karras, *Unmarriages*, chap. 3, 125–64.

7. Summary descriptions of cases are given in Dublin, Trinity College, Rare Book and Manuscript Library, Josiah Gilbart Smyly, *TCD MSS 1225–1228. A Calendar of Part of the Roman Inquisition Papers*, unpublished typescript, MS 1225, p. 26, and MS 1228, p. 28. Cf. MS 1228, pp. 14 and 18–19.

8. Ibid., MS 1225, pp. 33–34.

9. Marcocci, "Matrimoni omosessuali," 121 and 130.

10. See Rocke, *Forbidden Friendships*, 165–68; cf. 25, 37–38, 108, 183–84, and idem, "Sodomites," 13–15. Baldassari notes that youths would sometimes initiate encounters with adults in exchange for small sums of money or gifts, *Bande giovanili*, 13–14. There were also youths who essentially worked as prostitutes.

11. As will be seen later, however, in a different case involving the mimicking of religious ceremonies, white shirts were used to stand in for a priest's surplice.

12. "Gli uomini che si sposarono nella chiesa di San Giovanni erano consapevoli di commettere un atto sacrilego" (The men who married each other in the church of San Giovanni were conscious of committing an act of sacrilege) (Marcocci, "Matrimoni omosessuali," 124); cf. "il nodo più turpe del caso in cui era [Pinto] implicato: l'abuso del sacramento" (the most shameful crux of the case in which Pinto was involved: the abuse of a sacrament) (ibid., 123).

13. It might be noted that there were at the time in Rome, especially in Trastevere, taverns that harbored groups involved in both criminal activities and illicit sexual behavior. See Baldassari, *Bande giovanili*, 14, 54–56, and 72–79.

14. On the presence of courtesans in churches, see Storey, *Carnal Commerce*, 95–96.

15. See Romeo, *Amori proibiti*, and Scaramella, "Sodomia."

16. Despite this consideration, Marcocci's most recent argument is that the men were indeed seeking to legitimize their "forbidden love" ("Is This Love?," 46–47). For reasons discussed earlier, even if a form of shared love may well have characterized some of the men's evolving relationships at different points in time, the evidence concerning the "couples" Robles and Battista and Valez and Ribera does not seem to me straightforward. As far as we know, moreover, neither of these pairs was involved in a wedding ceremony. The hypothesis of a wedding between Pinto and Lopez is unsubstantiated.

17. John Jeffries Martin, *Myths of Renaissance Individualism* (Basingstoke, UK: Palgrave Macmillan, 2004). For the particular case discussed subsequently, see chap. 4, pp. 62–82.

18. Ibid., 63–64.

19. See, for example, ibid., 70–75.

20. Ibid., 80. We shall see later that *compagnonnage* organizations for journeymen in eighteenth-century France were characterized by similar practices, serving similar purposes.

21. Ruggiero, *Machiavelli in Love*, 21.

10. Looking Forward / Looking Back

1. The earliest of the cases examined here dates from 1706, the latest from 1748.

2. On London, see Bray, *Homosexuality in Renaissance England*; idem, "Homosexuality and the Signs of Male Friendship in Elizabethan England," in *Queering the Renaissance*, ed. Jonathan Goldberg (Durham, NC: Duke University Press, 1994), 40–61; Rictor Norton, *Mother Clap's Molly House: The Gay Subculture in England 1700–1830* (London: GMP Publishers, 1992); Randolph Trumbach, "The Birth of the Queen: Sodomy and the Emergence of Gender Equality in Modern Culture, 1660–1750," in *Hidden from History: Reclaiming the Gay and Lesbian Past*, ed. Martin Duberman, Martha Vicinus, and George Chauncey Jr. (New York: Penguin, 1989), 129–40; idem, "The Heterosexual Male in Eighteenth-Century London and His Queer Interactions," in *Love, Sex, Intimacy, and Friendship Between Men, 1550–1800*, ed. Katherine O'Donnell and Michael O'Rourke (Basingstoke, UK: Palgrave Macmillan, 2003), 99–127; idem, "London's Sodomites: Homosexual Behavior and Western Culture in the Eighteenth Century," *Journal of Social History* 11 (1977–78): 1–33; idem, *Sex and the Gender Revolution*, vol. 1, *Heterosexuality and the Third Gender in Enlightenment London* (Chicago: University of Chicago Press, 1998); idem, "Sodomitical Subcultures, Sodomitical Roles, and the Gender Revolution of the Eighteenth Century: The Recent Historiography," in *'Tis Nature's Fault: Unauthorized Sexuality During the Enlightenment*, ed. Robert Purks Maccubbin (Cambridge: Cambridge University Press, 1987), 109–21. On Paris, see Jeffrey Merrick and Bryant T. Ragan Jr., eds. and trans., *Homosexuality in Early Modern France: A Documentary Collection* (Oxford: Oxford University Press, 2001); Claude Courouve, *Les Assemblées de la Manchette, Paris—1720–1750* (Paris: C. Courouve, 2000), earlier versions published with some variations in content and title (1994, 1987, and 1978); Jeffrey Merrick, "Sodomitical Inclinations in Early Eighteenth-Century Paris," *Eighteenth-Century Studies* 30, no. 3 (1997): 289–95; idem, "Sodomitical Scandals and Subcultures in the 1720s," *Men and Masculinities* 1 (1999): 365–84; idem, "Sodomites and Police in Paris, 1715," *Journal of the History of Homosexuality* 42, no. 3 (2002): 103–28; idem, "'Nocturnal Birds' in the Champs-Elysées: Police and Pederasty in Prerevolutionary Paris," *GLQ: A Journal of Lesbian and Gay Studies* 8, no. 3 (2002): 425–32; idem, "Chaussons in the Streets: Sodomy in Seventeenth-Century Paris," *Journal of the History of Sexuality* 15, no. 2 (2006): 167–203; Michel Rey, "Les Sodomites Parisiens au XVIIIème Siècle" (MA thesis, Université Paris VIII–Vincennes, 1979–80); idem, "Parisian Homosexuals Create a Lifestyle, 1700–1750: The Police Archives," trans. Robert A. Day and Robert Welch, in *'Tis Nature's Fault: Unauthorized Sexuality During the Enlightenment*, ed. Robert Purks Maccubbin (Cambridge: Cambridge University Press, 1987), 179–91; idem, "Police and Sodomy in Eighteenth-Century Paris: From Sin to Disorder," in *The Pursuit of Sodomy: Male Homosexuality in Renaissance and Enlight-*

enment Europe, ed. Kent Gerard and Gert Hekma (New York: Harrington Park/ Haworth Press, 1989), 129–46, published simultaneously as the *Journal of Homosexuality* 16, nos. 1–2 (1988); Michael Sibalis, "Homosexuality in Early Modern France," in *Queer Masculinities, 1500–1800: Siting Same-Sex Desire in the Early Modern World*, ed. Katherine O'Donnell and Michael O'Rourke (Basingstoke, UK: Palgrave Macmillan, 2006), 211–31; idem, "Paris," in *Queer Sites: Gay Urban Histories Since 1600*, ed. David Higgs (London: Routledge, 1999), 10–37. For an overview, discussion, and bibliography, see Ferguson, *Queer (Re)Readings*, 1–37.

3. Cf. Rey, "Les Sodomites Parisiens," 70–71.

4. See Merrick, "Sodomitical Scandals," 381.

5. Paris, Bibliothèque de l'Arsenal, Archives de la Bastille, MS 10.257, "Baron," fol. 4. Rey, "Les Sodomites Parisiens," 65, gives some details concerning Baron.

6. Archives de la Bastille, MS 10.259, "Pinson."

7. Ibid., "Rousseau."

8. Ibid., "Harault."

9. Archives de la Bastille, MS 10.566. The case summary and two of the three interrogations (the second of Langlois and that of Bertault) are translated, though with occasional inaccuracies, some of which are signaled later, in *Homosexuality in Early Modern France*, ed. and trans. Merrick and Ragan, 52–59. Here said to be aged twenty-nine and a half, Langlois is elsewhere identified as being twenty-four; see Courouve, *Les Assemblées* (1994), 13; cf. *Homosexuality in Early Modern France*, 47.

10. This is obscured in the Merrick and Ragan translation since, in the second interrogation of Langlois, they render the first five occurrences of *societé* as *order*.

11. Bertault also refers to a gathering during *jours gras* at which they wore costumes and violinists provided music. Cf. Merrick and Ragan, *Homosexuality in Early Modern France*, 58.

12. The translation of Merrick and Ragan here is inaccurate and serves to increase the impression of a mysterious ceremony: "approached him and offered their hands to the candle he was holding" (*Homosexuality in Early Modern France*, 53).

13. Cf. ibid., 55 and 57.

14. "Et en effet le repondant s'en estant luy mesme informé dudit Lebel depuis sa sortie de St Lazare, ledit Lebel luy a confirmé que c'estoit pour ce sujet [sodomie] qu'il avoit esté arresté" (And in fact, the suspect himself having asked the said Lebel about it after his release from Saint-Lazare, the said Lebel confirmed to him that it was for this reason [sodomy] that he had been arrested). Merrick and Ragan read "n'en estant . . . informé," which gives a contradictory sense (*Homosexuality in Early Modern France*, 54). In 1703, at age twenty-five, Lebel had been detained in the Bastille and Saint-Lazare. He was said to have been debauched from his childhood, prostituting himself and others. His protestations of having been converted were not wholly convincing to the authorities. See ibid., 45. Later Langlois will admit to having heard that Lebel prostitutes youths to his master.

15. D'Argenson later asks Bertault about this ceremony, but the latter reveals no information. He denies having undergone anything similar or seen anyone else do so.

16. On the subject of *compagnonnage*, see Cynthia Maria Truant, *The Rites of Labor: Brotherhoods of Compagnonnage in Old and New Regime France* (Ithaca, NY: Cornell

University Press, 1994). The following discussion draws principally on this study. In relation to similar forms of sociability among itinerant pedlars, see *La Vie généreuse des Mercelots, Gueuz, et Boesmiens, contenans leur façon de vivre, subtilitez et gergon mis en lumière par Pechon de Ruby*, ed. Denis Delaplace (Paris: Honoré Champion, 2007). On the Company of the Griffarins, founded in opposition to the official Confraternity of Printers by nonitinerant journeymen printers in sixteenth-century Lyon, see Natalie Zemon Davis, "Strikes and Salvation at Lyon," in *Society and Culture in Early Modern France* (Stanford, CA: Stanford University Press, 1975), 1–16.

17. Typically aged between eighteen and thirty, these men had served their apprenticeship in a trade but not yet become masters. Some of them, however, would never accede to the higher status and would remain journeymen all their life. We recall that the three men interrogated by the Inquisition in Venice in 1582, discussed in the previous chapter, were also immigrant journeymen. The group at the Latin Gate was also made up, for the most part, of poor immigrants.

18. See Truant, *Rites of Labor*, and Davis, "Strikes and Salvation," esp. 14–15.

19. For example, the *Compagnons de la croûte* founded by Jacques-Louis Ménétra, who had been the head of a real *compagnonnage* group. See Truant, *Rites of Labor*, 151–52.

20. This is again mistranslated by Merrick and Ragan who substitute a plural for a singular ("il feroit") and have Bertault telling Langlois that "*they* would be husband and wife together" (*Homosexuality in Early Modern France*, 58, my italics), a rendering at odds with the context.

21. On marriages, marrying rooms, and chapels in the London molly houses, see Bray, *Homosexuality*, 81, 86, and 88, and especially Norton, *Mother Clap's Molly House*, 55–56, 61–62, and 100–102; cf. 188–89, 204–5, and 236–43. In many cases, marrying was a euphemism for having sex. On occasion, however, it seems to have referred to a more lasting bond. Actual wedding ceremonies performed by the Reverend John Church in Vere Street in the early nineteenth century included sexual consummation, but may well have been intended to form recognized unions. According to Norton, molly marriages involved two husbands, the term *wife* not being used to identify one of the partners as sexually passive. If this was indeed the case, it would constitute a significant difference from the Parisian evidence examined here.

22. On universalizing and minoritizing paradigms of same-sex desire, as defined by Eve Sedgwick, see chapter 3, note 15.

23. See Introduction note 7 in this volume.

24. Another interesting text from this point of view, offering representations of multiple forms of sexual pleasure, is Antonio Vignali's *La Cazzaria* (1525), ed. Pasquale Stoppelli, intro. Nino Borsellino (Rome: Edizioni dell'Elefante, 1984/1990); English translation by Ian Frederick Moulton, *La Cazzaria: The Book of the Prick* (London: Routledge, 2003).

25. See, for example, Rocke, *Forbidden Friendships*, 24–25 and 172; Ruggiero, *Boundaries of Eros*, 115–16; and Davidson, "Sodomy," 70–71.

26. Rocke, *Forbidden Friendships*, 88; cf. 79, 97–99, and 102–5. Rocke identified only one conviction of an older man who enjoyed passive anal sex.

27. For examples of exceptions to common patterns, see Ruggiero, *Boundaries of Eros*, 115–16 and 122–24, and Davidson, "Sodomy," 70–71.

28. Vienna, Österreichische Nationalbibliothek, Cod. 8951 Han, fol. 522v/scan 1053. See also chapter 12, esp. note 11.

29. See notably the work of Randolph Trumbach cited in note 2 of this chapter. Marcocci argues that the San Giovanni group calls for a reconsideration of the historiography of homosexuality on the basis of what he terms "the birth of homosexual love" ("Is This Love?," 47–49).

30. See Michel Foucault, *Histoire de la sexualité*, vol. 1, *La volonté de savoir* (Paris: Gallimard, 1976), esp. 59 and 90–91; and, generally, vol. 2, *L'Usage des plaisirs* (Paris: Gallimard, 1984), and vol. 3, *Le Souci de soi* (Paris: Gallimard, 1984). The same position was subsequently advocated most forcefully by David Halperin, whose work was criticized by Eve Sedgwick. See, notably, David M. Halperin, *One Hundred Years of Homosexuality and Other Essays on Greek Love* (New York: Routledge, 1990); Sedgwick, *Epistemology of the Closet*; David M. Halperin, *How to Do the History of Homosexuality* (Chicago: University of Chicago Press, 2002). Cf. John Boswell, "Revolutions, Universals, and Sexual Categories," in *Hidden from History: Reclaiming the Gay and Lesbian Past*, ed. Martin Duberman, Martha Vicinus, and George Chauncey Jr. (New York: Penguin, 1989), 17–36. For a detailed discussion, see Ferguson, *Queer (Re)Readings*, introduction and chap. 1.

31. On earlier discussions by historians and the evidence regarding the existence of subcultures or at least of networks in medieval and Renaissance Europe, see Ferguson, *Queer (Re)Readings*, 21–37. Cf. Ruggiero, *Boundaries of Eros*, 137–39.

32. Cf. Ferguson, *Queer (Re)Readings*, 49.

33. Here and later, cf. Sedgwick, *Epistemology of the Closet*, 44–48.

11. Ghost Stories

1. Hartman, *Lose Your Mother*, 115.

2. Freccero, *Queer/Early/Modern*, chap. 5, "Queer Spectrality," 70 and 78.

3. As Christopher Black writes, "Their roles in escorting the condemned to execution had as much to do with the living as with comforting the victim. A processional involvement, with the blessings of priests, has been interpreted as a ritual through which the living, seeing justice done, were protected against the revenge of the condemned from the next world" (*Italian Confraternities*, 217). Black refers to ideas put forward by Adriano Prosperi, "Il sangue e l'anima: Ricerche sulle Compagnie di Giustizia in Italia," *Quaderni storici* 51 (1982): 959–99 (esp. 961–64).

4. Michael Warner, *The Trouble with Normal: Sex, Politics, and the Ethics of Queer Life* (New York: Free Press, 1999), 117ff. The discussion of marriage is found, in general, on pp. 81–147.

5. George Chauncey, *Why Marriage? The History Shaping Today's Debate over Gay Equality* (New York: Basic Books, 2004).

6. See the opening pages of Dipesh Chakrabarty, *Provincializing Europe: Postcolonial Thought and Historical Difference* (Princeton, NJ: Princeton University Press, 2000).

7. Warner, *The Trouble with Normal*, 117ff. A similar concern drives James M. Bromley's reading of early modern English texts that, in the face of marriage's ever-growing valorization in terms of intimacy and futurity, "imagine, however briefly, alternatives to long-term monogamy grounded in interiorized desire," *Intimacy and Sexuality in the Age of Shakespeare* (Cambridge: Cambridge University Press, 2012), 27.

8. Judith Halberstam, *In a Queer Time and Place: Transgender Bodies, Subcultural Lives* (New York: New York University Press, 2005).

9. Cf. Beatriz Pastor, "Silence and Writing," discussed earlier in the Introduction of this volume.

10. Fondo di San Giovanni Decollato, busta 16, 34, fol. 54v. Cf. Orano, *Liberi pensatori*, but where the final word is mistakenly omitted. The resistance implied in this gesture finds confirmation in another occurrence of the same expression in the entry devoted to the heretical Greek Archbishop Macario of Macedonia, who refused to repent: "mai si volse confessare ne lassar memoria alcuna" (he refused to make his confession or leave any memory), Orano, *Liberi pensatori*, 13.

11. The final report on events sent to the Fugger family on August 23 states that other individuals have been apprehended, in addition to the seven boys referred to in the previous chapter. These include some who are being transferred from Naples and Milan, a hermit, and "il licentiado Boccadiglio." See Vienna, Österreichische Nationalbibliothek, Cod. 8951 Han, fol. 522v/scan 1053. Cf. Marcocci, "Is This Love?," 47–48. As Marcocci notes, Boccadiglio represents an Italianized spelling of the Spanish Bocadillo, probably a nickname with sexual connotations. On the other hand, I read *licentiado* as signifying not *licenzioso* (licentious) but rather *licenziato* (cf. the Spanish *licenciado*), attested in the sixteenth century and meaning "Che ha ottenuto il titolo accademico della licenziatura" (One who has obtained the academic degree of *licenziatura*). See *Grande Dizionario*, ed. Battaglia, sv. The degree in question was awarded after the bachelor's but before the doctorate and qualified the recipient to teach or practice a particular professional subject, such as law. Further archival research might reveal additional evidence concerning the arrests of these and other "accomplices."

12. I draw on the title of the pioneering collection of essays, *Hidden from History: Reclaiming the Gay and Lesbian Past*, ed. Martin Duberman, Martha Vicinus, and George Chauncey Jr. (New York: Penguin, 1989).

13. See Goldberg, "The History that Will Be."

14. Édouard Glissant, *Poétique de la relation. Poétique III* (Paris: Gallimard, 1990), 23–34; Gilles Deleuze and Félix Guattari, *Mille plateaux*, vol. 2, *Capitalisme et schizophrénie* (Paris: Éditions de Minuit, 1980), trans. Brian Massumi, *A Thousand Plateaus: Capitalism and Schizophrenia* (Minneapolis: University of Minnesota Press, 1987), introduction.

BIBLIOGRAPHY

Manuscript and Unpublished Sources

Dublin. Trinity College, Rare Book and Manuscript Library
MSS TCD 1224–1242. *Roman Inquisition Papers* (1564–1660).
Josiah Gilbart Smyly. *TCD MSS 1225–1228. A Calendar of Part of the Roman Inquisi-tion Papers.* Unpublished typescript.
Madrid. Archivo Histórico Nacional
Ministerio de Asuntos Exteriores y de Cooperación. Embajada de España cerca de la Santa Sede, legajos 4–6.
Naples. Archivio Storico Diocesano di Napoli
Sant'Ufficio, 856, c. 52.
Paris. Bibliothèque de l'Arsenal
Archives de la Bastille. MSS 10.257, 10.259, 10.566.
Rome. Archivio di Stato
Fondo della Confraternita di S. Giovanni Decollato. *Giornale*, busta 5, vol. 10; *Testamenti*, busta 16, vol. 34.
Tribunale Criminale del Governatore. *Processi*, busta 168, n. 2.
Simancas. Archivo General de Simancas
Estado. Roma, legajo 933.

Vatican City. Archivio della Congregazione per la dottrina della Fede
S. O. (Sanctum Officium), Decreta 1577–78; S. O., Decreta 1578–79.
Vatican City. Biblioteca Apostolica Vaticana
MS Urbinati Latini, 1046, *Avvisi di Venezia con notizie anche da varie località d'Italia
e d'Europa inviate da Girolamo Cortese e da altri raccoglitori al duca d'Urbino Fran-
cesco Maria II Della Rovere.* A microfilm copy can be consulted at Saint Louis
University, Saint Louis, MO, Pius XII Memorial Library, Knights of Columbus
Vatican Film Library, Roll 1401.
Venice. Archivio di Stato
Senato. Dispacci ambasciatori. Roma, filza 13.
Vienna. Österreichische Nationalbibliothek
Cod. 8951 Han, *Novellae Fuggerianae* (1578). A digital version can be consulted on-
line through the library's website: http://data.onb.ac.at/rec/AL00169821.

Primary Sources

Aretino, Pietro. *Pietro Aretino.* Edited by Carlo Serafini and Luciana Zampolli, intro-
duction by Giulio Ferroni. Cento Libri per Mille Anni. Rome: Istituto Poligrafico e
Zecca dello Stato, 2002.
———. *Ragionamenti.* Edited by Giovanni Aquilecchia, with French translation by Paul
Larivaille. 2 vols. Paris: Belles Lettres, 1998–99.
———. *Sonetti sopra i "XVI modi."* Edited by Giovanni Aquilecchia. Rome: Salerno Edi-
trice, 1992.
Bandello, Matteo. *Le novelle.* Edited by Delmo Maestri. 4 vols. Alessandria: Edizioni
dell'Orso, 1992–96.
Benserade, Isaac de. *Iphis et Iante.* Edited by Anne Verdier, with Christian Biet and Lise
Leibacher-Ouvrard. Vijon: Lampsaque, 2000.
Boaistuau, Pierre. *Histoires tragiques.* Edited by Richard A. Carr. Paris: Honoré Cham-
pion, 1977.
Boccaccio, Giovanni. *Decameron.* Edited by Vittore Branca, 6th ed. rev. Turin: Giulio
Einaudi, 1991; first pub. 1980.
———. *Le Decameron de Messire Jehan Bocace.* Translated by Antoine Le Maçon. Paris:
Estienne Roffet, 1545.
Canon Law, Code of. Roman Catholic Church. http://www.vatican.va/archive/ENG1104
/INDEX.HTM.
Castellani, Giacomo. *Avviso di Parnaso nel quale si racconta la povertà e miseria dove è
giunta la Republica di Venetia et il Duca di Savoia. Scritto da un curioso novellista spag-
nuolo. Con alcune annotationi molto importanti sopra le cose che in esso si contengono.
Per Valerio Fulvio, Savoiano.* "In Antopoli: Stamperia Regia," 1619.
Cellini, Benvenuto. *La Vita.* Edited by Lorenzo Bellotto. Parma: Fondazione Pietro
Bembo/Ugo Guanda Editore, 1996.
Crescimbeni, Giovanni Mario. *L'Istoria della Chiesa di S. Giovanni avanti Porta Latina.*
Rome: Antonio de' Rossi, 1716.

Due ambasciatori veneziani nella Spagna di fine Cinquecento. I diari dei viaggi di Antonio Tiepolo (1571–1572) e Francesco Vendramin (1592–1593). Edited by Luigi Monga. Moncalieri: Centro Interuniversitario di Ricerche sul "Viaggio in Italia," 2000.

Estienne, Henri. *Apologie pour Hérodote.* Edited by P. Ristelhuber. 2 vols. Geneva: Slatkine, 1969; first pub. Paris, 1879.

Five Comedies from the Italian Renaissance. Edited and translated by Laura Giannetti and Guido Ruggiero. Baltimore: Johns Hopkins University Press, 2003.

Gerson, Jean. *Œuvres complètes.* Edited by P. Glorieux. 10 vols. in 11. Paris: Desclée, 1961–73.

Henry III, King of France. *Lettres de Henri III, roi de France.* Edited by Pierre Champion, Michel François et al. Paris: Klincksieck/Honoré Champion, 1959–.

Homosexuality in Early Modern France: A Documentary Collection. Edited and translated by Jeffrey Merrick and Bryant T. Ragan Jr. Oxford: Oxford University Press, 2001.

La Mothe Le Vayer, François de. *Le Banquet Sceptique.* In [Orasius Tubero, pseud.]. *Quatre Dialogues faits à l'imitation des Anciens.* Frankfurt: Jean Sarius, 1604 [= France, c. 1630].

L'Estoile, Pierre de. *Registre-Journal du règne de Henri III.* Edited by Madeleine Lazard and Gilbert Schrenck. 6 vols. Geneva: Droz, 1992–2003.

Machiavelli, Niccolò. *Teatro. Andria, Mandragola, Clizia.* Edited by Guido Davico Bonino. Turin: Einaudi, 2001.

Montaigne, Michel de. *Œuvres complètes.* Edited by Albert Thibaudet and Maurice Rat. Bibliothèque de la Pléiade. Paris: Gallimard, 1962.

———. *The Complete Works: Essays, Travel Journal, Letters.* Translated by Donald M. Frame. New York: Alfred A. Knopf, 2003.

———. *Journal de voyage de Michel de Montaigne en Italie ... Avec des notes par M. de Querlon.* 1 vol. in 4°. À Rome, et se trouve à Paris, chez Le Jay, 1774.

———. *Journal de voyage. L'Italia alla fine del secolo XVI. Giornale del viaggio di Michele de Montaigne in Italia nel 1580 e 1581.* Edited by Alessandro D'Ancona. Città di Castello: S. Lapi, 1889.

———. *Journal de voyage.* Edited by Louis Lautrey. Paris: Hachette, 1906.

———. *Journal de voyage.* Edited by Charles Dédéyan. Paris: Belles Lettres, 1946.

———. *Journal de voyage.* Edited by François Rigolot. Paris: Presses universitaires de France, 1992.

———. "La Copie Leydet du 'Journal de Voyage' présentée et annotée par François Moureau." In *Autour du Journal de Voyage de Montaigne, 1580–1980,* Actes des Journées Montaigne, Mulhouse, Bâle, October 1980, ed. François Moureau and René Bernoulli, 107–85. Geneva: Slatkine, 1982.

Mutinelli, Fabio. *Storia arcana ed aneddotica d'Italia raccontata dai veneti ambasciatori.* 4 vols. Venice: Pietro Naratovich, 1855.

Pastorale, canones et ritus ecclesiasticos, qui ad sacramentorum administrationem aliaque pastoralia officia rite obeunda pertinent, complectens. Antwerp: ex officina Christophori Plantini, 1589.

Petrucci, Giovanni Battista. *Poema Latino Anepigrafo su S. Giacomo della Marca*. Edited and translated by Luigi de Luca and Girolamo Mascia. Naples: S. Francesco al Vomero, 1975.

Relazioni degli ambasciatori veneti al Senato. Edited by Eugenio Albèri. 15 vols. 1839–63. Vol. 10/Series 2, vol. 4. Florence: Società editrice fiorentina, 1857.

Rituale Romanum. Editio Princpes (1614). Edited by Manlio Sodi and Juan Javier Flores Arcas. Vatican City: Libreria Editrice Vaticana, 2004.

Thiers, Jean-Bapiste. *Traité des superstitions*. 4 vols. Paris: Compagnie des Libraires, 1741.

[Thomas, Artus?]. *L'Isle des Hermaphrodites*. Edited by Claude-Gilbert Dubois. Geneva: Droz, 1996.

La Vie généreuse des Mercelots, Gueuz, et Boesmiens, contenans leur façon de vivre, subtilitez et gergon mis en lumière par Pechon de Ruby. Edited by Denis Delaplace. Paris: Honoré Champion, 2007.

Vignali, Antonio. *La Cazzaria* (1525). Edited by Pasquale Stoppelli, introduction by Nino Borsellino. Rome: Edizioni dell'Elefante, 1984/1990.

——. *La Cazzaria: The Book of the Prick*. Translated by Ian Frederick Moulton. London: Routledge, 2003.

Vocabolario degli accademici della Crusca. 4 editions (1612–1738). http://www.lessico grafia.it.

Secondary Sources

Adichie, Chimamanda Ngozi. "The Danger of a Single Story." TED talk, recorded July 2009. http://www.ted.com/talks/chimamanda_adichie_the_danger_of_a_single _story.

Amelang, James S. *Parallel Histories: Muslims and Jews in Inquisitorial Spain*. Baton Rouge: Louisiana State University Press, 2013.

Amer, Sahar. "Cross-Dressing and Female Same-Sex Marriage in Medieval French and Arabic Literatures." In *Islamicate Sexualities: Translations Across Temporal Geographies of Desire*, edited by Kathryn Babayan and Afsaneh Najmabadi, 72–113. Cambridge, MA: Harvard Center for Middle Eastern Studies, 2008.

Archivo de la Embajada de España cerca de la Santa Sede. 4 vols. Vol. 1. *Indice Analítico de los documentos del siglo XVI*. Rome: Palacio de España, 1915.

Archivo General de Simancas, Catalogo XIV, Secretaría de Estado, Negociación de Roma. Primera Parte, Años 1381 a 1700. Valladolid: Imprenta Allén, 1936.

Aubenas, R. "Le Contrat d'"affrairamentum' dans le droit provençal du moyen âge." *Revue historique de droit français et étranger*, 4th ser., 12 (1933): 478–524.

Babayan, Kathryn, and Afsaneh Najmabadi, eds. *Islamicate Sexualities: Translations Across Temporal Geographies of Desire*. Cambridge, MA: Harvard Center for Middle Eastern Studies, 2008.

Baldassari, Marina. *Bande giovanili e "vizio nefando": Violenza e sessualità nella Roma barocca*. Rome: Viella, 2005.

Barbierato, Federico. *The Inquisitor in the Hat Shop: Inquisition, Forbidden Books and Unbelief in Early Modern Venice*. Farnham, UK: Ashgate, 2012.

Barthes, Roland. "L'effet de réel." *Communications* 11 (1968): 84–89.

Beck, William John. "Montaigne face à la [*sic*] homosexualité." *Bulletin de la Société des Amis de Montaigne*, 6th ser., 9–10 (1982): 41–50.

———. "The Obscure Montaigne: The Quotation, the Addition, and the Footnote." *College Language Association Journal* 34, no. 2 (1990): 228–52.

Benjamin, Walter. "Theses on the Philosophy of History." In *Reading the Past: Literature and History*, edited by Tamsin Spargo, 118–26. Basingstoke, UK: Palgrave, 2000.

Berco, Cristian. *Sexual Hierarchies, Public Status: Men, Sodomy, and Society in Spain's Golden Age*. Toronto: University of Toronto Press, 2007.

Black, Christopher. *Italian Confraternities in the Sixteenth Century*. Cambridge: Cambridge University Press, 1989.

Black, Christopher, and Pamela Gravestock, eds. *Early Modern Confraternities in Europe and the Americas: International and Interdisciplinary Perspectives*. Aldershot, UK: Ashgate, 2006.

Boggione, Valter, and Giovanni Casalegno. *Dizionario letterario del lessico amoroso: Metafore, eufemismi, trivialismi*. Turin: Unione Tipografico-Editrice Torinese, 2000.

———. *Dizionario storico del lessico erotico italiano: Metafore, eufemismi, oscenità, doppi sensi, parole dotte e parole basse in otto secoli di letteratura italiana*. Milan: Longanesi, 1996.

Boswell, John. "Revolutions, Universals, and Sexual Categories." In *Hidden from History: Reclaiming the Gay and Lesbian Past*, edited by Martin Duberman, Martha Vicinus, and George Chauncey Jr., 17–36. New York: Penguin, 1989.

———. *Same-Sex Unions in Premodern Europe*. New York: Villard Books, 1994.

Boudou, Bénédicte. "Le Mariage clandestin et la rupture du mariage dans la nouvelle de Violente et Didaco, chez Bandello et Boaistuau." *Cahiers de recherches médiévales et humanistes* 21 (2011): 343–58.

Boutcher, Warren. "'Le moyen de voir ce Senecque escrit à la main': Montaigne's *Journal de voyage* and the Politics of *Science* and *Faveur* in the Vatican Library." In "(Ré) interprétations: Études sur le Seizième Siècle," edited by John O'Brien, *Michigan Romance Studies* 15 (1995): 177–214.

Bravmann, Scott. *Queer Fictions of the Past: History, Culture, and Difference*. Cambridge: Cambridge University Press, 1997.

Bray, Alan. *The Friend*. Chicago: University of Chicago Press, 2003.

———. "Homosexuality and the Signs of Male Friendship in Elizabethan England." In *Queering the Renaissance*, edited by Jonathan Goldberg, 40–61. Durham, NC: Duke University Press, 1994.

———. *Homosexuality in Renaissance England*. London: Gay Men's Press, 1982.

Bromley, James M. *Intimacy and Sexuality in the Age of Shakespeare*. Cambridge: Cambridge University Press, 2012.

Brown, D. Catherine. *Pastor and Laity in the Theology of Jean Gerson*. Cambridge: Cambridge University Press, 1987.

Burshatin, Israel. "Written on the Body: Slave or Hermaphrodite in Sixteenth-Century Spain." In *Queer Iberia: Sexualities, Cultures, and Crossings from the Middle Ages to the Renaissance*, edited by Josiah Blackmore and Gregory S. Hutcheson, 420–56. Durham, NC: Duke University Press, 1999.

Canepari, Eleonora. "Cohabitations, Household Structures, and Gender Identities in Seventeenth-Century Rome." In "Gender in Early Modern Rome," edited by Julia L. Hairston, *I Tatti Studies in the Italian Renaissance* 17, no. 1 (2014): 131–54.

Cestaro, Gary P., ed. *Queer Italia: Same-Sex Desire in Italian Literature and Film.* New York: Palgrave Macmillan, 2004.

Chakrabarty, Dipesh. *Provincializing Europe: Postcolonial Thought and Historical Difference.* Princeton, NJ: Princeton University Press, 2000.

Chauncey, George. *Why Marriage? The History Shaping Today's Debate over Gay Equality.* New York: Basic Books, 2004.

Christensen-Nugues, Charlotte. "Parental Authority and Freedom of Choice: The Debate on Clandestinity and Parental Consent at the Council of Trent." *Sixteenth Century Journal* 45 (2014): 51–72.

Cipolla, Costantino, and Giancarlo Malacarne, eds. *El più soave et dolce et dilectevole et gratioso bochone: Amore e sesso al tempo dei Gonzaga.* Milan: FrancoAngeli, 2006.

Cohen, Thomas V., and Elizabeth S. Cohen. *Words and Deeds in Renaissance Rome: Trials Before the Papal Magistrates.* Toronto: University of Toronto Press, 1993.

Cole, Peter, trans. and ed. *The Dream of the Poem: Hebrew Poetry from Muslim and Christian Spain, 950–1492.* Princeton, NJ: Princeton University Press, 2007.

Colker, Marvin L. *Trinity College Library Dublin: Descriptive Catalogue of the Mediaeval and Renaissance Latin Manuscripts.* 2 vols. Aldershot, UK: Scolar Press for Trinity College Library, 1991.

Connell, William J., and Giles Constable. *Sacrilege and Redemption in Renaissance Florence: The Case of Antonio Rinaldeschi.* Toronto: Centre for Reformation and Renaissance Studies, 2005.

Coontz, Stephanie. *Marriage, a History: How Love Conquered Marriage.* New York: Penguin, 2005.

Courouve, Claude. *Les Assemblées de la Manchette, Paris—1720–1750.* Paris: C. Courouve, 2000.

Cristellon, Cecilia. "Does the Priest Have to Be There? Contested Marriages Before Roman Tribunals: Italy, Sixteenth to Eighteenth Centuries." *Österreichische Zeitschrift für Geschichtswissenschaften* 20, no. 3 (2009): 10–30.

———. "Marriage and Consent in Pre-Tridentine Venice: Between Lay Conception and Ecclesiastical Conception, 1420–1545." *Sixteenth Century Journal* 39, no. 2 (2008): 389–418.

———. "Public Display of Affection: The Making of Marriage in the Venetian Courts Before the Council of Trent (1420–1545)." In *Erotic Cultures of Renaissance Italy,* edited by Sara F. Matthews-Grieco, 173–97. Farnham, UK: Ashgate, 2010.

Dall'Orto, Giovanni. *Tutta un'altra storia: L'omosessualità dall'antichità al secondo dopoguerra.* Milan: il Saggiatore, 2015.

Dandelet, Thomas James. *Spanish Rome, 1500–1700.* New Haven, CT: Yale University Press, 2001.

Davidson, N. S. "Sodomy in Early Modern Venice." In *Sodomy in Early Modern Europe,* edited by Tom Betteridge, 65–81. Manchester: Manchester University Press, 2002.

Davis, Natalie Z. *The Return of Martin Guerre.* Cambridge, MA: Harvard University Press, 1983.

——. "Strikes and Salvation at Lyon." In *Society and Culture in Early Modern France*, 1–16. Stanford, CA: Stanford University Press, 1975.

Dean, Trevor. "Fathers and Daughters: Marriage Laws and Marriage Disputes in Bologna and Italy, 1200–1500." In *Marriage in Italy, 1300–1600*, edited by Trevor Dean and K. J. P. Lowe, 85–106. Cambridge: Cambridge University Press, 1998.

——, and K. J. P. Lowe, eds. *Marriage in Italy, 1300–1600*. Cambridge: Cambridge University Press, 1998.

Dekker, Rudolf M., and Lotte C. van de Pol. *The Tradition of Female Transvestism in Early Modern Europe*. New York: St Martin's Press, 1989.

Deleuze, Gilles, and Félix Guattari. *Mille plateaux*. Vol. 2. *Capitalisme et schizophrénie*. Paris: Éditions de Minuit, 1980.

——. *A Thousand Plateaus: Capitalism and Schizophrenia*. Translated by Brian Massumi. Minneapolis: University of Minnesota Press, 1987.

Desan, Philippe. "L'appel de Rome, ou comment Montaigne ne devint jamais ambassadeur." In *Chemins de l'exil, havres de paix: migrations d'hommes et d'idées au XVIe siècle*, edited by Jean Balsamo and Chiara Lastraioli, 229–59. Paris: Champion, 2010.

Dinshaw, Carolyn. *Getting Medieval: Sexualities and Communities, Pre- and Postmodern*. Durham, NC: Duke University Press, 1999.

Di Sivo, Michele. "Il fondo della *Confraternita di S. Giovanni decollato* nell'Archivio di Stato di Roma (1497–1870). Inventario." *Rivista storica del Lazio* 12 (2000): 181–225.

Duberman, Martin, Martha Vicinus, and George Chauncey Jr., eds. *Hidden from History: Reclaiming the Gay and Lesbian Past*. New York: Penguin, 1989.

Edgerton, Samuel Y., Jr. *Pictures and Punishment: Art and Criminal Prosecution During the Florentine Renaissance*. Ithaca, NY: Cornell University Press, 1985.

Epps, Brad. "Comparison, Competition, and Cross-Dressing: Cross-Cultural Analysis in a Contested World." In *Islamicate Sexualities: Translations Across Temporal Geographies of Desire*, edited by Kathryn Babayan and Afsaneh Najmabadi, 114–60. Cambridge, MA: Harvard Center for Middle Eastern Studies, 2008.

Ferguson, Gary. "Avant-goûts: (Homo)sexualités comparées au seuil de la modernité." In *Littérature et identités sexuelles*, edited by Anne Tomiche and Pierre Zoberman, Collection *Poétiques Comparatistes*, 105–22. Paris: Société Française de Littérature Générale et Comparée, 2007.

——. "Early Modern Transitions: From Montaigne to Choisy." In "Transgender France," edited by Todd W. Reeser, *L'Esprit Créateur* 53, no. 1 (2013): 145–57.

——. *Queer (Re)Readings in the French Renaissance: Homosexuality, Gender, Culture*. Aldershot, UK: Ashgate, 2008.

——. "(Same-Sex) Marriage and the Making of Europe: Renaissance Rome Revisited." In *What's Queer About Europe? Productive Encounters and Re-Enchanting Paradigms*, edited by Mireille Rosello and Sudeep Dasgupta, 27–47 and 190–95. New York: Fordham University Press, 2014.

Ferraro, Joanne M. *Marriage Wars in Late Renaissance Venice*. Oxford: Oxford University Press, 2001.

Firpo, Luigi. "La satira politica in forma di ragguaglio di Parnaso. I—Dal 1614 al 1620." *Atti della Accademia delle scienze di Torino*, Series 2, Classe di scienze morali, storiche e filologiche 87 (1952–53): 197–247.

Fosi, Irene. *Papal Justice: Subjects and Courts in the Papal State, 1500–1750*, translated by Thomas V. Cohen. Washington, DC: Catholic University of America Press, 2011.

——. "Pietà, devozione e politica: due confraternite fiorentine nella Roma del Rinascimento." *Archivio storico italiano* 149, no. 1 (1991): 119–61.

Foucault, Michel. *Histoire de la sexualité*. Vol. 1, *La volonté de savoir*. Paris: Gallimard, 1976. Vol 2, *L'Usage des plaisirs*. Paris: Gallimard, 1984. Vol. 3, *Le Souci de soi*. Paris: Gallimard, 1984.

——. "Lives of Infamous Men." In *The Essential Foucault: Selections from The Essential Works of Foucault, 1954–1984*, edited by Paul Rabinow and Nikolas Rose, 279–93. New York: New Press, 2003.

——. "Of Other Spaces." *Diacritics* 16, no. 1 (1986): 22–27.

Fraccari, Claudio. "Addendum. La chiave nella toppa: Repertorio lessicale e mappa per aree semantiche dei *Cicalamenti* del Grappa." In *El più soave et dolce et dilectevole et gratioso bochone: Amore e sesso al tempo dei Gonzaga*, edited by Costantino Cipolla and Giancarlo Malacarne, 327–40. Milan: FrancoAngeli, 2006.

——. "Le parole per dirlo. Glossario," In *El più soave et dolce et dilectevole et gratioso bochone: Amore e sesso al tempo dei Gonzaga*, edited by Costantino Cipolla and Giancarlo Malacarne, 341–54. Milan: FrancoAngeli, 2006.

——. "Per amor di metafora: Linguaggio erotico e travestimenti dell'osceno nella corrispondenza gonzaghesca," In *El più soave et dolce et dilectevole et gratioso bochone: Amore e sesso al tempo dei Gonzaga*, edited by Costantino Cipolla and Giancarlo Malacarne, 265–89. Milan: FrancoAngeli, 2006.

Freccero, Carla. *Queer/Early/Modern*. Durham, NC: Duke University Press, 2006.

Freeman, Elizabeth, ed. "Queer Temporalities," a special number of *GLQ: A Journal of Lesbian and Gay Studies* 13, nos. 2–3 (2007).

Gallucci, Margaret A. "ACTing UP in the Renaissance: The Case of Benvenuto Cellini." In *Queer Italia: Same-Sex Desire in Italian Literature and Film*, edited by Gary P. Cestaro, 71–82. New York: Palgrave Macmillan, 2004.

——. "Cellini's Trial for Sodomy: Power and Patronage at the Court of Cosimo I." In *The Cultural Politics of Duke Cosimo I de' Medici*, edited by Konrad Eisenbichler, 37–46. Aldershot, UK: Ashgate, 2001.

Gerard, Kent, and Gert Hekma, eds. *The Pursuit of Sodomy: Male Homosexuality in Renaissance and Enlightenment Europe*. New York: Harrington Park/Haworth Press, 1989. Published simultaneously as the *Journal of Homosexuality* 16, nos. 1–2 (1988).

Giannetti, Laura. *Lelia's Kiss: Imagining Gender, Sex, and Marriage in Italian Renaissance Comedy*. Toronto: University of Toronto Press, 2009.

Ginzburg, Carlo. *The Cheese and the Worms: The Cosmos of a Sixteenth-Century Miller*, translated by John and Anne Tedeschi. Baltimore: Johns Hopkins University Press, 1980.

Giorgio, Michela de, and Christiane Klapisch-Zuber, eds. *Storia del matrimonio*. Bari: Laterza, 1996.

Glissant, Édouard. *Le discours antillais*. Paris: Gallimard, 1997.

——. *Poétique de la relation. Poétique III*. Paris: Gallimard, 1990.

Goldberg, Jonathan. "The History that Will Be." In *Premodern Sexualities*, edited by Louise Fradenburg and Carla Freccero, with Kathy Lavezzo, 3–21. New York: Routledge, 1996.

Goldberg, Jonathan, and Madhavi Menon. "Queering History." *PMLA* 120, no. 5 (2005): 1608–17.

Grande Dizionario della lingua italiana. Edited by Salvatore Battaglia. 21 vols. plus index and supplement. Turin: Unione Tipografico-Editrice Torinese, 1961–2009.

Gravestock, Pamela. "Comforting the Condemned and the Role of the *Laude* in Early Modern Italy." In *Early Modern Confraternities in Europe and the Americas: International and Interdisciplinary Perspectives*, edited by Christopher Black and Pamela Gravestock, 129–50. Aldershot, UK: Ashgate, 2006.

Grieco, Allen J. "From Roosters to Cocks: Italian Renaissance Fowl and Sexuality." In *Erotic Cultures of Renaissance Italy*, edited by Sara F. Matthews-Grieco, 89–140. Farnham, UK: Ashgate, 2010.

Halberstam, Judith. *In a Queer Time and Place: Transgender Bodies, Subcultural Lives*. New York: New York University Press, 2005.

Halperin, David M. *How to Do the History of Homosexuality*. Chicago: University of Chicago Press, 2002.

——. *One Hundred Years of Homosexuality and Other Essays on Greek Love*. New York: Routledge, 1990.

Hammond, Nicholas. "Bavardages et masculinités." In "L'Homme en tous genres: Masculinités, textes et contextes," edited by Gary Ferguson, *Itinéraires. Littérature, textes, cultures* (2008/2009): 91–105.

——. "Bavards et bardaches: Relectures du XVIIe siècle." In *Queer: Écritures de la différence?*, edited by Pierre Zoberman. 2 vols. Paris: L'Harmattan, 2008, 1:133–41.

——. *Gossip, Sexuality and Scandal in France (1610–1715)*. Oxford: Peter Lang, 2011.

Hampton, Timothy. *Fictions of Embassy: Literature and Diplomacy in Early Modern Europe*. Ithaca, NY: Cornell University Press, 2009.

Hartman, Saidiya V. *Lose Your Mother: A Journey Along the Atlantic Slave Route*. New York: Farrar, Straus and Giroux, 2007.

Hetherington, Kevin. *The Badlands of Modernity: Heterotopia and Social Ordering*. London: Routledge, 1997.

"Historicism and Unhistoricism in Queer Studies." Letters to the editor from Carla Freccero, Madhavi Menon, and Valerie Traub. *PMLA* 128, no. 3 (2013): 781–86.

Karras, Ruth Mazzo. *Unmarriages*. Philadelphia: University of Pennsylvania Press, 2012.

King, Helen. *The One-Sex Body on Trial: The Classical and Early Modern Evidence*. Farnham, UK: Ashgate, 2013.

Klapisch-Zuber, Christiane. *Women, Family, and Ritual in Renaissance Italy*. Translated by Lydia G. Cochrane. Chicago: University of Chicago Press, 1985.

Laqueur, Thomas. *Making Sex: Body and Gender from the Greeks to Freud*. Cambridge, MA: Harvard University Press, 1990.

Larivaille, Paul. "Entre hédonisme et hermétisme: Notes sur l'équivoque érotique dans la littérature italienne de la Renaissance." In *Figures et langages de la marginalité aux XVIe et XVIIe siècles*, edited by Maria Teresa Ricci, 21–41. Paris: Champion, 2013.

Le Roux, Nicolas. *La Faveur du roi: Mignons et courtisans au temps des derniers Valois (vers 1547–vers 1589)*. Seyssel: Champ Vallon, 2000.

Leushuis, Reinier. "'Col publicamento del matrimonio sgannar ciascuno': Marriage and Betrothal in Bandello's *Novelle*." In *Marriage in Premodern Europe: Italy and Beyond*, edited by Jacqueline Murray, 307–31. Toronto: Centre for Reformation and Renaissance Studies, 2012.

Levin, Michael J. *Agents of Empire: Spanish Ambassadors in Sixteenth-Century Italy*. Ithaca, NY: Cornell University Press, 2005.

Levy, Allison, ed. *Sex Acts in Early Modern Italy: Practice, Performance, Perversion, Punishment*. Farnham, UK: Ashgate, 2010.

Lombardi, Daniela. *Matrimoni di antico regime*. Bologna: Il Mulino, 2001.

Love, Heather. *Feeling Backward: Loss and the Politics of Queer History*. Cambridge, MA: Harvard University Press, 2007.

Maccubbin, Robert Purks, ed. *'Tis Nature's Fault: Unauthorized Sexuality During the Enlightenment*. Cambridge: Cambridge University Press, 1987.

Marcocci, Giuseppe. "Is This Love? Same-Sex Marriages in Renaissance Rome." *Historical Reflections* 41, no. 2 (2015): 37–52.

———. "Matrimoni omosessuali nella Roma del tardo Cinquecento: Su un passo del 'Journal' di Montaigne." *Quaderni storici* 133 (2010): 107–37.

Martin, John Jeffries. *Myths of Renaissance Individualism*. Basingstoke, UK: Palgrave Macmillan, 2004.

Masi, Giorgio. "'Gente scapigliatissima e bizzarra': La poesia libertina di Curzio Marignolli." In *Extravagances amoureuses: L'Amour au-delà de la norme à la Renaissance / Stravaganze amorose: L'Amore oltre la norma nel Rinascimento*, Actes du Colloque international du groupe de recherche *Cinquecento plurale*, Tours, September 18–20, 2008, edited by Élise Boillet and Chiara Lastraioli, 341–414. Paris: Honoré Champion, 2010.

Matthews-Grieco, Sara F., ed. *Erotic Cultures of Renaissance Italy*. Farnham, UK: Ashgate, 2010.

Matthiae, G., A. Missori, et al. *S. Giovanni a Porta Latina e L'Oratorio di S. Giovanni in Oleo*. Le Chiese di Roma illustrate 51. Rome: Marietti, [1960?].

Mayer, Thomas F. *The Roman Inquisition: A Papal Bureaucracy and Its Laws in the Age of Galileo*. Philadelphia: University of Pennsylvania Press, 2013.

———. *The Roman Inquisition on the Stage of Italy, c. 1590–1640*. Philadelphia: University of Pennsylvania Press, 2014.

McClure, George. "Heresy at Play: Academies and the Literary Underground in Counter-Reformation Siena." *Renaissance Quarterly* 63 (2010): 1151–1207.

Menchi, Silvana Seidel, and Diego Quaglioni, eds. *Coniugi nemici: La separazione in Italia dal XII al XVIII secolo*. Bologna: Il Mulino, 2000.

———. *Matrimoni in dubbio: Unioni controverse e nozze clandestine in Italia dal XIV al XVIII secolo*. Bologna: Il Mulino, 2001.

———. *Trasgressioni: Seduzione, concubinato, adulterio, bigamia (XIV–XVIII secolo)*. Bologna: Il Mulino, 2004.

———. *I tribunali del matrimonio (secoli XV–XVIII)*. Bologna: Il Mulino, 2006.

Menon, Madhavi. *Unhistorical Shakespeare: Queer Theory in Shakespearean Literature and Film*. New York: Palgrave Macmillan, 2008.

Merrick, Jeffrey. "Chaussons in the Streets: Sodomy in Seventeenth-Century Paris." *Journal of the History of Sexuality* 15, no. 2 (2006): 167–203.

——. "'Nocturnal Birds' in the Champs-Elysées: Police and Pederasty in Prerevolutionary Paris." *GLQ: A Journal of Lesbian and Gay Studies* 8, no. 3 (2002): 425–32.

——. "Sodomites and Police in Paris, 1715." *Journal of the History of Homosexuality* 42, no. 3 (2002): 103–28.

——. "Sodomitical Inclinations in Early Eighteenth-Century Paris." *Eighteenth-Century Studies* 30, no. 3 (1997): 289–95.

——. "Sodomitical Scandals and Subcultures in the 1720s." *Men and Masculinities* 1 (1999): 365–84.

Moschini, Vittorio. *S. Giovanni Decollato*. Le Chiese di Roma illustrate 26. Rome: Danesi [1926/1930?].

Murray, Jacqueline, ed. *Marriage in Premodern Europe: Italy and Beyond*. Toronto: Centre for Reformation and Renaissance Studies, 2012.

Norton, Rictor. *Mother Clap's Molly House: The Gay Subculture in England 1700–1830*. London: GMP Publishers, 1992.

Nussdorfer, Laurie. "Men at Home in Baroque Rome." In "Gender in Early Modern Rome," edited by Julia L. Hairston, *I Tatti Studies in the Italian Renaissance* 17, no. 1 (2014): 103–29.

——. "The Politics of Space in Early Modern Rome." *Memoirs of the American Academy in Rome* 42 (1997): 161–86.

Orano, Domenico. *Liberi pensatori bruciati in Roma dal XVI al XVIII secolo*. Rome, 1904; Livorno: U. Bastogi Editore, 1971.

Orlando, Ermanno. "Il matrimonio delle beffe: Unioni finte, simulate, per gioco. Padova e Venezia, fine secolo XIV–inizi secolo XVI." In *Trasgressioni: Seduzione, concubinato, adulterio, bigamia (XIV–XVIII secolo)*, edited by Silvana Seidel Menchi and Diego Quaglioni, 231–67. Bologna: Il Mulino, 2004.

Ortalli, Gherardo. *La pittura infamante nei secoli XIII–XVI*. Rome: Società Editoriale Jouvence, 1979.

Paglia, Vincenzo. *La Morte confortata: Riti della paura e mentalità religiosa a Roma nell'età moderna*. Rome: Edizioni di Storia e Letteratura, 1982.

Pastor, Beatriz. "Silence and Writing: The History of the Conquest." Translated by Jason Wood. In *1492–1992: Re/Discovering Colonial Writing*, edited by René Jara and Nicholas Spadaccini, 121–63. Minneapolis: Prisma Institute, 1989; repr. University of Minnesota Press, 1991.

Pastor, Ludwig Freiherr von [Ludovico Barone von Pastor]. *Storia dei Papi dalla fine del Medio Evo*. Vol. 8. *Pio V (1566–1572)*. Translated by Angelo Mercati. Rome: Desclée & Ci, 1951. From *Geschichte der Päpste seit dem Ausgang des Mittelalters*. 16 vols. Freiburg im Breisgau: Herder, 1886–1933.

——. *Storia dei Papi dalla fine del Medio Evo*. Vol. 9. *Gregorio XIII (1572–1585)*. Translated by Pio Cenci. Rome: Desclée & Ci, 1955. From *Geschichte der Päpste seit dem Ausgang des Mittelalters*. 16 vols. Freiburg im Breisgau: Herder, 1886–1933.

Pastore, Stefania, Adriano Prosperi, and Nicholas Terpstra, eds. *Brotherhood and Boundaries. Fraternità e barriere*. Pisa: Edizioni della Normale, 2011.

——. *Faith's Boundaries: Laity and Clergy in Early Modern Confraternities.* Turnhout: Brepols, 2012.

Peters, Edward. *Torture.* Rev. ed. Philadelphia: University of Pennsylvania Press, 1996; first pub. 1985.

Petitjean, Johann. *L'Intelligence des choses: Une histoire de l'information entre Italie et Méditerranée (XVIᵉ–XVIIᵉ siècles).* Rome: École française de Rome, 2013.

Poirier, Guy. *Henri III de France en mascarades imaginaires: Mœurs, humeurs et comportements d'un roi de la Renaissance.* Quebec City: Presses de l'Université Laval, 2010.

——. *L'Homosexualité dans l'imaginaire de la Renaissance.* Paris: Champion, 1996.

Prosperi, Adriano. *L'Inquisizione romana: Letture e ricerche.* Rome: Edizioni di storia e letteratura, 2003.

——. "Il sangue e l'anima: Ricerche sulle Compagnie di Giustizia in Italia." *Quaderni storici* 51 (1982): 959–99.

Prosperi, Adriano, with Vincenzo Lavenia and John Tedeschi, eds. *Dizionario storico dell'Inquisizione.* 4 vols. Pisa: Edizioni della Normale, 2010.

Reeser, Todd W. "Re-Reading Platonic Sexuality Sceptically in Montaigne's 'Apologie de Raimond Sebond.'" In *Masculinities in Sixteenth-Century France: Proceedings of the Eighth Cambridge French Renaissance Colloquium, 5–7 July 2003*, edited by Philip Ford and Paul White, 103–26. Cambridge: Cambridge French Colloquia, 2006.

Rey, Michel. "Parisian Homosexuals Create a Lifestyle, 1700–1750: The Police Archives." Translated by Robert A. Day and Robert Welch. In *'Tis Nature's Fault: Unauthorized Sexuality During the Enlightenment*, edited by Robert Purks Maccubbin, 179–91. Cambridge: Cambridge University Press, 1987.

——. "Police and Sodomy in Eighteenth-Century Paris: From Sin to Disorder." In *The Pursuit of Sodomy: Male Homosexuality in Renaissance and Enlightenment Europe*, edited by Kent Gerard and Gert Hekma, 129–46. New York: Harrington Park/Haworth Press, 1989. Published simultaneously as the *Journal of Homosexuality* 16, nos. 1–2 (1988).

——. "Les Sodomites Parisiens au XVIIIème Siècle." MA thesis, dir. Jean-Louis Flandrin, Université Paris VIII–Vincennes, 1979–80.

Reynolds, Philip L. "Marrying and Its Documentation in Pre-Modern Europe: Consent, Celebration, and Property." In *To Have and to Hold: Marrying and Its Documentation in Western Christendom, 400–1600*, edited by Philip L. Reynolds and John Witte Jr., 1–42. Cambridge: Cambridge University Press, 2007.

Reynolds, Philip L., and John Witte Jr., eds. *To Have and to Hold: Marrying and Its Documentation in Western Christendom, 400–1600.* Cambridge: Cambridge University Press, 2007.

Robinson, David M. *Closeted Writing and Lesbian and Gay Literature: Classical, Early Modern, Eighteenth-Century.* Aldershot, UK: Ashgate, 2006.

Rocke, Michael J. *Forbidden Friendships: Homosexuality and Male Culture in Renaissance Florence.* Oxford: Oxford University Press, 1996.

——. "Sodomites in Fifteenth-Century Tuscany: The Views of Bernardino of Siena." In *The Pursuit of Sodomy: Male Homosexuality in Renaissance and Enlightenment Europe*, edited by Kent Gerard and Gert Hekma, 7–31. New York: Harrington Park/

Haworth Press, 1989. Published simultaneously as the *Journal of Homosexuality* 16, nos. 1–2 (1988).

Romeo, Giovanni. *Amori proibiti: I concubini tra Chiesa e Inquisizione. Napoli 1563–1656.* Bari: Editori Laterza, 2008.

Rothstein, Marian. *Reading in the Renaissance: "Amadis de Gaule" and the Lessons of Memory.* Newark: University of Delaware Press, 1999.

Ruggiero, Guido. *The Boundaries of Eros: Sex Crime and Sexuality in Renaissance Venice.* Oxford: Oxford University Press, 1985.

———. *Machiavelli in Love: Sex, Self, and Society in the Italian Renaissance.* Baltimore: Johns Hopkins University Press, 2007.

Russo, Francesco. *Nostra Signora del Sacro Cuore (Già S. Giacomo degli Spagnoli).* Le Chiese di Roma illustrate 105. Rome: Marietti, 1969.

Sander-Faes, Stephan Karl. *Urban Elites of Zadar: Dalmatia and the Venetian Commonwealth (1540–1569).* Rome: Viella, 2013.

Saslow, James M. *Ganymede in the Renaissance: Homosexuality in Art and Society.* New Haven, CT: Yale University Press, 1986.

Scaramella, Pierroberto. "Sodomia." In *Dizionario storico dell'Inquisizione*, edited by Adriano Prosperi, with Vincenzo Lavenia and John Tedeschi. 4 vols. Pisa: Edizioni della Normale, 2010, 3:1445–50.

Sedgwick, Eve Kosofsky. *Epistemology of the Closet.* Berkeley: University of California Press, 1990.

Shannon, Laurie. "Nature's Bias: Renaissance Homonormativity and Elizabethan Comic Likeness." *Modern Philology* 98, no. 2 (2000–2001): 183–210.

Sherberg, Michael. "Il potere e il piacere: la sodomia del *Marescalco*." In *La Rappresentazione dell'altro nei testi del Rinascimento*, edited by Sergio Zatti, 96–110. Lucca: Maria Pacini Fazzi Editore, 1998.

Sibalis, Michael. "Homosexuality in Early Modern France." In *Queer Masculinities, 1500–1800: Siting Same-Sex Desire in the Early Modern World*, edited by Katherine O'Donnell and Michael O'Rourke, 211–31. Basingstoke, UK: Palgrave Macmillan, 2006.

———. "Paris." In *Queer Sites: Gay Urban Histories Since 1600*, edited by David Higgs, 10–37. London: Routledge, 1999.

Soyer, François. *Ambiguous Gender in Early Modern Spain and Portugal: Inquisitors, Doctors and the Transgression of Gender Norms.* Leiden: Brill, 2012.

Steinberg, Sylvie. *La Confusion des sexes: Le Travestissement de la Renaissance à la Révolution.* Paris: Fayard, 2001.

Storey, Tessa. *Carnal Commerce in Counter-Reformation Rome.* Cambridge: Cambridge University Press, 2008.

———. "Courtesan Culture: Manhood, Honour and Sociability." In *Erotic Cultures of Renaissance Italy*, edited by Sara F. Matthews-Grieco, 247–73. Farnham, UK: Ashgate, 2010.

Stow, Kenneth. *Jewish Dogs: An Image and Its Interpreters. Continuity in the Catholic–Jewish Encounter.* Stanford, CA: Stanford University Press, 2006.

Tedeschi, John. *La dispersione degli archivi della Inquisizione Romana.* Florence: Leo Olschki, 1973.

——. "A 'Queer Story': The Inquisitorial Manuscripts." In *Treasures of the Library, Trinity College Dublin*, edited by Peter Fox, 67–74. Dublin: Royal Irish Academy for the Library of Trinity College Dublin, 1986.

Terpstra, Nicholas, ed. *The Art of Executing Well: Rituals of Execution in Renaissance Italy*. Kirksville, MO: Truman State University Press, 2008.

Terry, Allie. "The Craft of Torture: Bronze Sculptures and the Punishment of Sexual Offense." In *Sex Acts in Early Modern Italy: Practice, Performance, Perversion, Punishment*, edited by Allison Levy, 209–23. Farnham, UK: Ashgate, 2010.

Tinguely, Frédéric. *Le voyageur aux mille tours: Les ruses de l'écriture du monde à la Renaissance*. Paris: Honoré Champion, 2014.

Traub, Valerie. "The New Unhistoricism in Queer Studies." *PMLA* 128, no. 1 (2013): 21–39.

Truant, Cynthia Maria. *The Rites of Labor: Brotherhoods of Compagnonnage in Old and New Regime France*. Ithaca, NY: Cornell University Press, 1994.

Trumbach, Randolph. "The Birth of the Queen: Sodomy and the Emergence of Gender Equality in Modern Culture, 1660–1750." In *Hidden from History: Reclaiming the Gay and Lesbian Past*, edited by Martin Duberman, Martha Vicinus, and George Chauncey Jr., 129–40. New York: Penguin, 1989.

——. "The Heterosexual Male in Eighteenth-Century London and his Queer Interactions." In *Love, Sex, Intimacy, and Friendship Between Men, 1550–1800*, edited by Katherine O'Donnell and Michael O'Rourke, 99–127. Basingstoke, UK: Palgrave Macmillan, 2003.

——. "London's Sodomites: Homosexual Behavior and Western Culture in the Eighteenth Century." *Journal of Social History* 11 (1977–78): 1–33.

——. *Sex and the Gender Revolution*. Vol. 1, *Heterosexuality and the Third Gender in Enlightenment London*. Chicago: University of Chicago Press, 1998.

——. "Sodomitical Subcultures, Sodomitical Roles, and the Gender Revolution of the Eighteenth Century: The Recent Historiography." In *'Tis Nature's Fault: Unauthorized Sexuality During the Enlightenment*, edited by Robert Purks Maccubbin, 109–21. Cambridge: Cambridge University Press, 1987.

Tulchin, Allan A. "Same-Sex Couples Creating Households in Old Regime France: The Uses of the *Affrèrement*." *Journal of Modern History* 79 (2007): 613–47.

Vatican Archives: An Inventory and Guide to Historical Documents of the Holy See. Supplement 1, The Archives of the Congregation for the Doctrine of the Faith. Edited by Francis X. Blouin Jr., Peter Horsman, Leonard A. Coombs, and Elizabeth Yakel. Ann Arbor: Bentley Historical Library, University of Michigan, 2003.

Warner, Michael. *The Trouble with Normal: Sex, Politics, and the Ethics of Queer Life*. New York: Free Press, 1999.

Weinstein, Roni. *Juvenile Sexuality, Kabbalah, and Catholic Reformation in Italy:* Tiferet Bahurim *by Pinhas Barukh ben Pelatiyah Monselice*. Leiden: Brill, 2009.

White, Hayden. *Tropics of Discourse: Essays in Cultural Criticism*. Baltimore: Johns Hopkins University Press, 1978.

INDEX